Reef Madness

Charles Darwin, Alexander Agassiz, and the Meaning of Coral

DAVID DOBBS

Pantheon Books • New York

Pantheon Books and colophon are registered
trademarks of Random House, Inc.

Library of Congress Cataloging-in-Publication Data

Dobbs, David, [date]
Reef madness : Charles Darwin, Alexander Agassiz,
and the meaning of coral/David Dobbs.—1st ed.
p.   cm.
Includes bibliographical references and index.
ISBN 0-375-42161-0 (hardcover : alk. paper)
1. Coral reefs and islands.   2. Science—History—19th century.
3. Agassiz, Alexander, 1835–1910.   4. Natural history—Philosophy.   I. Title.
QE565.D63 2005
551.42'4—dc22   2004040131
www.pantheonbooks.com

Book design by Robert C. Olsson

Printed in the United States of America
First Edition

2 4 6 8 9 7 5 3 1

Reef Madness

For my father,
Herman Allen Dobbs, Jr.

CONTENTS

PART III

LIST OF ILLUSTRATIONS

Reef Madness

A coral island in the Pacific. From Charles Darwin's
Structure and Distribution of Coral Reefs.

Introduction

In the last half of the nineteenth century, Alexander Agassiz, the smart, quiet son of the brilliant, famously talkative naturalist Louis Agassiz, entangled himself in an argument over the genesis of coral reefs that grew into one of the most heated and vital debates in science. To enter such a dispute went against a deeply ingrained caution. Despite a difficult childhood, the challenge of emigrating from his native Switzerland to the United States, and staggering personal losses, Alexander had become one of his generation's most respected scientists and, by solving the key engineering problems in a copper mine he partly owned, one of America's richest men. But such was his reserve that many colleagues had no idea he was rich, while few business acquaintances knew he spent most of his time studying starfish and coral reefs.

His modest course was quite unlike the highly public path his father had taken. Louis Agassiz, a lecturer of fantastic eloquence, stunning memory, and beguiling charm, had won immense popular fame with his spellbinding account, given in countless talks, books, and articles, of how zoology's wonders reflected a divine plan. (A species, said Louis, was "a thought of God.") Louis paid a high price for this renown, however, when in 1859 Charles Darwin's *Origin of Species* displaced his creationist explanation of species. Louis's fierce resistance to Darwin's evolution theory cost him his scientific credibility, and his fall was painful to watch. Alexander tried to avoid scientific debate and any sort of spotlight ever after.

Yet Alexander, who loved the ocean, found the question of coral reefs irresistible. How did these huge, beautiful forms, composed of the skeletons of tiny animals that could survive only in shallow water, come to rise on foundations that emerged from the Pacific's greatest depths? Did these creatures somehow build these foundations? It seemed unlikely. Yet if not, how did so many of these platforms—thousands of them reaching just shy of the surface—come to be? Though this mystery drew the attention of great scientists for decades, a satisfactory answer proved elusive. Today, of course, the main argument about coral reefs is how to save them, and only scientists might recall the debate that once raged about their origin. But in the 1800s, particularly from the 1870s onward, the "coral reef problem," as it was known, stood as one of the most difficult and contentious in science. Only the 1860s clash over evolution seemed comparable.

One reason the coral reef debate reached such a pitch is that it in many ways reprised the evolutionary debate, engaging many of the same people and ideas. It played out as an eerie coda to the battle over Darwinism, with strange dissonances, inverted themes, and prominent soloists playing different instruments, their lines of music sometimes unexpectedly reversed or turned upside down, as if Bartók had rearranged an operatic score by Wagner. The coral reef problem did not concern species origin or humankind's descent. But it posed again the evolutionary debate's confounding questions about the importance of evidence, the proper construction of theory, and the reliability of powerful but abstract ideas.

These were not marginal issues. Indeed, their reexamination during the Victorian era allowed and often drove the great advances science made in the nineteenth century (and the twentieth, for that matter) and helped solidify science as a separate discipline. For the five centuries before the Victorian era, what we now call science—the analysis of how nature works—had been known as natural philosophy, and it held strong links to theology; for many, natural philosophy was simply the study of God's natural works. It was only in the 1800s that the word *scientist* was coined, for it was only then that people began to think of science as an endeavor driven by its own, particularly rigorous set of rules. As science moved inexorably away from the realm of religious philosophy (a break that had started with Copernicus), its rules increasingly stressed empiricism, the reliance on observable dynamics rather than mythic explanations. This growing empiricism stirred a more self-conscious consideration of how scientists should draw conclusions from what they observed.

These changes produced great rewards. Indeed, the story of the advance of Western science—at its best, a search for knowledge that can be communally pursued, readily shared, and rigorously checked with data culled from replicable observation—is largely the story of the development of reliable empirical methods, and many of those methods were developed or greatly refined through the tortuous debates of the nineteenth century. But the era's great changes in method and philosophy meant that its scientists were playing a game the rules of which were constantly being revised.

The coral reef problem involved virtually all of these methodological and philosophical issues and difficulties, and its solution taxed all methods then available, both technical and theoretical. On a technical level, the absence of sonar, deep-drilling equipment, or other means of seeing what lay below the ocean's surface left much of the most relevant evidence (most notably the contours of the ocean bottom and the composition of its underlying strata) out of reach. This elusiveness of definitive evidence forced an intense dispute over how to weigh what evidence *could* be observed and how much liberty of imagination to allow in the absence of more data.

That these were precisely the questions considered most vital to science is one reason the coral reef problem grew so intractable. The other reason, especially cogent for Alexander Agassiz, was that the problem involved the legacy of Charles Darwin. Darwin, of course, had not merely unseated Alexander's father from the pinnacle of American science; he was the single most controversial and influential figure in nineteenth-century science. And as it happened, the prevailing theory of coral reefs throughout the mid-1800s had been published by Darwin in 1836, only a few months after the twenty-six-year-old naturalist returned from his five-year *Beagle* voyage, twenty-three years before the *Origin of Species,* and a year after Alexander was born.

Like his later theory of evolution, Darwin's theory of coral reefs imaginatively explained an array of forms with a vision of incremental change through time. Unlike his evolution theory, the coral reef theory was published after Darwin had seen only a modest amount of evidence—in this case, a handful of the world's thousands of reef structures. Its explanatory power soon made it the textbook theory, however, and Darwin quickly moved on to a much more exhaustive research of material for his evolutionary thesis. But in the decades after he published his coral reef theory, the sparseness of the observable data supporting it, along with the accrual of significant contradictory evidence, cast it into doubt.

Alex found himself among the doubters. The sweeping nature of Darwin's theory had unsettled him since the early 1850s, when as a very young man he accompanied his father on a Caribbean trip in which they saw reefs that seemed to defy Darwin's theory. Then, in 1876, three years after his father died, Alex learned of new findings on sea-bottom formation from the freshly completed *Challenger* oceanographic circumnavigation. Talking with the scientists who sailed on that trip, the forty-year-old Alex became convinced that Darwin's coral reef thesis, posed before Darwin had become the cautious and thorough scientist who wrote *Origin,* conflicted not just with the *Challenger's* findings but with most of what had been observed about coral reefs in the forty years since Darwin published his thesis. Meanwhile, Darwin's evolutionary theory, particularly its displacement of Louis's creationist vision of species, had made Darwin a hero of the empirical method. Alex felt Darwin's coral reef theory fell short of the very empiricism he had championed.

For Alex, of course, the entire question was complicated (to put it mildly) by being connected with the man who had all but destroyed his father. That he liked Darwin only made it worse. They had met in 1869, when Alex twice visited Darwin as part of a research trip to Europe. Darwin had by then become a gray eminence of sixty, while Alex was an up-and-coming scientist of twenty-four. At the time, the dispute between Darwin and Alex's father, over a decade old, had cooled enough that Louis could write his son a friendly letter of introduction to Darwin. Alex and Darwin took to each other immediately. They had much in common. They both liked to work alone, away from society. Because Darwin had an inheritance and Alex his copper money, neither had to teach or publish to live comfortably; they could concentrate on science, and they took great pleasure in doing so. More personally, both came from highly accomplished and ambitious fathers who threw long shadows, and both lost their mothers at tender ages—Darwin at eight, Alex at twelve. Both were mentored by adoring and prominent maternal uncles. And in their thirties, both would suffer deeply scarring familial losses. The warmth they discovered in each other was likely amplified for rising amid the ideological and political debate that had pitted Darwin against Louis. Alex left England with an affection for Darwin that heightened his admiration for him as a scientist, and for several years afterward they corresponded amiably.

This mutual regard and respect, and Alex's recognition that Darwin was in many ways the founder of the biology that he and his peers now practiced, made the coral reef question even more troublesome for Alex. In a way, the issue caught him between two fathers, giants of the age, who embodied the polarities of thought and method that all of science was struggling to reconcile. He recognized that, and it tormented him. Yet if anything this bind made him even more careful, exacting, and thorough. He would spend thirty years and a sizable fortune to build a case against the theory he thought Darwin had published too quickly.

Alexander Agassiz's quest has since been forgotten, buried in time, much as the evidence he sought was buried in stone. But the epistemological dilemma he tried to resolve still stands, and Alexander's attempt—his singular position in one of science's last great epistemological debates—reveals much about both an era's greatest questions and the timeless difficulty of squaring our personal legacies with the world's mysteries.

It's an oddity of this story that of its three main figures, Alexander, its most central, is in many ways the least exciting and, on the surface anyway, the least endearing. Alexander was introverted and dour and could be gruff, an intimidating figure. His father, by contrast, was charismatic; and Darwin, though less gregarious than Louis, exuded in his letters and published writings a quiet charm that seemed to magnify his understated genius. Alexander did not possess or even wish for the grandeur of the men whose legacies he tried to unravel. He shared his father's extraordinary powers of memory and work but not his boldness of imagination and character. He could and did work harder than Darwin, and he could grasp as much; but he lacked, perhaps in reaction to his father's excesses of imagination, Darwin's conceptual daring.

It is precisely his lack of the imaginative or inspirational fire we call genius that makes Alexander Agassiz's struggle with the coral reef problem so compelling. Here we see someone distinctly mortal, smarter and more determined than most of us yet still on the same plane, striving to see the world in a way he can trust. Like many of us he must sometimes squint through the fog left by his ancestors. The light shifts and dims. At critical points he must find his way not by the serene conviction of genius but by tenuous instinct and a few tested maxims. And even at his most certain, when the light is most clear, he's not quite sure where he will end up.

Part One

CHAPTER ONE

Magpie

I

THE NAME AGASSIZ, from the southern, Francophone area of what is now Switzerland, means magpie—a bird, of course, but also a person, as *Webster's* puts it, "who chatters noisily." If this did not hang well on the reserved man that Alexander Agassiz would become, it fit his father snug. Louis Agassiz talked as voluminously and engagingly as anyone ever has about science, or for that matter about almost anything. He could mesmerize a room full of scientists, an auditorium flush with factory workers, or a parlor pack of literati, including his salon companions Oliver Wendell Holmes, Ralph Waldo Emerson, and Henry Wadsworth Longfellow, the sharpest talkers in a smart and garrulous town. He was one of those brilliant, babblative sorts whose immense skill in their main work is nearly eclipsed by their gift for talk.

The orative urge can serve teachers well, scientists poorly. Yet if it distracted him from work, Louis's eloquence accounted for much of his renown, throwing a glow around his theories and accomplishments that made them appear more illuminating than they were. His reputation grew much larger than justified by a sober look at his work. In Louis's American prime, from the mid-1840s to the late 1850s, the clerisy considered him the country's supreme scientist and one of its greatest intellectual talents. The public granted him that status even longer, well beyond his death in 1873. When he passed away, the major newspapers carried the news in huge type on their front pages, as if a president had died, and the nation's vice president attended the funeral. The country's top literary figures wrote aggrieved elegies; Oliver Wendell Holmes composed one for the *Atlantic Monthly*, a sort of house organ for Louis, adding to the several Agassiz odes he had already printed there. Even today, though time and Louis's lost battle against Darwin have diminished his reputation, he stands as one of

Louis Agassiz in 1844, during a time when he felt he would realize his ambition and become the world's greatest naturalist

the giants of American science. Of scientists (rather than inventors) working in America, only Albert Einstein ever gained a similar combination of professional respect and public adoration. Yet Louis Agassiz's work never remotely approached the originality, importance, or practical implications of Einstein's. With one exception, his ice age theory, the main theories he promoted fell obsolete, at least among scientists, even before he died. Yet he still stands as a scientific icon.

His fame comes in part from his establishment of the Harvard Museum of Comparative Zoology, a highly productive institution that trained many good scientists and, through example, competition, and direct mentorship, helped spur the development of other leading institutions. This and his ice age work would rightly place Louis Agassiz among the significant figures of American science. But those accomplishments don't explain his exalted status.

How did a man who made few enduring original scientific contributions become a lasting symbol of American science? As his early biographer, Jules Marcou, a French protégé who followed Louis across the Atlantic to work with him for several decades at Harvard, noted, "He was one of those very few men whose works are not sufficient to make him entirely known; one must meet him face to face. . . . Agassiz himself was more interesting than his works."[1] This can read as both praise and damnation, of course, reflecting the ambivalent tone of Marcou's biography. (Marcou's book, published after Louis had died, would enrage Alexander, who tried to have its more critical and personal passages suppressed.) But Marcou knew Louis well. He recognized in him that intangible quality that enables some people to move others to adoration, action, and a permanent change in thinking. Louis Agassiz thrillingly personified a Romantic ideal that combined deep learnedness with avid curiosity—and flattered his followers by emphasizing the latter. Though his own best work rested as much on reading as on observation, he urged his students to "study nature, not books." It was a delicious invitation to a young country in a Romantic era. With his childlike enthusiasm, acute eye, mongoose-quick mind, and charming mispronunciations, Louis sold beautifully the primacy of clear-eyed observation over bookish learning. To an audience eager to claim its own intellectual legitimacy he insisted that vigorous, hands-on study of nature would not only strengthen mind, body, and soul but yield a knowledge greater than any library could hold. It was as if Louis's mentor Georges Cuvier, the learned taxonomist and brilliant lecturer of early-nineteenth-century European science, had fused with Walt Whitman and Teddy Roosevelt.

Was ever another like him? His son, Alex, must have asked himself that, as virtually everyone who knew Louis did at some point. The obvious answer was no. He threw a hell of a shadow.

2

When he was twenty-one, Louis Agassiz wrote his father, "I wish it may be said of Louis Agassiz that he was the first naturalist of his time. . . . I feel within myself the strength of a whole generation to work toward this end, and I will reach it if the means are not wanting."[2]

Even for someone just past twenty, this ambition, particularly its sense of possessing the power of an entire age, is stunning in its confidence, scope, and focus. Yet young Louis had good reason to feel so strong. He was an accomplished, determined, and stupendously energetic prodigy. The son of a pastor, raised near the Jura Mountains in southwestern Switzerland (then a loose collection of cantons under Prussian rule), Louis showed from his earliest days a precocious brilliance. As a boy he spent countless hours hunting, fishing, and gathering bugs, small mammals, and fish, keeping many of the survivors in cages and aquaria at home. (*Magpie* also denotes an obsessive collector.) When he was fifteen, he composed a ten-year plan for himself requiring rigorous collecting and dissection of specimens; wide reading in science, literature, and philosophy; and eventual study at leading natural history institutions in Germany and then Paris before launching his career as a naturalist at twenty-five. He would follow this program with remarkable faith. During his adolescence (which he spent mainly at a boarding school twenty miles from home), he not only carefully classified his finds but studied the logic behind the different classification systems then in use—a concern, as we'll see, central to nineteenth-century zoological studies in general and to Louis's career in particular.

He was prodigious in talk as well. At boarding school he attracted a circle of fellow bright gabbers, and by the time he entered university at fifteen, he hosted a student salon, known as the Little Academy, which convened in his rooms several evenings a week to discuss science, art, and culture. "Agassiz knew everything," recalled a fellow Little Academician. "He was always ready to demonstrate and speak on any subject. If it was a subject he was not familiar with, he would study and rapidly master it; and on the next occasion he would speak in such brilliant terms and with such profound erudition that he was a constant sourse of wonder to us."[3]

When his salon mates went home, Louis would resume studying, then go to bed late. The next day he would rise at six, spend most of the morning working in the lab, fence (at which he excelled), eat lunch, take a walk, study until dinner, and then reconvene his Little Academy and talk till the wee hours. He seemed never to tire (Alex and his friends would later call him "the steam engine"), and he appeared to retain all he heard, read, or saw. Once, asked to identify a fish, he recalled by drawer number a similar specimen he had seen more than a decade before at a natural history museum in Vienna. A subsequent letter verified both the identification and the drawer number.

He possessed a brash confidence that he could generally back up. According to one story (of many he would spawn), Louis, affronted by some perceived slight given his Swiss fencing team by a German team while he was studying in Munich, challenged the German team to a match in which he alone would take on the entire squad, one at a time. The Germans laughingly agreed. Louis dispatched first their best fencer and then their next-best three before the Germans threw in the towel.

He carried this competitive exuberance to friendships. He and his close friend Alexander Braun (who would become both a prominent botanist and Louis's brother-in-law) once became so caught up in a conversation about fencing that they took up rapiers and sparred without thinking to put on their masks. They did not stop until Louis, the quicker of the two, had slashed his friend's face.

He pursued education and career with similar zeal. His self-designed program ran into trouble early in his college years, when his parents made it clear they expected him to be a physician. He solved the problem (and retained his family's financial support) by executing both his own and his parents' plans, earning a medical degree even as he followed his own agenda by studying natural history in Lausanne, Zurich, Heidelberg, Vienna, and Munich. He took both degrees in early 1830, at the age of twenty-two. Then he returned home for a few months to finish his first book, a catalog of fish, and planned the next stage of his campaign: Paris.

Louis's ambitions had included Paris from the beginning, for Paris was then Europe's most important center of natural history study, outranking both London and Munich. At its heart was the Muséum d'Histoire Naturelle, the largest and most prestigious institution in natural science, where Jean-Baptiste Lamarck and Georges

Cuvier headed an illustrious and rivalrous staff. Their primary preoccupation was identifying, dissecting, and cataloging the many biological specimens of living and extinct species being sent to the museum from around the world. This discipline of classification, also known as taxonomy, had been essentially founded a century before, when the Swede Carolus Linnaeus roughed out the classification hierarchy of kingdom, class, order, genus, and species (phylum and family were added later) that has served so well and flexibly ever since. Linnaeus also invented binomial nomenclature, by which each species is known by its genus and species names (*Homo sapiens, Falco peregrinus*).

Linnaeus's system furnished a treelike organization in which to place new species. But it did not settle how many branches that tree should have at each level or how to decide on which branch a new species should reside. Those questions remained open, and the many scientific expeditions sent around the globe in the eighteenth and early nineteenth centuries had quickened the debate on how to answer them. Explorers were discovering species at an unprecedented rate, and the emerging science of paleontology was complicating things further. You had to figure out where to place not just an iguana but an iguanodon, a pterodactyl, and a platypus. You had to define categories broad enough to accommodate these species but narrow enough to be meaningful. What physical differences should divide categories at the most basic levels? How heavily should structural considerations weigh versus physiological? Was a crab, for instance, more like a spider or a starfish? A starfish more like a crab or an anemone?

Underlying these questions, and giving taxonomy the air of grand endeavor, was the sense that the discipline was not merely distinguishing among creatures but limning the order of God's work. Taxonomy rose mainly from the practical need to identify all the species being discovered. But its emergence offered a great theological and political convenience, for it came at a time when those in Western science—funded and conducted largely by institutions and people who were either pious or under pressure to seem so—were glad to find a way to reinforce Judeo-Christian tenets. Discoveries about the earth's age, like Copernicus's and Galileo's work two centuries before regarding our place in the universe, had forced a looser, more metaphorical interpretation of the Bible's account of creation, making science once again seem a doubter of religion. Geological findings made it clear the earth was older than the Bible said it was, and the fossil record seemed to contradict the story of Noah's flood. Although these discoveries didn't turn Christian dogma upside down the way Copernicus's work did and Darwin's would, they forced a reworking of the biblical version of creation, a process that discomfited many and threatened some.

By placing all life into a systematic structure, however, taxonomy could glorify God by showing the order of his work. The binomial system did this beautifully, for its bifurcating-branch system graphically brought all life-forms back to the same tree trunk. This organizational scheme need not be theistic, of course; the same taxonomic system later readily described a nature created by evolution. But the tree of life described by Linnaean taxonomy could be easily offered and accepted as the work of God. Who or what else could create an array so marvelously complex and interconnected? Taxonomy allowed naturalists to elaborate rather than undermine the notion of a world made by a single, omnipotent Creator.

All this, along with the many new species being discovered, made taxonomy one of the most exciting disciplines in all of science. And Paris was the center of the taxonomic world, with Cuvier, Lamarck, Etienne Geoffroy Saint-Hilaire, and other taxonomists competing ferociously to parse God's order. Cuvier had claimed the greatest renown among them through a combination of strong science, shrewd politicking, and bold showmanship. He had fundamentally transformed taxonomy by rejecting the notion of an animal kingdom that merely ranged from the simple to the complex and dividing it instead into four broad categories that he called "embranchments": vertebrates, radiates, mollusks, and articulates. These same categories, which today we know as phyla, have (with about thirty additional phyla discovered since Cuvier's time) headed the animal-kingdom framework ever since. This innovation created a far more logical and useful classification of the animal kingdom. In addition, Cuvier's 1812 *Recherches sur les ossements fossiles des quadrupèdes* pioneered the science of paleontology and the classification of fossils. Cuvier even claimed to have developed a system, which he called the "correlation of parts," for extrapolating an animal's entire anatomy from almost any bone. Presented with just one bone from a newly discovered skeleton, he would wow audiences by predicting the structure of the remainder. He once did this with a fossilized opossum embedded in rock, successfully predicting, from what he could see of a tiny portion of the skeleton, that it would be an animal of the marsupial family.

Early in his career, Cuvier invented the term "balance of nature," a coinage reflecting his belief that every piece of nature had a traceable link to every other. "Nature makes no jumps," he wrote in one of his early papers, a 1790 *Journal d'Histoire naturelle* article about wood lice. He was essentially quoting Aristotle, but the idea served his purposes well. A wood louse was related to a snail and a whale, and if you worked long enough, you could trace the links.

This connected-web idea rose from Cuvier's flirtation with the concept of a "chain of being" that connected all entities—animal, mineral, vegetable—in a single, unbroken sequence of related forms. This idea was central to the Romantic school of philosophy and science known as *Naturphilosophie*. Cuvier signed on to the chain-of-being idea for a time, then distanced himself from it because it played into the hands of pre-Darwin evolutionists, including his colleagues and rivals Lamarck and Geoffroy, and because he felt growing unease with anything that seemed conjectural. Soon after dropping the chain-of-being idea, in fact, he forswore any notion that seemed speculative or even explicitly theoretical. Instead he put his faith in a presumably clear-eyed empiricism, in what could be actually seen or otherwise observed. From then on he would subscribe to facts alone, recognizing only what order he could discern from ostensibly disinterested, assumption-free observation and description. "We know how to limit ourselves to describing," he said, ignoring that in categorizing species he was imposing distinct ideas about how the world was organized. His supposed humility—his assertion that humans should not offer ideas about how God worked but should merely describe that work—hid the arrogance of his presumption that he could discern that work's precise nature. He would have said the definition of a given species or other taxonomic category was not *his* idea but God's; he just happened to be able to see it.

He had little doubt that he could see this order far better than could anyone else. He argued ferociously with Lamarck and others about how to divide the animal kingdom, usually prevailing (even though he was actually the weaker taxonomist in areas outside his beloved fish) because of his extensive publications and, more important, because his system of embranchments (or phyla) and his insistence on identifying specimens through dissection rather than external features were such useful tools for organizing the animal world. His taxonomic theory flourished and survived, of course, the same way a successful species does, through adaptability. Yet in Cuvier's eyes his theory of biological organization, particularly the identification of embranchments, rose not from an idea but as the simple product of accurate observation: He did not invent the branches of the animal kingdom; he merely recognized them. Taxonomy—the description of the categories as well as the placement of species within them—was strictly empirical. The good scientist was content to see what things were, not to pose ideas about how they worked. Never mind that the notion of empirical truth was a pretty audacious idea itself.

3

Cuvier's ambitious taxonomy, his certitude regarding his work and its significance, and his pinnacled status all appealed immensely to Louis. His example must have seemed replicable, for he was very much like Louis: the impeccable memory, the sharp eye and quick mind, the boundless ambition, the flair for the dramatic. They even shared the same taxonomic passion, cataloging fish.

Louis had decided early on that Cuvier was the only biologist who could complete his education. While still in Munich, Louis had begun cataloging a collection of fishes that one of his professors had brought back from Brazil, and he corresponded with Cuvier about them, seeking and getting guidance. Cuvier, as Louis well knew, was then cataloging all the known fish on the *planet*. He was glad to make Louis's acquaintance. Louis worked hard on the book and did a solid job. When he finished it he sent Cuvier a copy with a humble note—and the book's dedication page devoted to the master. Cuvier sucked in the bait. When Louis later wrote to say he wanted to come to Paris and to catalog the fossil fish of central Europe, Cuvier invited him to visit. Louis was quite excited. He saw the invitation as the beginning of something grand. Then, shortly before arriving, Louis heard that Cuvier had recently started work on some piscine paleontology of his own, cataloging all the fossil fishes of the world. (Like Louis, Cuvier rarely planned small.) Louis began worrying that his own work might be overrun by Cuvier's, and when Cuvier received him politely but guardedly, not as an equal, Louis was at first disappointed.

Still, Cuvier was receptive enough, giving Louis lab space and access to some of the Muséum d'Histoire Naturelle's samples. Louis, determined to make the best of it, put in fifteen-hour days, quitting only when the light failed. He worked so hard that he regularly dreamed about fossil fish. In one case he dreamed three nights running of a fish that he was trying to extract from its encasing stone. On the third night, seeing its full form, he awoke and drew it. When he finished extracting the fish that day at the lab, he found it looked exactly as in his sketch. He had in his sleep performed a Cuvierian correlation of parts.

Cuvier, perceiving in Agassiz a rare acuity and power, soon granted him complete access to the museum's fossil collections and asked other Paris curators to do the same. He began inviting Louis to his home for Saturday-night salons, then weekday dinners. He showed him the ropes of professional Paris, encouraged and praised him, even recommended him and his coming fossil fish monograph to the Académie des Sciences, a virtual guarantee of prominent publication. Most significant, Cuvier passed to him his project cataloging all known fossil fishes—and not, as Louis had feared, in the role of underling coauthor but as lead researcher and author. Cuvier too gained from this gift, for with much of a museum to run, other taxonomy and paleontology work waiting, and a project under way to describe the geology around Paris, he was badly overextended. Nonetheless, the gesture carried incalculable value. It erased the potential conflict between Louis's European project and Cuvier's global project, so Louis would not have to choose between subjugating his work to the master's or offending him (and risking obscurity) by offering a competing work. And it represented a show of faith and even affection, for fossil fish were among the subjects closest to Cuvier's heart.

Cuvier took on many protégés, for he always had more projects than he could handle. (Louis would later imitate him in this as in many things.) But the fossil fish project, along with all the time the two spent together, made it clear that Louis Agassiz was Cuvier's brightest young star, the golden boy who matched the master's powers. It seemed almost as if Cuvier was preparing him as successor. He introduced him to Paris's scientific and cultural elite, taught him taxonomy, showed him how to manage a large museum and, by example, how to cultivate and wield influence and authority.

One such demonstration, a formative experience for Louis, was a debate that Cuvier was conducting with Etienne Geoffroy Saint-Hilaire, the museum's professor of vertebrate zoology and another leading taxonomist, over the nature and relationships of the animal kingdom's organization. While Cuvier divided the animal kingdom into different embranchments distinguished by mutually exclusive "ground types," Geoffroy insisted that all animals were variations on one essential form. This idea had philosophical underpinnings in the chain-of-being theory, which, ironically, Geoffroy had learned first from Cuvier, and, more deeply, from *Naturphilosophie,* which held that all life-forms were variations on a few essential archetypes. Geoffroy, as his late colleague and mentor Lamarck had before him, now explained those variations as the results of some sort of evolutionary force that moved them away from the original archetype and argued that their common heritage gave them a "unity of composition" (that is, fundamental likenesses).

It was a nice tautology, completely untestable, and exactly the sort of speculation Cuvier despised. The notion of evolving species also clashed with Cuvier's creationist conviction that the earth's creatures were God's work. Geoffroy and Cuvier debated the issue tirelessly. By the time Agassiz witnessed their final rounds, they had been hammering at each other for a quarter century. Twenty-five years before, in 1807, Geoffroy had seemed to disprove Cuvier by showing an essential skeletal similarity between the forelimbs of terrestrial vertebrates and the pectoral fins of fish. Cuvier countered by finding in fish the apparently unique structure of the operculum, a bony flap covering the gills. This set Geoffroy back a spell. But after considerable work (ten years of comparative anatomy) he was able to draw a plausible connection between this supposedly unique operculum and several mammalian auditory bones, thus reasserting unity of composition. Along the way, the two managed to embarrass each other many times. Geoffroy, for instance, once caught Cuvier misclassifying a certain reptile fossil as a close crocodile relative, while Cuvier had great fun ridiculing Geoffroy's assertion that anemones and mollusks rose from the same basic form as vertebrates.

The two were now trading jabs through alternating lectures at the Académie des Sciences and the Collège de France. In the face of Cuvier's repeated attacks on the speculative nature of his arguments, Geoffroy seemed to be losing the larger arguments about both taxonomy and evolution, and for good reason. Cuvier's notion of embranchments simply seemed to make more sense, particularly in its division of vertebrates from other animals. Anemones and centipedes, after all, strike anyone as different from squirrels and birds. And while evolutionary theory would eventually displace Cuvier's notion of fixed species, Geoffroy, like all pre-Darwinian evolutionists, could offer no plausible explanation of how evolution occurred. He could only point to results. He had a body—piles of bodies—but no smoking gun. He failed to make a solid case for evolution because he could not identify a process by which it worked. With no dynamic to point to, he lost to the prevailing explanation: Animals were the way they were—variations, similarities, and all—because God made them that way. So Cuvier won, at least for a time.

For Agassiz, who had found the chain-of-being idea attractive while in Munich (his friend Alexander Braun would sign on permanently), the Cuvier-Geoffroy feud revealed how readily an empirically based argument could triumph over abstract theory. This did not mean that empirical arguments lacked grand meaning, at least in taxonomy, for there was significance aplenty in delineating God's order. Rather it meant that any claim to a large idea, such as the existence of embranchments, should rest on a wealth of tangible, observed evidence showing the idea's close, demonstrable correspondence to physical reality. If it did, it would beat speculation about hidden dynamics every time.

4

Cuvier's example confirmed most of Louis's prejudices and ambitions. The rewards of being "first naturalist" seemed great indeed. Cuvier, a baron by now, enjoyed numerous commissions, titles, and positions, abundant income, and enormous influence. He consumed heartily (his nickname, "the Mammoth," referred to more than just paleontological interest) and had the world at his feet. Temperamental and impatient, he was said to hold an enlightened despotism as his own political ideal. Yet he knew when to take a knee. When Napoléon rose to power in 1804, Cuvier seamlessly transferred his allegiance to this new ruler, tempering certain religious views accordingly. He did the same when the monarchy replaced Napoléon in 1814 and then a third time when the 1830 revolution deposed the crown. "What servility and baseness has not been shown toward those in power by M. Cuvier!" wrote Stendhal. But it worked. Over the first three decades of the 1800s, no scientist lived better or wielded more clout. He not only stood atop the scientific establishment but held an influential position as a councillor of state (a combination advisor and judge) in France's administrative judicial system. Cuvier loved it. He exercised his authority with a largesse and ruthlessness that reflected back to him, in both the gratitude of those he helped and the pain of those he hurt, the scope of his own power.

Louis seemed to absorb, as a healthy thing, Cuvier's entire example. Holding his own in conversation with the city's most prominent scientists and citizens, eating beyond his means, standing alongside Cuvier at the pinnacle of Paris's social and scientific worlds, he enjoyed the heady feel of extreme prominence. Here was a model to emulate: an intellectual stance that combined painstaking rigor with a view of the big picture, and a position of power and influence that provided the space, money, materials, and assistance his ambitions demanded.

He was still soaking it up when Cuvier suddenly died of cholera in May 1832. Louis had known him just six months. The relationship ended when it was at its most exciting, expansive, infatuated stage. But rather than fall to earth, Louis would self-consciously continue along that exhilarating arc of encouragement and possibility. Cuvier had confirmed Louis's opinion of himself as his generation's greatest talent, and Louis saw no need to seek a second opinion. While he accepted the friendship and guidance of Alexander von Humboldt for a few months after Cuvier's death, he would never meet another scientist he considered his superior. The torch had been passed. Louis, feeling born to the job, gladly took it in hand.

CHAPTER TWO

Neuchâtel

Alexander Agassiz at age twelve,
from a drawing by his mother

I

A LEXANDER AGASSIZ first appeared in a scientific work at age four, when a pen-and-ink drawing of him fishing graced the cover of a volume in his father's series about central European freshwater fish, *Histoire naturelle des poissons d'eau douce de l'Europe central.* The illustration was executed by Joseph Dinkel, an artist who worked faithfully and effectively for Louis for more than fifteen years, adding much to Louis's reputation; his kind disposition also made him beloved company to young Alex. It's a happy picture, suggesting, as Louis surely recognized, a creative, independent life integrating aesthetic, physical, and intellectual pleasures with family and work. Louis's letters make it clear that he believed he had created such a life. But as is so often the case with the family pictures we choose to share, Dinkel's drawing reflected Louis's most flattering self-conception. Events would prove this bucolic happiness illusory. Covering as it does a work whose authorship was contested and whose production strained Louis's home life, the picture subverts its own imagery. And the fishing child, this embodiment of innocence and curiosity, would soon find himself cast on inhospitable shores.

2

Most of Louis's preeminent biographers—people like Jules Marcou, who knew him well personally, and Edward Lurie, who researched him exhaustively—mark Cuvier's death as a great loss in Louis Agassiz's career, for it removed at a critical time the one figure who might have taught him to discipline his energies and restrain his wilder theoretical impulses, things both Louis's father and Humboldt tried but failed to teach him. While the insight seems accurate, one wonders, given the effusiveness of Louis's energies, compulsions, and narcissism, if even Cuvier could have curbed him.

It seems safe to say, however, that at least Louis's earlier career might have gone differently. Had Cuvier lived longer, he probably would have helped Louis secure a position in Paris, where he might have risen to replace Cuvier as a leader of European science, not to mention salon life. As it was, the weeks after Cuvier's death found Louis in a Paris packed with ambitious prodigies. His only offer was an invitation from Cuvier's publisher to work with Achille Valenciennes, another Cuvier protégé, to complete the master's immense fish-classification project. Louis passed, for he was not eager to collaborate on anything when he had Cuvier's fossil fish project all to himself. (The sheer size of the Valenciennes project may have daunted him too. It would grow to twenty-two volumes, and Valenciennes would die thirty-three years later not having completed it.) Collaboration was not to be Louis's style. What he wanted were protégés of his own.

As Louis's luck would have it, his mother soon relayed word of a new college and museum of natural history being formed in Neuchâtel, a small city near his hometown of Môtier. Aided by an introduction from Humboldt and an artful letter of his own hinting at pressing offers in Paris, he won the directorship of the museum and the college's natural history curricula. His position would be funded partly by the Prussian king and partly by contributions from the town's aristocracy, who had been rallied by Louis's uncle, François Mayor.

So in September 1832 Louis Agassiz, twenty-five years old, returned home having realized many of his early academic and professional goals. He eagerly took up his new duties. He found he could give brilliant lectures with minimal preparation. This left him more time for writing *Poissons fossiles,* the study Cuvier had passed him, and to establish a natural history society into which he invited many of the town's leading citizens—an astute move in generating more excitement about his presence. He also organized children's outings and evening lectures for the public at the museum, making it a vital and exciting new civic institution.

In the relatively small arena of Neuchâtel—a regional market center of around six thousand people—this brilliant young professor instantly stood out; if he wasn't yet first naturalist of Europe, he certainly was of Neuchâtel. Agassiz enjoyed this experience so much that he turned down an offer, only a few weeks into his new job, to take a professorship at the University of Heidelberg, a more prestigious institution where he had been a student six years earlier. He realized he liked starting things. Besides, he and Neuchâtel were infatuated with each other. Louis had charmed the town's financial and civic leaders, and for the time he felt he could get anything he wanted. Few could engender enthusiasm for the future as readily as Louis Agassiz did, and few enjoyed being adored more than he.

He had been working a more personal charm for several years on Cécile Braun, the sister of his old classmate and fencing partner Alexander Braun. He'd fallen for Cécile while a guest at the Braun house, in Carlsruhe, Germany, when he and Alexander were studying in nearby Heidelberg. Having grown closer on subsequent visits over the years, the two had been waiting only for Louis to find stable employment to marry. The time had come.

Their engagement initially raised mixed emotions in Cécile's family. Alexander Braun, who had spent several years around Louis, recognized that while he was generous, affectionate, and rarely short on cheer, he also held an inflated view of himself and what he could take on, traits that could overwhelm a spouse, particularly one as gentle and shy as Cécile. Yet Braun, succumbing to the charm to which no one seemed immune and impressed by Louis's rise in Paris, swallowed those worries, and in the fall of 1832 he and his parents endorsed the engagement. The couple married a year later in Carlsruhe, and Cécile joined Louis in Neuchâtel.

Their prospects seemed good. Though Louis earned only a free apartment, board, and the equivalent of around four hundred dollars a year (about eight thousand dollars today), his potential seemed unlimited. Both his and Cécile's families and the town's leaders seemed to share his ambitions for himself and the new museum. In a pattern that would hold throughout his life, his optimism and the proven generosity of others made him confident that he could raise any necessary resources. Both his own family and his mentors, including Cuvier and Humboldt, had already thrown money his way when he ran short of funds to pay the artist Dinkel or obtain specimens. He kept making big plans and, through a combination of hard work, good luck, and charm, realizing them; he thus convinced himself and others that he could execute ever larger plans.

His home life held similar promise. In Cécile, Louis had found a woman and a family that broadened his world both culturally and financially. Cécile, raised in a cultured upper-middle-class family, had experience in music, art, and literature that Louis coveted. He was enchanted by her home in Carlsruhe, a large house with spacious grounds where an afternoon might be spent studying botanical specimens from the nearby oak forest and the evening singing four-part Bach chorales. Cécile's talent as an artist enthralled him. In an early bonding experience, he sat (one must guess cheerfully) while she drew his portrait. And though he already employed Dinkel to draw his specimens, that work expanded with every new research or publishing project. The idea of Cécile's helping with specimen illustration excited them both and gave them a sense of joint endeavor. It hurt not a whit that her family had money.

Alexander von Humboldt, one of the few people Louis looked up to, approved. In a letter congratulating Louis on his engagement, he wrote, "It is not enough to be praised and recognized as a great and profound naturalist; to this one must add domestic happiness as well." In the same note he gave Louis a prod, by way of positive reinforcement, to curb his megalomania: "It is a pleasure to watch the growing renown of those who are dear to us; and who should merit success more than you, whose elevation of character is proof against the temptations of literary self-love?"[1] If there was a hint and a warning in that compliment, Louis seemed to miss it.

3

Over the next decade or so, amid the distractions of running a curriculum and establishing a new museum, Louis Agassiz performed the best and most substantial scientific work of his career, making major contributions with his fish fossil study and then his famous ice age theory.

Louis worked hard on *Poissons fossiles,* the taxonomic survey of fossil fish he published in five installments beginning in 1833. Having mastered the collections in Paris, Munich, and Heidelberg, he traveled Europe examining those elsewhere, a tour that gave him a comprehensive knowledge of virtually all known fossil fish and the museums that housed them—and let him impress everyone with his sharp eye, quick mind, flawless memory, and tremendous gift for talk. These travels created keen anticipation for the book.

The first volume seemed to confirm these expectations. Louis's descriptions and classifications, illustrated with Dinkel's exquisite drawings, beautifully realized the taxonomist's task. And if the book's gentle insistence that this order contradicted any notions of evolution seems archaic today, it did not then; rather, the work's synthesis of taxonomy, comparative anatomy, and paleontology added weight to Louis's assertion that the evidence he had gathered, with significant gaps between seemingly similar species, showed that "species do not pass insensibly one into another" but "appear and disappear unexpectedly, without direct relations with their precursors."[2] The project met warm reception in all quarters. Adam Sedgwick, a leading geologist and a vital early mentor to Charles Darwin, would write Charles Lyell, the world's most prominent geologist, that he thought *Poissons* "by far the most important work now on hand in the geological field."[3]* Lyell, whose *Principles of Geology* was causing a reevaluation of geological history contrary to Agassiz's view, also praised the work, saying that Agassiz's "knowledge of natural history surprises me the more I know of him."[4]

Poissons, emerging over the following decade, made a strange document. Despite its taxonomic breadth and descriptive acuity, Agassiz's use of a taxonomic shortcut—he categorized fish using the external features and scales, rather than by the more laborious but exacting method of comparing their internal anatomy—somewhat compromised the long-term value of the classifications. But if its taxonomy did not hold up as well as Cuvier's, the book greatly advanced fish paleontology. The work's essay portions, meanwhile, used an early version of the circular creationist argument that Louis would later stick to so ferociously, an argument that, despite his professed allegiance to a strict inductivism, climbs far out on a speculative limb. Like any decent scientist or curious human, Louis could not resist seeking patterns in what he saw. And like Cuvier, he believed the taxonomic evidence showed no sign of transmutation and proved that species "changed" only by a series of mass extinctions and subsequent re-creations—a sort of global delete-and-replace pattern left by a God who revised his own work.

This vision raised an obvious and troubling question: What did God use for these waves of extinction and creation? Noah's flood could account for only one such revision (and hardly explained fish extinctions), and the fossil record showed at least several successions of similar species. This suggested either a continuous evolution-like progression or (if you were inclined to see waves of extinction and re-creation) at least several massive, worldwide revisions. If you wanted

* Sedgwick was not uniformly impressed, however. In the same letter in which he praised *Poissons,* he complained that Louis sometimes speculated too freely:

> Agassiz joined us at Dublin, and read a long paper to our section [the geological division of a conference]. But what think you? Instead of teaching us what we wanted to know, and giving us of the overflowing of his abundant ichthyologic wealth, he read a long, stupid, hypothetical dissertation on geology, drawn from the depths of his ignorance. . . . I hope we shall, before long, be able to get this moonshine out of his head, or at least prevent him from publishing it.

Adam Sedgwick to Charles Lyell, 20 Sept. 1835, *Life and Letters of Sedgwick,* vol. 1 (Cambridge, 1890), p. 44, as quoted in Jules Marcou, *Life, Letters, and Works of Louis Agassiz* (New York: Woodworth, 1915).

to buttress creationism with science, as Agassiz did, you had to come up with more than just a single catastrophe.

Agassiz soon stumbled on what seemed a likely answer. In one of his greatest contributions, he pioneered the idea of the ice age, expanding it from glacial studies in the Alps and receiving primary credit (albeit disputed) for a concept that would explain a huge range of phenomena. His development of the theory also showed a penchant for drama and controversy that would emerge repeatedly thereafter.

In the summer of 1836, Johann de Charpentier, a mining engineer and amateur geologist who ran a salt mine in the Rhône Valley, invited Louis to vacation at his house in nearby Vaud. He said he had some geology he wanted to show him. Louis had heard about Charpentier's odd ideas: that the grinding action of glaciers was responsible for turning the Alps and surrounding areas into such grooved terrain, and that glaciers also created the landscape features that we now know as glacial moraines and erratics, the fields of detritus and huge boulders, respectively, that in many areas seem to have fallen from the sky, so detached are they from any likely point of origin. Charpentier had been introduced to this theory in 1829 by a younger colleague, Ignace Venetz, who had first heard it in 1820 from a chamois-hunter named Jean-Pierre Parraudin; Parraudin had hit upon a rough glacial-age theory as the answer to why so many boulders sat perched on hilltops. Charpentier had resisted this notion when Parraudin pitched it to him years before, but he converted when Venetz, having taken it up, elaborated it convincingly at a lecture Charpentier attended. In his subsequent walks around the Alps he became utterly convinced that glaciers had once covered most of the Alps, carving deep valleys and leaving boulders and moraines strewn about. Over the early 1830s he expounded the idea as widely as he could in talks and meetings.

In a series of hikes that summer of 1836, Charpentier slowly sold the idea to Louis, who was also initially quite skeptical. Agassiz slowly overruled his reservations because, as many would experience in the years ahead, the glacial theory provided convincing explanations—a shock of recognition and clarity—for numerous landscape phenomena. It radically altered one's view of the earth. Striated and polished rocks, boulders left in strange places, gravel ridges, block-shaped depressions, and countless other oddities all suddenly made sense. The ice age was one of those ideas that make everything fall into place and let you see things you hadn't seen before. In that sense, it met the standard we generally apply today for a useful theory: It provided the most plausible explanation for a breadth of data.

As Charpentier showed him around, Louis found the theory increasingly attractive, and when he got back to Neuchâtel he pondered it excitedly. Glaciers, he realized, could explain not only scratched rocks, erratic boulders, and kettles (the depressions where ice blocks had melted), but the question of how God cleaned house and rebuilt. They were "God's great plough," as he would put it in his lectures, a biological eraser as effective as any flood, and their repeated, massive occurrences in successive ice ages (the term *Eiszeit* was coined by his friend and colleague Karl Schimper as they discussed what Agassiz had seen) explained the gaps that he and other paleontologists had found in the fossil record. In these ice ages, he theorized, glaciers covered not just the mountains but all of temperate earth in huge sheets, reshaping the land and extinguishing almost all life.

It was a brilliant insight, and Agassiz's application of it to the fossil record was inspired. This creative extension would have thrilled Cuvier. It ingeniously reconciled creationism with recent scientific principles such as uniformitarianism (also known as gradualism). First articulated by geologist James Hutton in 1795 and then skillfully deployed by Charles Lyell in his 1830 *Principles of Geology,* uniformitarianism was the argument that natural science must base its theories on forces presently and observably in effect. It was the latest step in science's march toward empiricism—that is, toward theories based on demonstrable ties to observation. Western scientists (or "natural philosophers," as they were called then) had practiced an increasingly self-conscious devotion to empiricism since at least Galileo's time, and empirical principles had been especially boosted in Britain by the philosophy of John Locke in the 1700s. Hutton's uniformitarianism was merely the geological expression of these principles. Just as Newtonian math rationalized physical phenomena in the 1600s and chemistry rose in the 1700s to replace alchemy, the gradualism of the 1800s offered a rational alternative to the prevailing catastrophism, which relied on spectacular, hypothetical, onetime past events to explain the landscape.

This move toward empiricism had repeatedly threatened religious views of the world, for observations sometimes clashed with
theological explanations. Thus Galileo paid dearly for elaborating
Copernicus's observations proving that the earth circled the sun
rather than vice versa. Louis's ice age theory, however, posed no such
threat. Instead, it reconciled gradualism with catastrophism, for it
provided a catastrophe you could observe in action, in small scale, in
every alpine glacier. It therefore seemed to support a central creationist dynamic with evidence drawn from direct observation. In a career
built on reconciling empirical method with creationist vision, the ice
age was Louis Agassiz's first great stroke.

Louis lost no time developing the idea. He immediately began
buttressing it with his own observations and set about making the
theory his. A year after visiting Charpentier, at the July 1837 meeting
of the Swiss Society of Natural History, he gave a talk announcing his
discovery that in a prehistoric ice age a huge sheet of ice had covered
the earth from the North Pole at least as far south as the Mediterranean, and that this accounted for much of Europe's physiognomy.
This lecture significantly extended Charpentier's theory, which
mainly concerned central and western Europe.

Louis began spending most of every summer in the Alps studying glaciers. In his frequent travels around Europe to look at fossil
fish, he took every chance to seek more evidence of glaciation and to
publicize his new ideas about the ice age. His lectures and field trips
fascinated everyone, spreading his reputation spectacularly. (For
Agassiz, a visit and a field trip threw far more influence than any
number of published papers—one reason he talked more than he
published.) After one of his trips to England, the British biologist
Edward Forbes wrote him, "You have made all the geologists glacier-
mad here, and they are turning Great Britain into an ice-house."[5]
Though his ideas met some resistance in Britain because they contradicted Charles Lyell's flood-based theories, Lyell himself as well as
other leading geologists and naturalists soon agreed that Louis's ice
accounted for much of what they saw in the landscape. In a country
thick with geologists, Louis's ice age insights made him one of the
most renowned.

One of his more intriguing triumphs came from applying the ice
age theory to the mystery of the "parallel roads" of Glen Roy. These

"roads," so called because local lore pegged them as ancient trade or hunting paths, consisted of a series of three parallel terraces running along both sides of the Scottish valley of Glen Roy. Each terrace is roughly sixty feet wide and dead level. The highest lies eighty feet above the middle one, which runs about two hundred feet above the lowest. British scientists had been puzzling over them since the 1700s. Given the roads' lack of slope and sand-and-gravel composition, most scientists agreed they were shorelines. But how did lake or seawater reach several hundred feet above the valley floor and almost two thousand feet above sea level? The puzzle drew guesses from all quarters.

Passing judgment on Glen Roy, in fact, had been a rite of passage for British geologists for almost a century. Charles Darwin took his turn in 1838, when he visited it not long after returning from the *Beagle* voyage. "I wandered the mountains in all directions," he wrote Lyell, "and . . . without any exceptions, not even the first volcanic island [he saw on the *Beagle* voyage], the first elevated beach, or the passage of the [Andean] Cordillera, was so interesting to me as this week. It is by far the most remarkable area I ever examined."[6] In the Andes three years before, Darwin had found seashells at eight thousand feet, convincing him that those mountains had risen from the sea, and he had been fascinated ever since with geological uplift and subsidence. Even as he walked Glen Roy, this fascination was leading Darwin to the subsidence theory of coral reef formation that Alexander Agassiz (just three years old at this point) would grapple with years later.

Here at Glen Roy, however, Darwin saw not subsidence but uplift. Specifically, he theorized that the entire valley had once been at or under sea level and that the three sets of terraces were former shores that rimmed a saltwater sea or inlet as the land rose in three subsequent surges. This complemented a larger theory of changing sea levels that Lyell had posited to explain phenomena such as erratic boulders, moraines, and other out-of-place items, and it fit nicely into Darwin's own obsession with rising landforms.

Darwin promptly wrote a ninety-page paper detailing this theory. It was his first paper of length—the first time he'd exercised his theoretical imagination and published the results—and it brought him much satisfaction and recognition. The Royal Society accepted the paper early in 1839 and elected him a fellow a week later. The paper secured his entry, independent of his *Beagle* investigations, into the upper strata of British science.

A year later, Louis Agassiz toured Britain for the third time to examine fish fossils and talk *Eiszeit*. On visiting Glen Roy he declared that it was not a raised seabed but a valley that had been blocked at its ends by ice during an ice age, creating a freshwater lake that left shorelines (the "roads") as it drained in three warming events—somewhat like a filled tub with its plug thrice pulled and replaced. This explanation had roots only marginally less speculative than Darwin's, rising as much from Louis's belief in glaciation as Darwin's did from his belief in uplift. However, Louis cited substantial evidence that Darwin had either underplayed or overlooked—a complete absence of marine fossils, for instance, which Darwin had noted but discounted, and signs of ancient outgoing streams that Darwin had missed.

Louis's better-supported argument triumphed, though only after a debate that burned hot at first and then flared sporadically over the next two decades. The originality of Agassiz's argument impressed everyone immediately, but in Britain it initially convinced only a few. Fortunately for Louis, these few included some of the country's most prominent scientists, such as William Buckland, an Oxford professor and Lyell mentor who wrote two papers supporting Agassiz's view. Others came around more slowly. Lyell and Sedgwick, for example, initially resisted Louis's Glen Roy account even though they generally accepted his ice age theory. But as observations made by other investigators in the subsequent twenty years seemed to support Agassiz's explanation over Darwin's, most of the doubters, including Lyell, came to agree with him about Glen Roy. Darwin eventually did as well.

Louis's insight at Glen Roy accelerated acceptance of his ice age theory. It also greatly distressed Darwin, who watched in agony as his first child, as he once called his Glen Roy theory, stumbled and fell. He suffered less from shame of error than from horror at the realization that he had speculated too freely. An imaginative theorist all his life, Darwin was at this stage still learning to rigorously test his creative ideas. (He was thirty when he published his Glen Roy paper.) His shorter coral reef paper, presented in 1837 to the Geological Society, had met little criticism precisely because he had tested it sharply against the available evidence before publishing. (It helped too that though he had seen only a few coral reefs, few Brits had seen more.) Now he feared that he had grown too bold. He feared in particular that he had too readily dismissed a shortage of supporting evidence, such as the lack of marine fossils at Glen Roy, as a meaningless absence. At a time when he was struggling to test and develop his theory of natural selection—a view he knew would be profoundly controversial—the thought that he was using faulty logic terrified him. He had left himself out on a limb, and Louis Agassiz had sawn it off.[7] What faults might he be overlooking in his nascent evolution theory?

These doubts did not hit Darwin all at once. They accumulated sickeningly over a twenty-year span. For a time, he tried to fend Agassiz off, arguing that while both his seashore theory and Agassiz's glacial-lake theory had problems, his had fewer. But as most scientists moved to Agassiz's view, Darwin slowly let go of his theory. After two decades he finally surrendered completely when a comprehensive review by the respected geologist Thomas Jamieson found for Agassiz. Even then, he wrote Lyell, he was pained: "I am smashed to atoms about Glen Roy. . . . My paper was one long gigantic blunder. Eheu! Eheu!"[8]

Years before, however, he had surrendered to Agassiz on the larger point of glaciation, and as often occurs, the defeat taught more to the loser than the winner. In 1842, at the time Louis was turning England into an ice house, Darwin had undergone a sort of *Eiszeit* conversion when he took a long walk in Wales and, in an area he had walked a decade before with Adam Sedgwick, saw signs of glaciation everywhere. He was stunned that he could have missed them before. "Eleven years ago I spent a whole day in [this] valley," he wrote a friend, "where yesterday everything but the ice of the glacier was palpably clear to me, and then I saw nothing but plain water and bare rock."[9] As he later recalled in his autobiography, "Neither [Sedgwick nor I] saw a trace of the wonderful glacial phenomena around us [on the earlier trip]; we did not notice the plainly scored rocks, the perched boulders, the lateral and terminal moraines. Yet these phenomena are so conspicuous that . . . a house burned down by fire did not tell its story more plainly than did this valley."[10]

Thus Louis's glacial theories brought Darwin an epiphany on one hand and, several years later, humiliation on the other. These were the first in a strange, irony-laced series of encounters between the minds and legacies of these two men, and their reactions to these early clashes are revealing. For Darwin, the explanatory power of Louis's larger glacier theory, witnessed so starkly on his Wales walk, confirmed a vital lesson: Productive observation actually rises from sound theory—not the opposite, as Louis would assert. A mere idea could transform the world, making palpable features and dynamics previously hidden. Later, Darwin's long, slow defeat on Glen Roy led him to test his theories more rigorously and hold himself to a higher level of proof. This lesson, added to his habitual caution, doubtless contributed to his twenty-three-year hesitation in publishing his theory of evolution. But both the Glen Roy reversal and the revelations he saw in the *Eiszeit* hypothesis helped Darwin forge the distinctive theoretical approach—imaginative in spawning ideas, rigorous in testing them—that let him develop the evolution theory that would negate much of Louis's work.

Thus Darwin learned both boldness and caution from his encounters with Louis's ice age work. Louis took from Glen Roy an opposite lesson: He felt emboldened to push his speculative theories ever further. At Glen Roy Darwin had stumbled, collected himself, and adjusted his gait. Louis had sprung across a valley and landed safely. He would soon put so much faith in his leaps that even when his support was delusory, he would land and feel solid ground.

4

When he wasn't sorting fish or visualizing glaciers, Louis headed an increasingly busy household. On December 17, 1835, with Louis in the thick of *Poissons,* Cécile gave birth to Alexander Emmanuel Rodolphe Agassiz—the first name coming from Cécile's brother, Rodolphe from Louis's father.*

---

* Alex's actual legal name is uncertain. Alexander Emmanuel Rodolphe Agassiz is the name by which Alex went all his life and under which he immigrated to America and later took citizenship. But late in life he found among old family papers a birth certificate, apparently valid, naming him Alexander Rodolphe Albert Agassiz.

Relatively little from Alex's early years has survived his move to the United States and (later) his own careful tending of family history. Alexander never wrote a memoir, and as an adult he actively sheltered himself and his family from the sort of scrutiny his father had invited. His surviving letters reveal little of his personal history, for while there are many, he destroyed those more intimate. His letterpress letter books have crucial pages razored out, and the papers lack diaries and letters mentioned elsewhere. At some point he (and perhaps his secretary and heirs) did a lot of cleaning up. However, enough descends via his childhood family and its many hangers-on to reveal a child who inherited his father's sharp intelligence and taste for work but who lacked his father's ebullient confidence that all would work out. For Alex, things usually didn't.

Things started well enough. Cécile, a healthy twenty-seven when she bore Alex, was still infatuated with Louis and the life she was establishing with him in Neuchâtel. Though less sophisticated than the Heidelberg area in which she was raised, Neuchâtel, in the heart of Swiss chocolate-, wine-, and clock-making country, was the cultural and market center for the surrounding region of valley farms and vineyards. Across the town's namesake lake stood the Alps; behind it rose the Juras. Like her native Carlsruhe, Neuchâtel was a physically beautiful place, and Cécile likely thought she could re-create there the happiness her parents had at home. Her parents were highly educated and cultured. Her father, the postmaster general of the grand duchy of Baden, was a distinguished amateur geologist who had installed an extensive library, mineral collection, and natural history laboratory in their home, and Cécile had grown up happily with three brothers with whom she explored, read, and sang. A gifted musician and artist, she now found herself married to a prominent young scientist in another small, picturesque city. It remained only to create a convivial mix of family, art, and science.

She began by assuming some of the drawing duties for Louis's *Poissons* and other publications. She had done botanical illustrations for her brother for several years, and as her grandson would later observe, she now brought "an unusual combination of delicacy and vigor" to the illustration of Louis's fish and marine fossils.[11] Decades later, her daughter Ida was looking at some of these original drawings at the British Museum (which had purchased them during one of the many times that Louis needed cash) when the curator who was showing her the drawings remarked, "I noticed that those signed by the artist 'C.A.' are much the most beautiful."[12]

Though Alex's arrival interrupted this work, the baby gave Cécile immense pleasure. By this time she had begun to miss Germany acutely, and her occasional visits there only sharpened the pang. The foreign world she occupied in Neuchâtel, of Swiss sensibility, French language, and full of scientists and students trying to impress her husband, began to seem provincial. She especially missed music. Alex gave her the chance to remedy some of this, for he was hers to form. From his youngest days she taught him drawing, music, and German, determined that he grow up cultured.

Alex, however, also felt a strong pull from his father's world. Collecting small animals thrills most young children; Alex's interest was further focused and fired by Louis's enthusiasm and the growing "scientific factory" he was creating in the house. By the time Alex was born, the Agassizes had moved from the apartment the university gave them into a house that was increasingly devoted to lab and work space. With Louis and his assistants constantly unpacking and working up specimens, the place offered an ever-changing display of oddities that must have fascinated young Alex. He soon became an avid young collector. A cousin later remembered seeing, in a drawer in Alex's wardrobe, a collection of mysterious creatures, plants, and parts thereof, all preserved in small bottles. If a playmate got too near the wardrobe, Alex would cry, "Please don't touch my anatomy!"[13]

The house hosted a rotating cast of intriguing figures. The artist Joseph Dinkel, a warmhearted, thoughtful, and entertaining soul, had lived with the family since before Alex's birth. Like a combination of mother and father but issuing fewer demands, Dinkel shared with Alex the intricate pleasures of both the specimens he was drawing and the drawings themselves. Another artist, Jacques Burkhardt, soon joined the operation and, like Dinkel, befriended Alex and his sisters. (Burkhardt would eventually move with Louis to America.) Alex spent much time with both these men and later attributed his great drawing talent to them as well as to his mother.

This cast expanded as Alex began to study the world in earnest. A secretary, Edward Desor, joined the operation in 1836, and Karl

Schimper, a close college friend of both Louis's and Alexander Braun's, arrived in 1837 to teach at a nearby college and worked frequently with Louis until 1840. Though these men distracted Louis, Alex enjoyed the clear, devoted attention of his mother, so their presence was likely more that of kindly uncles than unwelcome competitors.

This core group included one of the stranger characters in nineteenth-century science, Amanz Gressly. Gressly, a Swiss six years older than Louis, had studied geology and took a special interest in paleontology. When he joined Louis in the mid-1830s, he had just developed what would prove his most lasting scientific contribution, the theory of stratigraphic facies. This was the recognition that most geological strata, or layers, contain within their lateral expanses distinct zones, or facies, that differ according to the environmental conditions present at the times they were formed. One key difference was what sort of fossils each facies contained. This discovery held tremendous value, for it enabled a knowledgeable person like Gressly to match particular communities of fossils with particular facies, greatly aiding the classification and aging of the fossils.

When Gressly, painfully shy, came to Louis with his still unpublished facies paper, Louis saw instantly how much Gressly's knowledge would add to his classification and paleontological work. He promptly published the paper, bought Gressly's specimen collection, and hired him. Gressly would later help engineer many of the alpine train tunnels. But in his years with Agassiz, he was completely absorbed in finding fossils and solving the puzzle of what facies they represented. He seemed to care about nothing else. The man was ever outdoors. Leaving in spring, he would spend months at a time tramping all over the Juras and the Alps, unheard from until he would return one day to empty his numerous, large pockets (he often wore several shirts as well as an overcoat) of the rare and beautiful fossils he had chiseled from the mountains. When traveling he usually lodged with farmers. They learned to receive him gladly, for in the course of dinner he could tell them where to drill a well or find a spring or unearth clay, stone, or gravel. After dinner he would retire to a spare bed, couch, or even the barn. He always slept in his clothes, shoes included. He spent almost nothing. Louis, usually cashless himself, would sometimes scare up a few francs to send Gressly off with, and Gressly would live for months on what others might spend in a week-end. Once, emptying his pockets after a two-month trek, Gressly pulled from the bottom of one pocket, with a surprised exclamation, a few coins Agassiz had given him before his departure—and which in eight weeks he had never thought to pull out and spend. While in Neuchâtel he stayed at a third-rate inn run by the sister of the artist Burkhardt, in a "small bedroom, poorly furnished" as Agassiz's colleague Marcou later put it, "which soon became a true pandemonium of the most sordid kind." This odd wanderer was a great hit with Alex and his sisters. "Like a child, as he was all his life," wrote Marcou, "he played with the children, making cocks and boats and dancing frogs out of pieces of old almanacs or newspapers."[14]

With characters like that around—and with sisters born when he was two and then four—a curious boy like Alex was seldom bored. He also had his formal education to absorb, attending classes at the Neuchâtel *Gymnasium;* studying German, Latin, and French; learning drawing from Dinkel and Burkhardt and his mother; and taking the violin lessons his mother insisted on. He sometimes accompanied his father or his assistants on field outings so that he could fatten his own collections. When he was four, his summers came to include trips to the Aar glacier, where Louis had established the "Hôtel de Neuchâtel," a field camp from which he and his retinue studied glaciers. An early lithograph shows young Alex being ferried up to the camp in a basket atop a guide's back. Through the rest of his life he liked walking, preferring it to any transport save horseback.

This childhood, full of stimulation and entertainment and engaging study, can appear idyllic through the prism of two centuries, our romanticized view of preindustrial Europe, and the filter of family history. But even by the early 1840s the gloss was starting to wear off the Agassizes' life in Neuchâtel. Louis's profligate spending of time, money, and his family's privacy had eroded his marriage. Though opposites may attract, they don't necessarily thrive in the same environment. Cécile, quieter and more private than Louis, resented her husband's absences (for he traveled frequently to examine specimens, lecture, and hobnob) and the constant presence of his retinue. By 1840 she shared their house with at least five people outside the immediate family—artists Dinkel and Burkhardt, secretary Desor, assistant Karl Vogt, and Louis's mother, Rose (for Adolphe had died), who lived there full-time; with many others who stayed for a few nights or weeks; and with a stream of daytime and evening visitors—students, colleagues, admirers. Tired of paying others to print his monographs, Louis had started a publishing company, and that too demanded his attention and (though originally meant to make money) drained funds. Neither her home nor her money, not even her own dinner table, seemed to belong to Cécile. Dinner typically included not only all houseguests but anyone who happened to drop by near mealtime. The table often hosted more than a dozen of Louis's assistants, colleagues, protégés, and admirers, and they frequently stayed late into the evening. Quiet by nature, Cécile could hardly get in a word with her husband, and the talk at her table was what her guests rather than she desired. She particularly despised Edward Desor, Louis's secretary, who she believed took advantage of Louis, pushing him to overextend himself financially and professionally. She also disliked Karl Vogt, who joined Desor at dinner in slinging off-color jokes and antireligious jibes that Cécile (rather devout, and trying to raise three young children) found offensive.

This was not exactly the cultured harmony of music, work, and familial collaboration she had imagined. Her house was a zoo, and she could scarcely get the keeper's attention. She pleaded with Louis to scale back. His mother and brother did likewise. But Louis was not to be reached. He only further expanded his activities, taking on ever more projects and traveling frequently to study or lecture. Summers he was gone altogether, hot on the trail of the ice age.

Louis was in fact now overdrawn professionally, financially, and in the goodwill of friends and colleagues. His love of lecturing and of the big idea had led him to test, in his presentations around Europe, an early version of the "Plan of Creation" lectures he would later give in America—his own elaboration of Cuvierian special creationism. This new focus struck some, especially his new, empirically minded British colleagues, as an unfortunate departure from his more rigorous taxonomy and geology. Lyell was among those who found his creationist vision a stretch. On hearing Agassiz's lecture on the topic, Lyell reportedly told Darwin that he found it "so delightful, that he could not help all the time wishing it was true."[15]

Closer to home, Louis's years of overspending on staff, travel, and the hemorrhaging publishing operation had led him to borrow repeatedly from family (including Cécile's), friends, and his benefac-

tors in town. As his debts mounted high enough for even the infatuated to see, those funds dried up. By 1845 he faced sharp deficits with
no way to pay them.

He had also alienated several friends, assistants, and colleagues
who felt he had used their ideas without proper credit. Most of these
disputes concerned the ice age theory that Agassiz had so successfully
adopted. The first aggrieved party was Karl Schimper, who left
Neuchâtel in a huff in 1840 because he thought Agassiz had inade-
quately acknowledged the contributions (including the term *Eiszeit*)
he had made to the ice age theory in their many long discussions
about it. A year later Agassiz infuriated Charpentier, who had introduced Louis to glacial studies (and hosted him that first summer), by
publishing his major volume on the ice ages a mere few weeks before
Charpentier published his; Charpentier received Louis's published
book as he was reviewing his own final page proofs. Though Louis
acknowledged him in the book, Charpentier was livid that Agassiz
did not grant him the courtesy of first publication. It probably didn't
help that Louis had already claimed the subject as his own in his
many lectures around Europe. Then in 1844 Karl Vogt broke with
Agassiz because he felt Louis wasn't giving him enough credit on
publications Vogt had helped write.*

---

* Some of Louis's admirers stuck with him in the face of astonishing insults and trials; for
them his magnetism apparently matched his boundless self-absorption. This applied even to
those who recognized his faults in general. Humboldt, for instance, who was generous to Agassiz, often warned Louis of the dangers of overextending himself, of "literary self-love," and of
neglecting his home life; yet he overlooked a self-centeredness that led Louis to all but ignore
one of Humboldt's greatest personal losses. Only two years after Humboldt had helped Louis
in Paris and secured him the Neuchâtel job, he wrote Louis a distraught letter telling, in most
affecting terms, of the loss of his brother William:

> I have seen the being I loved most, who alone gave me some interest in this arid
> land, slowly decline. For four long years my brother had suffered . . . [In the end]
> he died . . . with a strength of character and a serenity of mind worthy of the great-
> est admiration. It is cruel to see so noble an intelligence struggle . . . against physi-
> cal destruction. We are told that in great grief we should turn with redoubled
> energy to the study of nature. The advice is easy to give; but for a long time even the
> wish for distraction is wanting.

Louis responded, "I cannot express to you my pleasure in reading your letter. . . . To
know that I have occupied your thoughts a moment, especially in days of trial and sorrow such
as you have had to bear, raises me in my own eyes, and redoubles my hope for the future. And
just now such encouragement is particularly cheering under the difficulties which I meet in
completing my task in England. I have now been here nearly two months. . . ." He continues
with two pages of what he has been up to and hopes to do next, and not another word about
Humboldt or his brother.

Though Cécile was glad to see Vogt leave, it was not enough. In the early spring of 1845, convinced that Louis would not curb his excesses as long as Desor was around to encourage expansionary habits, she told him that either Desor went or she did. Convinced that he couldn't escape his financial jam *without* Desor, Louis refused to fire him. Cécile made good on her threat. She took the girls—leaving ten-year-old Alex in the local academy—and moved to her brother's house in Carlsruhe.

The dissolution of this once burgeoning home can be seen as a sudden explosion of Alex's world, and perhaps in fact he never saw it coming. The accounts that have been passed down through the Agassiz family leave it hard to tell. Yet even the thin, laundered version that has survived shows the residue of great distress. One of the few stories about Alex from the last months his father and mother were together, passed off by his own son George in *Letters and Recollections of Alexander Agassiz* as a boyish prank, evinces a ferocious hostility toward Louis. For in a most spectacular and personally risky way, Alex struck at Louis's most important benefactor.

Neuchâtel's governor at the time served the king of Prussia, who at the behest of Humboldt had funded the Neuchâtel job and to whom Louis had applied, even as things began to unravel in Neuchâtel, for funding for the trip that would take him to the United States. Louis both enjoyed and greatly needed the favor of both king and governor, and he courted the governor at every opportunity.

Alex regarded the governor less fondly, and in an escalation that his own son credits implausibly to politics, he expressed this dislike in a way that badly embarrassed his father. As George relates it, the king's Neuchâtel governor was

> a retired Prussian general, and a martinet who liked to show his authority in the smallest details, [and] was so lacking in the rudiments of humor as to complain to Louis Agassiz that his little son was not saluting him politely, and Alex was punished. Meeting the Governor on the street the next day, the boy saluted him in the most abject possible manner. The Governor complained again, whereupon the elder Agassiz, much incensed, gave his son a sound thrashing. . . . Not content with this, the Governor singled out his diminutive adversary at a

school celebration and held him up for reproof before a large audience.

When it was Alexander's turn to receive his prizes from the Governor, he was so angry that he refused them with scorn, turned his back on the representative of the King, and . . . walked out of the room. This led to further difficulties at home. Infuriated at the Governor's treatment, this youthful patriot collected a band of confederates of his own age, stormed the [Governor's] castle on the night of a large dinner party at which his father was present, and smashed all the windows of the state dining-hall. Louis Agassiz, suspecting the instigator of this outrage, rushed home, but found his son safely in bed and apparently asleep.

He would not sleep there long. When Cécile moved out a few months later, Alex moved from home to a boarding school in Neuchâtel run by a cleric, Frederic Godet. Louis, meanwhile, began dismantling his scientific factory, selling off the publishing operation and its assets and laying off some of his retinue but retaining Desor, Dinkel, and Burkhardt. Within a few weeks Alex got the news that his father had indeed won funding from the king for what was to be a two-year collecting trip throughout North America. Louis's departure dragged on, however, as he had much to clean up before he left—classes to finish, debts to rearrange, publications to complete, and groundwork to lay for what would prove a permanent move to the United States.

Alex watched this long leavetaking from the boarding school. Though placing his son decisively would seem a high priority for a father departing overseas, Alex was still at Godet's in March 1846 when Louis left Neuchâtel for good. It was not until the following school year that Alex joined his mother in Germany. Of the intervening year we know little. He stayed at Godet's boarding school, and he may have traveled a few times to visit his mother and sisters, first in Carlsruhe, then in Freiburg after Cécile moved there to follow her brother, who had taken a post as director of the botanical gardens there. After Cécile and Alex's sisters Ida and Pauline had settled in, Alex finally joined them sometime in the second half of 1847.

CHAPTER THREE

Freiburg

O F T H E Y E A R that Alexander lived in Freiburg, so few facts
survive that it's hard to know what to make of them. Not yet
twelve, he arrived to find his mother living "in most straitened circumstances," as George Agassiz would later put it, in a tiny apartment near the Schwaben Tour, a tower over one of the city gates.

Apparently never robust, Cécile was now ailing. Still, she reportedly loved Freiburg, an extraordinarily charming town that was then
perhaps at its most alluring. "She greatly loved the quaint old walled
cathedral town and its beautiful surroundings," her grandson George
relates from the distance of two generations and an ocean, and
"although now an invalid, she was still able to take short excursions
into the country," where she would draw the flowers brought to her
by her daughters or the beetles, caterpillars, and butterflies captured
by Alex. "The Freiburg winter," he continues, "with its bracing and
sunny air, was an especially happy time for the children. Alexander
now became a proficient skater, an art in which as a young man he
excelled. . . . The boy and his mother spent many happy hours, while
she sat in one of the high-backed sleds of that region, which he skillfully guided through the gay crowd of all ages who glided gracefully
over the ice."

This is hard to credit. Having spent the previous eighteen
months in limbo as his parents parted ways, by all reports sensitive
and prone to melancholy anyway, Alex probably felt something short
of "especially happy" that winter. He did go on botanical outings

with his uncle Alexander and enjoyed consultations with Braun's colleague the zoologist Carl von Siebold, who helped Alex classify his bugs, extracting as a fee an occasional choice beetle. These stimulations, along with being reunited with his mother and sisters, must have lifted Alex's spirits. But the transition from the window-smashing youth to the smiling skater seems forced. Possibly Alex

Cécile Braun Agassiz, from a self-portrait in 1829,
four years before she married Louis

himself held to that memory and passed it down because his skating supplied a pleasure rare in what otherwise must have been a dark winter.

The winter was grim enough to spoil forever his love of music—a significant loss, given his mother's cultivation of his taste for it. His bane that winter, he later recalled, was his violin tutelage. He had never loved to play the instrument, and he took his lessons now in the early morning in a cathedral so cold, he later told his children, that he could scarcely hold his bow. His teacher, perhaps frustrated by Alex's lack of enthusiasm, would correct his worst mistakes by rapping him on the knuckles with his bow.

As spring ripened, Cécile's health worsened. The lethargy and cough of early tuberculosis expanded to the fever and bloody hack of the disease's lethal bloom. The children almost certainly absorbed the bacilli as well, but as is often the case with older children, they remained healthy, though doubtless increasingly frightened. Alex assumed the running of the household, keeping the simple accounts and going to market each day, dutifully continuing his studies and violin practice. But the disease had Cécile. She died that summer of 1848.

Cécile's brother took in Alex and his sisters, and an exchange of letters across the Atlantic soon settled their fates. Louis, busy convincing Harvard to build him a museum, could not come fetch his children. The girls went to live with their aunts in Neuchâtel while Alex stayed in Freiburg with his uncle. What would have become of Alex had his mother lived? Quite possibly he would have stayed in Freiburg, become a naturalist, likely quite prominent, and had a distinguished and perhaps even a brilliant career in Europe.

In spring of 1849, however, Alex's cousin on his father's side, Dr. Charles Mayor, decided to move to the United States, and it was arranged that Alex would meet him in Paris and sail with him from Le Havre to Boston. Though his feelings on leaving Freiburg can only be imagined, his actions as reported by his son George seventy-five years later provide some hint. At the Freiburg train station, he removed his violin from its case, set it on the platform, and smashed it beneath his feet.

CHAPTER FOUR

Cambridge

I

A RRIVING IN New York in June 1849, thirteen-year-old Alexander Agassiz entered a world sharply different from the one he had left. Though Boston, to which Louis immediately took him, resembled European cities more than did most American towns (Louis generously likened it to Paris and London), it remained a far cry from Freiburg. And Alex, shy to start with, knowing hardly a word of English, must have felt the language barrier keenly.

He found his father, however, glowing from his seduction of his new country. For Louis Agassiz had conquered the United States faster and more thoroughly than perhaps any foreigner ever had. He loomed large almost from the instant he arrived, and while he made a sensational impact, it proved lasting, exerting an intellectual and cultural influence well beyond his initial fame and beyond even his death a quarter century later. Much of the initial fervor was created by his brilliance, eloquence, and charm. But his wider, more enduring impact spread not simply because he was irresistible, but because he offered a set of ideas for which his new country was ripe. His reconciliation of Christianity and science stood at the center of this appeal. But equally vital was that his particular marriage of learning and spirit—his elegant synthesis of the scholarly world of facts and ideas with a Whitmanesque sensual attentiveness—suggested a way for his vibrant but insecure adopted nation to establish its intellec-

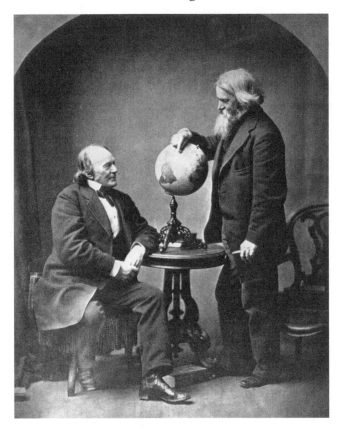

*Louis Agassiz with his friend and ally Benjamin Peirce, the
Harvard mathematician. Peirce is pointing out the location of
Cambridge, Massachusetts, on the globe. In the 1850s, the two men
were unchallenged in the world of American science.*

tual heritage. As a result, his appeal overran bounds of fashion, politics, interest, and time. His contemporary admirers included virtually all of his scientific and intellectual peers, the country's financial and social elite, and cultural luminaries ranging from Henry Wadsworth Longfellow to Henry David Thoreau. Among later generations, his devotees spanned the spectrum from Teddy Roosevelt to Ezra Pound and included virtually every naturalist trained in the United States. These admirers saw in Louis something vitally American. As William James (who traveled to Brazil with Louis as a Harvard undergrad and became friends with Alex) wrote in a moving and insightful tribute almost twenty-five years after Louis's death, no American since Benjamin Franklin had so embodied the country's spirit or captured its imagination.[1]

2

Louis's American renown actually preceded him. The textile magnate and Harvard supporter John Amory Lowell, founder of the Lowell Institute and its already famous lecture series, first heard of Louis in detail in 1842 when Charles Lyell, in Boston to give that year's Lowell Lectures, gushed about Louis's eloquence and agility of mind. Bolstered with that and other recommendations (a composite portrait suggesting a gregarious fusion of Cuvier and Lyell), Lowell invited Louis to give the lectures over the winter of 1846–1847, then excited his many friends in the national press into trumpeting Louis's arrival.

The accolades grew as Louis spent his first month in the United States visiting universities and science centers in New Haven, Albany, New York City, Princeton, Philadelphia, and Washington. He completely seduced the country's intelligentsia. He seemed to know the particulars of almost everything going on in all current natural science and could readily discuss the philosophical questions raised. He showed a flattering curiosity about everyone's work and seemed instantly to grasp the possibilities, problems, and fascinations of every scientific inquiry—and often offered observations that expanded the investigator's horizons. Benjamin Silliman, Jr., a second-generation Yale chemistry professor who knew pretty much everyone in American science, offered a typical effusion after Louis's first visit to New Haven:

> He is full of knowledge on all subjects of science, imparts it in the most graceful and modest manner and has, if possible, more of *bonhomie* than of knowledge. He has a more minute knowledge of his subject and at the same time a more wonderful generalizing power and philosophical tone than any man I have ever met. . . . It is not yet agreed whether the Ladies more liked the *Man* or the Gentlemen the *Philosopher*.[2]

Louis cemented this impression of amiable savant with the Lowell Lecture series he gave beginning that December. By that time the talks were so keenly anticipated that the organizers offered a second lecture most days, and Louis packed the house—some five thousand seats—again and again. The lectures, which he titled "The Plan of Creation in the Animal Kingdom," elaborated Cuvier's vision of nature as divine design, but with a panache that only Louis could bring. In talks rich with facts, oddities, and charming asides, he described how the preceding century's zoological discoveries had revealed a natural order so intricately patterned that only a supreme intelligence could have created it. Some of nature's patterns, he explained, announced themselves—witness the prevalence of symmetry in body type or other major traits shared by closely related species. Other patterns revealed themselves only through close observation—the way developing embryos of advanced species, for instance, seemed to mimic successively the forms of "lower" species, so that a chimpanzee fetus resembled first a fish and then a pig before coming to look something like a chimp. He chose examples so astutely and described them so evocatively that while a textile worker could understand them, the country's most advanced scientists, such as the botanist Asa Gray or Benjamin Silliman, Jr., learned something new.

He described the discovery of unexpected and often beautiful patterns in highly different life-forms, such as spiral structures found in both plants and animals, food-catching tentacles found in sea animals and terrestrial plants, and the radiate patterns found in both flowers and marine invertebrates. About the time he had everyone slack-jawed in wonder, he would provide comic relief by explaining how even the apparent breaks from this pattern—what he called "God's leetle jokes," such as the turtle or the narwhal—fit into the plan. Working without notes, he delivered all this with great animation and humor. When he was stumped for the right word in English (fumbling always oh so endearingly through a few candidates), he would draw on the blackboard, describing as he went.

Such a vast, complicated, highly structured scheme, he said, could only be the work of God. What else could account for such variety of form unified by so many patterns? True, some scientists and philosophers had suggested that some undocumented dynamic called evolution, or transmutation, might play a hand. But evolution was not only unfounded (no one had ever shown how one species could change to another); it was unneeded, for divine design could explain all of nature's wonderful diversity. A species did not emerge from some mysterious transmuting force. It rose, said Louis, as "a thought of God."

Thus Louis Agassiz sold a view of nature that seemed at once enticingly progressive and safely devout. Like the Cuvierian taxonomy from which it sprang, Louis's plan of creation seemed to push science forward without threatening prevailing religious views about the world's genesis. He appeared to resolve the tension between science and religion that had haunted scientists since Copernicus. Here was a rigorous science that not only tolerated belief in God but actually required it.

It was an alluring vision. Louis made it even more so by insisting that the observant amateur could discover these patterns as readily as the learned scholar. "Study nature, not books," he urged his audience, espousing a seductively egalitarian notion of what it takes to master a discipline. Like a music teacher who kindly insists that *feeling* the music is the main thing—never mind all this theory, technique, and note reading—he appealed both to the democratic spirit and to the romantic notion that formal education is less important than enthusiastic application.

Louis's elevation of nature above books ignored the exhaustive formal study underlying his own knowledge. It also clashed with an elitism that showed in his clubbiness and his later development of exclusive scientific societies such as the National Academy of Sciences. Yet it stood in perfect accord with his romanticism. Perhaps because he discovered his love of biology tramping in fields, Louis had long lectured and led field trips not just for advanced students but for dedicated amateurs, especially teachers and children. He insisted that any smart person could become a proficient naturalist. Now, as he lectured before large lay audiences as well as professionals painfully mindful that they lacked the institutional resources that Louis had tapped in Europe, both his message and his manner—his affable approachability; his encouragement of amateurs; even his self-effacing, out-loud search for the right word, as if showing the thinness of his own education—insisted that an elastic mind, a sharp eye, and direct contact with nature ranked as the natural scientist's most vital assets. As his years in America strengthened this belief, it came to imbue every aspect of his teaching. He expressed it most notably in his sink-or-swim introduction to comparative anatomy, in which he would give a new student a strange specimen, usually from the sea, to examine for several days during which the student was to observe everything possible but never consult a book. He sometimes forbade books from dissection rooms altogether. The truth lay not in books or inherited knowledge; it stood before you, a work of God.

For a country eager to claim intellectual parity with Europe but keenly aware that it lacked a comparable intellectual history or institutional infrastructure, these ideas held immeasurable attraction—the more so, of course, for coming from one of Europe's top scientists.

So it was that Louis Agassiz satisfied America's hunger for someone to raise the torch that Franklin and Jefferson had once carried—a learned figure of international stature who was a peer to Europe's best, yet distinctly and unapologetically American in spirit. Strange that a new immigrant should be the one to fill this role. Yet Louis Agassiz's immediate understanding and embrace of America's energy and independence suited him for the task, while his European training ensured credibility.

Louis could thus resolve, as perhaps no one else could (and as enthusiastically as anyone could hope), Americans' mixed feelings regarding European learning. On one hand, as many observers (most famously Alexis de Tocqueville) noted, America in the early 1800s exuded confidence that its homegrown vigor could best European sophistication in any arena, military, political, economic, or cultural. Yet anyone paying attention recognized that America lagged Europe horribly in scholarly and scientific pursuits and institutions. Virtually all leading American scholars and scientists of the time went to Europe for their advanced training, and many native observers bemoaned the lack of any vital American intellectual or cultural spirit. Henry Adams, for instance, complained that Americans "had no time for thought; they saw, and could see, nothing beyond their day's work; . . . their attitude to the universe outside them was that of the deep-sea fish."[3] Americans' appreciation of beauty and culture, he felt, was succinctly expressed in Grant's lament that Venice would be a nice city if it were drained. Adams and others blamed this cultural myopia on the industrial age's growing materialism. A more prickly assessment came from the Spanish-born Harvard philosopher George Santayana, who found the American imagination not merely suppressed but geriatrically sterile. The established strain of American culture at the time—the Euro-imitative arts and sciences against which Whitman, Melville, Emerson, and others rebelled—Santayana saw as a "harvest of leaves" by a culture holding "an expurgated and barren conception of life . . . without native roots [or] fresh sap."

"[Even when Americans] made attempts to rejuvenate their minds by broaching native subjects," Santayana wrote, "the inspiration did not seem much more American than that of Swift or . . . Chateaubriand. . . . If anyone, like Walt Whitman, penetrated to the feelings and images which the American scene was able to breed out of itself, . . . he misrepresented the minds of cultivated Americans; in them the head as yet did not belong to the trunk."[4]

Louis's vision of nature study, however, presented a way to connect head, trunk, and soil. Drawing on native materials with energy, optimism, and initiative, naturalists both amateur and professional could create a homegrown alternative to stale high culture and debased mass culture while making a liberating asset of the country's lack of educational infrastructure. It was a neat trick, applying to science the celebration of endemic American energy that found literary voice in Whitman. Louis sang a song of scientific self.

Everyone ate it up—even future opponents like the Yale geologist James Dwight Dana and Harvard's Asa Gray. Though these men knew perfectly well that book learning was as vital as observation, they were enthralled by Agassiz's stunning memory, quickness of mind, and unrivaled power to rouse interest in natural science. Gray, who accompanied Agassiz on his initial tour down the coast, wrote a friend that Agassiz "charms all, both popular and scientific" and was "as excellent a man as he is a superb naturalist."[5] The man who would later battle Agassiz over Darwin's theory of natural selection wrote now that his lectures on embryology showed clearly that nature was formed by something other than just disinterested physical processes.

Reviews like this spurred tremendous demand for Agassiz's lectures. He had originally planned to give the Lowell Lectures and then tour the continent researching its natural history (thus fulfilling his duty to King Ferdinand). But even before he finished the Lowell series, he was getting offers from other institutions vying to land what Jacob Bailey, the naturalist at West Point, called "the big fish Agassiz." A bidding frenzy ensued, and Louis soon abandoned his plans for King Ferdinand's continental survey and concentrated on lecturing. In his first year in the United States, he earned more than eight thousand dollars—a huge sum at the time, more than he'd made in the previous decade in Europe—and was able to pay off all the debts he'd run up over fifteen years at Neuchâtel. Celebrity paid well.

Louis Agassiz, of course, was not merely famous. He was a genuinely distinguished scientist with a singular ability to inspire. This was not lost on John Lowell and the other members of Harvard University's corporation (its equivalent of a board of trustees). The university had been hoping to establish a school of science, and here arrived the perfect man to lead it—dynamic, energetic, internationally renowned, and able to raise money effortlessly. Lowell, inquiring gently with Louis and getting a warm response, convinced a fellow textile magnate, Abbott Lawrence, to underwrite a new science school. The Lawrence Scientific School (later absorbed into Harvard's school of arts and sciences) was thus created in 1847, and Louis became its first professor and effective director.

Eighteen months into his American tenure, then, Louis Agassiz had achieved goals of which he had long dreamed but so far fallen short: He had a prestigious and well-paid teaching position at a major institution; the ability to earn almost unlimited amounts of money and adulation; and near official status as his adoptive country's first naturalist.

3

When Alex arrived to join him, he found his father riding the headiest surge of his American success. Louis was also elated over the woman he introduced to Alex as his stepmother-to-be, Elizabeth Cabot Cary.

Well educated, musical, bilingual, attractive, warmhearted, and twenty-seven years old (as near in age to Alex as to Louis), Liz Cary was about the best thing that could have happened not just to Louis but to Alex. By all accounts she took Alex to heart immediately, and he, grateful after his recent trials for such an unequivocal commitment, remained dedicated to her all his life. In later years he called her his best friend as well as his mother. As for Louis, marrying Liz Cary furnished private stability and happiness for himself and his children and secured his acceptance into the highest layers of Boston society. For Elizabeth Cabot Cary was born of the Cabot family, one of the richest and most established of the oft-mingled clans (Cabots, Lowells, Feltons, Shaws, and others) who dominated Boston finance and society.

Liz Cary also possessed astonishing grace, intelligence, empathy, strength, and energy, and she managed to enhance and enjoy Louis's ambitions while curbing his domestic excesses. She greatly stabilized (one is tempted to say civilized) the home in which Alex lived. Upon his son's arrival, Louis's house held a menagerie that included snakes, an eagle, and a bear that was a gift from Henry Thoreau. Presumably a symbol of nature's noble simplicity, the bear simplified nothing, though it did offer unpredictable entertainment, as when during a dinner party it slipped its chains in the basement, raided the wine cask, and stumbled upstairs to disrupt the party. (It soon graced the dissecting table.) When Cary moved in, the animals and all of Louis's aides save Burkhardt moved out, and Alex, soon joined by his sisters, settled into the best-regulated home they ever had. (Some animals eluded immediate capture. Several weeks after moving in, Cary found a fugitive snake in one of her shoes. Louis, hearing her shout of protest, said he was wondering where that snake had got to.)

Even *sans animaux,* the place remained busy, for Cary and Agassiz, a sort of elite dream couple, became a node of Cambridge and Boston's social world. With Cary's help, Louis had conquered Brahmin Boston as thoroughly as he had Harvard. Ralph Waldo Emerson, in for a Boston visit from his own web in Concord, had heard enough of Louis from Thoreau and others that he knew him at first sight: "I saw in the cars a broad-featured, unctuous man, fat and plenteous as some successful politician, and pretty soon divined it must be the foreign professor who has had so marked a success in all our scientific and social circles, having established unquestionable leadership in them all; and it was Agassiz."[6]

4

Emerson soon joined the circle, becoming part of Louis's elite Saturday Club. On other nights, Cabots, Feltons, and Lowells came for dinner, and the place often swarmed with less formal visitors. Alex sometimes came home from school to find his father jawing with the great mathematician Benjamin Peirce, who lived across Quincy Street from Agassiz and became a close friend. Their bond seemed one of opposites. Peirce was a ferociously unapologetic intellectual elitist (he once delighted in being publicly called a nabob), a notoriously opaque lecturer, and a brilliant mathematician, while Louis espoused intellectual egalitarianism, lectured with singular lucidity, and could scarcely add. But they agreed that the universe was a divine creation, that it could be understood by those few who could perceive the rules of God's order, and that they ranked high among those few. Peirce, amused that his computationally challenged friend had a mathematically talented son, would often conjure some math puzzle for Alex. Alex usually solved it, which suggests both his intelligence and Peirce's feelings for him, for Peirce could stump anyone and usually chose to. Alex would witness an even more unpredictable mixture of lucidity and obscurity when the Saturday Club gathered, with Agassiz and Peirce joined by John Lowell, Longfellow, Emerson, and other luminaries who would talk deep into the night.

In this setting Alex began a part of his life more peaceful and productive, though hardly boring or routine. Once past his initial shyness and difficulties with English, he quickly made friends with his fellow students and the children of Cary's friends. In winter he liked to skate, and in summers he accompanied his father, stepmother, and sisters to Nahant, an island northeast of Boston where the Cabots and other blue bloods summered. There he developed a love of marine biology that grew all his life. He and his sisters sometimes accompanied their father and Cary on collecting or lecturing trips farther afield. In his first years in the United States, Alex traveled up and down the eastern seaboard; to the Gulf Coast; to the Florida Keys for the 1851 reef study; to South Carolina the following two winters when his father had lecturing stints in Charleston; and to many universities and scientific institutions between Boston and Washington,

D.C. By the time he was halfway through college, he was an accomplished field worker and had met most of the country's scientific elite.

Alex took great advantage of the opportunities this new world offered, resisting distraction and showing remarkable resilience and concentration. Already he could work as few others could. The youth was showing the characteristics that would distinguish the man: "The thoroughness and ease with which he worked, his great reserve, his sudden explosions of indignation, his quiet and entire devotion to those he loved, his occasional outbursts of mirth, as delightful as they were unexpected, his unfailing charm—all these belonged to the Swiss boy no less than to the scientific man of cosmopolitan friendship and fame."[7]

Enrolling at Cambridge High School soon after he arrived, he graduated two years later, in spring 1851, at fifteen. That fall he entered Harvard. He excelled in all sciences and in math, having more luck than most in following Peirce's lectures. Yet while he spoke five languages, he showed little interest in studying any of them, and he assiduously avoided philosophy. Like Peirce, who loved math because it was the most rigorous instrument for testing theories, Alex sought knowledge where it could be found and confirmed with most certainty. As his son would later phrase it, "He devoted himself to the knowable, and left groping among the intangibles to others."[8]

We can only wonder how much of this agnosticism was a reaction to his father's promiscuous theorizing. Each side of Alex's family had harbored doers as well as thinkers (Cécile had a second brother who was a mining engineer, and Louis's brother was a merchant), so perhaps Alex merely inherited a practical bent. Yet it invites speculation that a youth so exposed to philosophical inquiry should seem averse to it. His uncle Alexander, Alex's most substantial intellectual influence in the years before he came to America, was an adherent of *Naturphilosophie,* and Louis, though claiming a strict empiricism, spun elaborate speculative structures from his findings and talked to no end of philosophical matters.

Alex steered decidedly clear of all this, even as an undergraduate, when such musings come most naturally. This hard-nosed literal-mindedness, which he would retain all his life, fit firmly into an apparent abjuration of his father's excesses. Where Louis was loud, impulsive, expansive, and distractible, Alex was quiet, steady, held his cards close, and worked with a diligence—actually finishing things—that his father had sustained only briefly and only in his youth. Perhaps when one has a father as flamboyant as Louis Agassiz, the best rebellion is quiet conservatism. Or perhaps Alex simply saw the trouble Louis's extravagance created and chose a more controlled path. He had certainly suffered enough shocks riding Louis's.

In any case, Alex approached his schoolwork with remarkable energy and discipline. While not the bon vivant his father was, he had a quieter sort of charm beneath his subdued, acutely attentive demeanor. One friend he made in South Carolina the winter of 1851–1852, a young woman four years older than he (twenty to his sixteen), recalled later that "he was so different from other boys, and so delightful, a most charming boy—just at the age when boys are so seldom charming."[9] Though reserved, he was confident socially. Having long produced small plays with his sisters, he joined Harvard's Hasty Pudding theatrical club, and he rowed bow on a famed crew that also included Charles William Eliot, who as president of the university from 1869 to 1909 would become one of the most important figures in American higher education. (At only medium height and around 140 pounds, Alex would seem an unlikely oarsman, but he had impressive physical strength all his life.)

Living in the big Quincy Street house with his family, going to class across the street with his father and his father's colleagues during the day, Alex did not exactly move beyond his father's sphere while attending college, nor beyond the complications arising from Louis's chronic overextension. As his college years ended, Alex found himself teaching in a girls' prep school that Liz Cary had founded. Cary started the school partly out of a strong interest in education (she later became Radcliffe College's first president) but also because Louis, even with his new salary and lucrative speaking calendar, was again spending more than he earned. Cary, determined to provide a household income independent of Louis's, set up the Agassiz Girls' School and recruited Alex to teach there. He dutifully took the job even while he studied chemistry briefly and then reenrolled in the Lawrence Scientific School for another graduate degree, this one in natural history. For the next two years, he fit a half-time teaching position at the girls' school amid his studies.

Many twenty-year-old men would relish holding forth before

rooms full of bright young women, but Alex hated it. Unlike his father, he found teaching neither easy nor enjoyable. In fact he seemed increasingly resistant to the charms of both academe and natural history as professions. He told his close friend and classmate Theodore Lyman that he had entered engineering school because he didn't want to be a poor biologist or have to teach all his life. Now, as he finished his natural history degree, that sense of entrapment seemed to resurface: He had his degree (three, in fact—an undergrad degree in zoology and master's equivalents in engineering and natural history) but faced the sort of underfunded, overextended existence he so hated seeing in his father. He was also in love, having fallen for one of his students, Anna Russell, the daughter of blue-blooded family friends. He wanted to marry her, but the thought of doing so and then staying on at the museum and making ends meet by teaching, either at the girls' school or at his father's school, felt constricting.

Louis set up an escape route: Alexander Dallas Bache, a good friend of his who was the director of the U.S. Coast Survey, happened to need a capable, sea-legged scientist and engineer to help survey the Pacific Northwest coast. It was a connection job, but Alex, educated in geology, oceanography, and engineering and an experienced coastal cruiser, was superbly qualified. The position sounded promising. Bache, emphasizing the military and commercial advantages of well-surveyed waters, had drawn massive government resources to the survey, and its work was highly regarded. But the cruise Alex went on during the fall of 1859 suffered such bad weather, and Alex so resented the bureaucratic inefficiencies of a government operation, that when cold weather halted operations for a time he took a leave rather than seek another immediate assignment.

In San Francisco, waiting for a boat to start the long trip home via Panama (which still had to be crossed overland), he spent almost a month catching, drawing, and cataloging perch and medusae. He became so absorbed that he didn't want to leave, and indeed he did not leave until he had written dozens of pages of description to "mon cher papa" and a monograph on West Coast perch.[10] Then, perhaps deterred by the thought of returning to Boston's winter, he accepted an invitation from the superintendent of the Pacific Mail Steamship

Company, whom he had befriended on his westward passage over the isthmus, to be his guest in Acapulco and Panama. In both places he did yet more collecting and wrote more long letters to Louis, scores of pages of lovely pen work and maps and drawings of sea creatures—medusae, crabs, crustaceans, sea worms and sea slugs, shrimp—each numbered and tied to a description at letter's end. They were casual, newsy letters home, but they were also natural history papers almost ready for publication, and he in fact later revised and published several.

His Coastal Survey job, meanwhile, remained available. But as the weeks passed, the job held less attraction. Though the work was sometimes exciting, the pay was poor, and he missed his fiancée. As he collected, cataloged, drew, and described, it became clear that engineering, whatever its practical and pecuniary attractions, would never hold him the way biology did. Like a boat coming around, his thoughts and plans turned toward home, and more seriously toward marriage.

The only problem was money. Anna Russell came from yet another rich merchant family, but she and Alex had agreed they should live independently. She had even reduced her spending in his absence, as if in preparation for a naturalist's budget. But though she was willing to sacrifice some comfort, neither she nor Alex was ready to live penniless. He needed a salary.

Here Theodore Lyman stepped in. Like many of the friends Alex had made through family and school, Lyman was rich, and as a fellow zoologist and graduate of the Scientific School he saw natural history as a vital enterprise. He also felt (as Henry Adams would echo years later) that Alex was the best of the class both at Harvard and the Scientific School. It bothered him that a lack of funds should keep his gifted friend from pursuing science. Lyman knew of Louis's chronic, maddening overextension and his erratic ways, and he felt sad to see how Alex suffered them. So he proposed a solution. Louis Agassiz had finally talked Harvard, along with the Massachusetts legislature and several private donors (including the Lyman family), into financing the establishment of a permanent museum for the Scientific School's growing collections. Construction on the Museum of Comparative Zoology had in fact begun while Alex was away. This new museum would need curators to organize its collections, and Lyman had already volunteered to serve as a curator of mollusks. Facing an arduous task (for Louis had acquired many, many mollusks), Lyman convinced Alex to let him fund another curatorial position so that Alex could work alongside him. Lyman put up fifteen hundred dollars a year (the sum Harvard had offered Louis just ten years before). This was not a plush salary and would require that Alex (and Russell, after they married) live with Louis and Liz Cary for a while to make ends meet. But it was a start.

CHAPTER FIVE

Fixity

I

ALEXANDER AGASSIZ assumed his duties at the Museum of Comparative Zoology in the spring of 1860, at the age of twenty-four, and spent the next decade or so as fruitfully as anyone his age could reasonably ask. He married well and happily; fathered three children; made himself rich; and established himself as a scientist of real importance. He was not the wunderkind his father had been. Yet despite immense distractions on every front, he managed not only to emerge from Louis's shadow without alienating him (a feat accomplished by only a few Agassiz protégés) but to reconcile his father's best methods with the seemingly incompatible perspective of a new scientific era. This last achievement was far more radical than even Alex realized.

He began by returning to zoology. Writing up his work on Pacific perch and starfish had revived his passion for taxonomy, and he applied himself to it energetically as soon as he got home from Panama. He spent much of that summer of 1859 and many thereafter at the seaside cottage in Nahant that Liz Cary owned with her sister, where Alex and Louis had converted a small shed into a field lab. Alex kept a dory in a bight nearby. In the mornings he would drag the heavy boat across the sand and launch it through the surf, then row out past the breakers or into coves so he could dive for sea urchins and starfish and scoop up medusae and other plankton. He particularly liked gathering these small creatures that float at the current's mercy: translucent pteropods, or "winged snails"; tiny, ghost-like ctenophores resembling minuscule jellyfish; and the embryos of starfish, urchins, and anemones. Bobbing in immense numbers near the surface, these animals usually go unnoticed, for they offer but flecks to the naked eye. Alex collected them with a silk dip net so he could watch them, alive and awriggle, under a microscope or in a glass bowl over a light table. Summers he collected busily, working the boat in the morning and examining and classifying his finds in the afternoon. He filled notebooks with observations, measurements, and exquisite sketches and watercolors.

Back in Cambridge for autumn and winter, he expanded these notes into the papers with which he made his first marks in the scientific world.* With titles like "Function of the Pedicellariae," "On the Young Stages of a Few Annelids," and "The Mode of Development of the Marginal Tentacles of the Free Medusa of Some Hydroids," these were thorough, painstaking papers bespeaking excruciatingly persistent microscope work. They described with scrupulous accuracy, and they occasionally divulged findings that excited other biologists. In "Function of the Pedicellariae," for instance, Alex revealed his discovery that the tiny, tulip-shaped stalks growing between the spines of sea urchins, thought to be mere ornament, served a function after all: They cleaned, passing debris in bucket-brigade fashion off the animal. (They were later found also to contain a stinging poison that repelled predators.) Work this demanding (some would say tedious) suits few. Alex loved it. It met his compulsion to organize and confirmed his conviction, learned from his father's rhetoric if not his work, that the most meaningful knowledge springs from meticulous observation.

He also enjoyed, most of the time, his job cataloging the museum's starfish and sea urchins, classifying them into known taxa and crying a small eureka at the infrequent new find. This was taxonomy at its most pleasurable: precise, protracted work revealing an accumulating pattern and the occasional discovery.

His home life echoed this, taking an increasing order leavened by the unexpected. In the fall of 1860 he finally married Anna Russell.

---

* Like most naturalists, he was catholic in his interests; his first published paper was on the flight mechanisms of butterflies.

Anna's father, George Russell, was a prominent textile merchant, and her mother was sister to Quincy Adams Shaw, who with his cousin Francis Parkman had published *The Oregon Trail* and who with his siblings and cousins would inherit the vast Shaw and Parkman fortunes. Anna's sister Mimi, meanwhile, married Alex's friend and benefactor Theo Lyman. Theo had actually played matchmaker between his wife's sister and his good friend, and his desire that Alex and Anna marry, along with his wish to see his friend pursue work he liked, had helped motivate his contribution to the museum of Alex's fifteen-hundred-dollar salary. (Alex never felt completely comfortable with this arrangement during the seven years it was in effect, but he accepted it because Theo reassured him, truthfully on all points, that the contribution was really to the museum and to science, not to Alex; that Alex more than earned it; and that Theo "had to give money away somewhere" and felt the money's departure not a whit.) In addition, Alex's sister Pauline married Quincy Adams Shaw himself (Anna's uncle); and Quincy's brother Gardner in turn married Theo Lyman's sister Cora. Alex's place in this spiderweb arrangement is dizzying to contemplate. By marrying Anna he made himself brother-in-law to his best friend; brother-in-law to his wife's (and his new) uncle; brother-in-law to his best friend's wife (Mimi); and, naturally, a cousin to himself a couple times over and at least once removed. More important, he was now related, in some cases several times over, to three of Boston's wealthiest families: the Russells, the Lymans, and the Shaws.

But though money lay all about, Alex and Anna remained determined to live on what Alex could earn. They made their first home in a set of rooms at Louis and Elizabeth's big house on Quincy Street, just across from the Harvard campus and a half mile from the museum. The girls' school was in its last couple of years, and while Alex sidestepped further teaching duties, the school was one more activity, along with the many visitors, colleagues, protégés, hangers-on, and sycophants, that made Louis's house, no matter how large, feel eternally full. Even so, the big, rambling home allowed Alex and Anna a small apartment of their own.

Eighteen months after marrying, in July 1862, Anna gave birth to a son, George Russell Agassiz. Another son, Maximilian, would follow in 1866, and a third, Rodolphe, in 1871. Despite living with their in-laws, the young couple grew to be quite affectionate. Anna's brother, Harry, reported to their sister Mimi after a six-week stay that "Alex is better the more you see of him and Annie seems to think so too. . . . When they were engaged they were icebergs to each other, compared to . . . now."[1]

This assessment is confirmed by letters of other relatives and friends, as well as Anna's, that consistently portray a marriage that must have brought an exhilarating sense of both expansion and safety to the much-buffeted Alex. Anna, four years younger than Alex, greatly admired his intelligence and steadiness while gently challenging his caution and reserve and encouraging his efforts to find his own place in the world. Likewise, Alex seems to have been a solicitous and affectionate husband who respected Anna's independence of thought and the persistent but politic ways in which she held her own (even asserting some relatively liberal leanings) in a household headed by two dominating, politically conservative personalities.

Alex also took growing pleasure and strength from his friendship with his brother-in-law Theo. It's probably hard to overstate the emotional and practical importance of this kinship. The money Theo provided—the museum salary and later some crucial loans— was the least of it. The two had become good friends as undergraduates, then grew closer over the years as they each took advanced degrees in zoology in the late 1850s (spending much time together at the Nahant lab) and worked together as curators and de facto managers of the new museum. (Alex handled the sea urchins and starfish, while Theo looked after their close cousins the brittle stars. Both spent time tending the museum's administration and finances.) This common history gave Theo an appreciation of Alex's position and difficulties unrivaled by anyone's except perhaps Anna's. Being married to sisters only tightened the bond. And as Theo esteemed Alex's intelligence, discipline, and gruff generosity, so Alex found in Theo (as in Anna, and as Louis had found in Cécile Braun and then Liz Cary) an example of a life more open to emotional and cultural pleasures than that of the cloistered researcher.

Theo thus became one of the few intimates Alex ever allowed himself, a role enhanced by his place outside the immediate family. Even early in their friendship, when both men were in their twenties and starting families, Alex would confide in Theo as in no one else.

Later, when they shared cruelly similar losses, Alex would lean on Theo, and Theo—more garrulous and introspective and, unlike Alex, a devoted diarist and letter writer—would express much that Alex could not bear to articulate.

In these early days of the 1860s, however, their conversation and correspondence tended toward their shared family and their labors at the museum. It also covered, unavoidably, the Civil War. Though the war affected Alex less than many men his age, it hardly went unfelt. New England had long been the region most opposed to slavery, and many Bostonians were radicalized in 1856, when native son and U.S. senator Charles Sumner, who had enraged many Southerners with his denunciations of slavery (and who, incidentally, had been court-ing Liz Cary when Louis Agassiz showed up), suffered a near fatal beating by South Carolina representative Preston Brooks. Brooks, finding Sumner working at his desk on the Senate floor one evening, attacked him with a brass-headed cane, striking him more than thirty times before the bloody and unconscious Sumner, his legs trapped beneath the bolted-down desk, uprooted the desk and fell back onto the floor. When Southerners hailed Brooks as a hero (he received scores of canes as gifts), Bostonians concluded the South would stop at nothing to defend and expand slavery. Several subse-quent incidents in which fugitive slaves were captured in Boston and returned south sharpened Bostonians' disgust. When war broke out in April 1861, many, including members of Boston's aristocracy, rushed to answer Lincoln's call for volunteers.

Throughout the war Alex agonized over whether to join them. Many of his former classmates served, as did several of his acquain-tances, friends, and family. Theo, for instance, though he first com-pleted an eighteen-month sojourn in Europe that he started just before the war broke, enlisted on his return in 1863, eventually serv-ing as an aide to General George Meade and publishing a well-regarded book about Meade's Virginia campaigns. Anna's cousin Robert Gould Shaw served in the Massachusetts Second Regiment and then took first command of the famed black regiment, the Fifty-fourth, and died leading a charge against Fort Wagner. Henry Lee Higginson, a childhood friend of Alex's who was wounded in 1862, proposed to Alex's sister Ida in 1863 and married her that December before returning to battle. And Anna's brother Harry was taken prisoner for a time (and thought dead for a few days) in 1862, and when released spent six weeks with Alex and Anna at Quincy Street before returning to the front. A number of other family friends had sons and brothers who did not come home. The war felt near indeed.

Surrounded by those who served, Alex several times nearly enlisted, particularly in 1864, a low point of the war for the North. But in the end—and partly because the museum had already suffered so many losses to enlistment—he heeded his father's call to tend the museum. Louis, notwithstanding some racist views he shared with many Southerners (and not a few Northerners), was, like many conservative Northerners, ardently pro-Union once the war started. Yet he felt that his own patriotic duty was to save science from being a war casualty. He vigorously preached the need at such times to move forward with science—and, naturally, with vital projects such as the Museum of Comparative Zoology. He thus managed to convince the state legislature to help fund the museum's expansion despite the war.

It was in managing this expansion that Alex saw a duty he could not neglect. As ever, Louis had more plans than he could execute, more promises than he could keep, and more specimens arriving than the staff and students (who were drafted as part-time curators) could process. It fell to Alex, as de facto manager of the museum's day-to-day operations, to compensate for these excesses. He scrambled for money, arranged specimen swaps in lieu of payment, and sometimes embarrassedly returned specimens the museum could not afford. He felt (with good reason) that if he left for the war, the museum would implode.

Louis wanted the Museum of Comparative Zoology to be not only a center of study that would advance knowledge but a place of public enlightenment that would diffuse that knowledge through educational displays. This dual-purpose museum would require many, many specimens. The scholars and taxonomists would need their own sets—ideally, several specimens showing different stages of development of each taxa, so that several scholars could simultaneously make comparative studies. The museum displays would require another full set showing each stage of development for each species. Accordingly, Louis spent much of the 1850s and early 1860s soliciting specimens from collectors all over North America—everyone from professionals at academic centers to amateur naturalists working out west. They had responded energetically, sending thousands of dead animals in boxes, barrels, and jars. Now that he had a museum, a budget (no matter how overstretched), and a store of specimens he could swap for others, Louis solicited yet more specimens.

From Alex's first day of work, then, he, Theo, and the other curators and students faced a daunting backlog of corpses that awaited unpacking, cleaning, classification, description, and preservation. As they were often packed in cheap whiskey, this was a chore that grew old quickly. More arrived weekly.

It was Alex's job to oversee this administrative and curatorial work. Struggling to impose order on a rapidly expanding situation while constantly fighting rearguard actions to keep the budget from glowing red, he often found himself under great strain. Theo's departure for Europe in early 1861 made this lonely task more so. Across the Atlantic he shared his woes. In June of that year, asking Theo to keep this to himself, he said he had discovered four thousand dollars' worth of storage and display cases still unpaid for, and that fall he wrote a letter "blue to the very depths" about his frustrations at the museum. A few months later he turned from a long passage about the war to "a subject not less disgusting, the Museum," and after a plaint about staffing inefficiencies and slow progress on curatorial work declared,

> When I speak to father about it I can get no satisfaction. He has a thousand excuses always ready . . . so that all my attempts at introducing any kind of system . . . have most signally failed. . . . [Meanwhile] he is killing himself by inches with the Museum, his book, the lectures he has to give for money to keep the machine going. . . . I tried all I could to make matters easier for him but all my efforts are wasted. . . . I must say it is rather discouraging not to be able to do any good and to be obliged to see things going on the way they do, when with very little delay everything could be put on a good footing.[2]

Such despair visits anyone struggling to curb a squanderous superior. For Alex, with his love of order, it clouded an otherwise happy time. Though he took satisfaction in what progress he could make organizing the museum, his father's excesses would gradually drive him to such exasperation that he would rage and then grow blue— and then distance himself from it, declaring that it was "not worth it" to worry.[3] For a time, he would let it roll off, then mounting frustration or a crisis would again make the situation seem untenable.

2

Alex was hardly the only underling frustrated by Louis. One of the museum's biggest problems in its first years was a swelling discontent among Louis's students. Though Louis could spark early enthusiasm like no one else, his authoritarianism would soon emerge to smother the flame. With the museum's founding in 1859, he had brought in a new crop of particularly promising students, his first, other than Alex and Theo, of doctorate caliber. However, they entered not a formal graduate-school track with established requirements pursued under a faculty's collective guidance (a system then still under development) but a master-apprentice arrangement modeled on the academies of Europe. A student's education, directed almost entirely by his mentor, would advance not by set criteria but at his master's discretion.

Louis's students soon found that their inspiring, charming, and generous master could be overbearing and capricious. Even more discouraging, he acknowledged progress reluctantly. He scolded and berated, changed the requirements for advancement, and expanded the students' curatorial duties, further slowing their progress. Sometimes he failed to credit students who had authored significant portions of works published under his name. He usually found their own papers not quite worthy of publication and often found the students themselves not quite ready for graduation or recommendation for positions elsewhere. Louis also badly hurt his reputation among his students during this period by resisting the efforts of Henry Clark, a former student and longtime aide whom he had recently made an assistant professor, to receive authorial credit for extensive passages he researched and wrote for Louis's monumental *Contributions to the Natural History of the United States*. Clark grew so frustrated that he published a "Claim for Scientific Property." Louis responded by banning Clark from the museum and squeezing him out of the Harvard faculty. The episode suggested disturbing things for his more independent and motivated students.

Inevitably, some rebelled. As early as 1861, several students began arguing with Louis, demanding pay rather than just scholarships for their curatorial work and pressing him to publish their papers in the museum's publications. (These oft-promised publications were repeatedly delayed by Louis's chronic budget and time overextensions.) When he resisted, several published their papers elsewhere. One, Albert Bickmore, showing he had learned much from the master, solicited subscriptions to his papers from the same wealthy Bostonians Louis so often tapped for cash. (Several signed on before Louis discovered the scheme and squashed it.) Bickmore and a few others, despairing of ever getting Louis's blessing to graduate, began putting out job feelers. Meanwhile, and most painful to Louis, some of the students began to badmouth him outside the museum's once tight circle. They accused him of behaving dictatorially, of treating students as assistants rather than as junior colleagues, and of practicing antiquated science. They even formed a secret club, the Society for the Protection of American Students from Foreign Professors, that was a combination scientific salon and kvetching parlor. Just four years before, most of its members had been infatuated founders of the Agassiz Zoological Club.

Louis learned of the secret society, of course, along with the publishing schemes, the job hunts, and the nasty talk. Over much of 1863 he bickered with the rebels individually and sometimes as a group. Their recalcitrance provoked several rages. Sometimes shouting, he reminded them that he had worked hard to gather a vast collection for their study; built a museum to house it; secured funds for scholarships and stipends—in short, had offered them every resource he could muster, including his own unrivaled expertise—and they had responded by defying, deceiving, and even taunting and belittling him. He pointed out that science was a vast field not learned overnight, that they were students and he the master, and that most of them were not yet qualified to publish on their own, much less take their place among the discipline's mature practitioners. He

accompanied these tirades with new, tighter rules of authorial control, specimen use, and publication permissions, forbidding, for
example, the publication of any research done using the museum's
materials unless he gave his blessing.

These edicts were not much stricter in principle than most at
similar institutions then or, for that matter, today. But the authoritarian tone Louis used in asserting them chafed. "Has anyone told
you about the . . . Napoleonic-tyrannic-Papalistic set of regula-
tions?" one student wrote to an assistant who had already defected.[4]
Within six months after the new rules went into effect, most of
Louis's brightest students—over half the total—had left. To his cha-
grin, most quickly landed jobs at other top institutions. Yale hired
one. The newly founded Peabody Institute in Salem, Massachusetts
(a threat in his own backyard, as Louis saw it), hired several others.
Albert Bickmore, whom Louis had caught soliciting private sub-
scribers, went to New York and helped establish what became the
American Museum of Natural History.

The student rebellion of 1863–1864 (also known as the "Salem
secession," for all the rebels who went to Salem's Peabody Institute)
left the Museum of Comparative Zoology a poorer, quieter place.
The few students remaining were both less capable and less bold, and
though Louis bid the rebels good riddance, Alexander recognized
that the museum had lost valuable people. Professional curators took
on much of the students' work at the museum, a stabilizing move
that Alex had long pressed for. But the students' accumulated taxonomic expertise had departed with them, as did some of the place's
spirit. The dorm that hosted beer-fueled philosophical discussions
stood empty; the Agassiz Zoological Club met no more; and the
sense of excited, youthful endeavor that had imbued the museum
was permanently dampened. Nothing, Louis said later, ever pained
him as much as this insurrection.

3

The uprising of 1863 and 1864 stung badly enough on Oedipal
grounds. Louis might have wished to blame it on the disruptive spirit
of wartime. But as he well knew, his students' discontent was sharpened not so much by the Civil War as by another war as momentous,

if less bloody. For the years of the student rebellion coincided with those in which Louis fought most of his battle against Darwinism. His resistance destroyed his credibility among peers and knocked him from his perch as an idol of the young. Louis, exquisitely sensitive to his standing, felt the loss keenly.

As with his students, Louis's stock among colleagues fell partly because they tired of his egotism and authoritarianism. But his colleagues lost respect primarily because his fight with Darwin exposed not just his megalomania but his unscientific science. In a way this was no fault of Louis's, for he used methods and principles long considered sound. But Darwin's theory caused an extensive reevaluation of what it meant to do good science—one that took decades to complete but that crystallized and created sharp effects quite abruptly, like the revolution it was—and Louis showed himself unable or unwilling to adjust.

It meant everything, of course, that the theory prompting this reexamination directly addressed the subject on which Louis based his reputation. Darwin's concept of species creation could hardly have contradicted Louis's more thoroughly. Whereas Louis held that God had created all species exactly as we know them, whole and immutable, Darwin proposed that all species had descended from common ancestors through an evolutionary process that favored the individuals of each generation who happened to inherit the traits most advantageous for their time. Species were produced not by divine design but by opportunistic exploitation of chance advantages. God's will, in short, had nothing to do with it, and there was no plan to speak of. We got here by dumb luck and ruthless competition.

Darwin's evolutionary theory is actually a set of several key concepts.[5] The most central and vital are that all species descend from a single common ancestor; that the number of species has multiplied in branching fashion as different varieties and populations have evolved into new species; and that the mechanism driving this change is natural selection—the "survival of the fittest" (or luckiest) individuals of each generation by virtue of the advantages granted by their genetic makeup. To oversimplify just slightly, one can view Darwin's construct as a theory of evolution *of* multiple species *via* common descent *by means* of natural selection.

This set of ideas threatened not just the creationist theory of species origin of the 1850s but almost every key principle of what constituted good science. It could hardly have been more radical. The very idea that species changed, for instance, insulted the concept of essentialism, which held that nature's variety could be sorted into categories distinguished by immutable essences. This view, central to Western science since Aristotle, saw variations within a species as imperfect reflections of that species' essence, not as potential first steps toward new species. Though its grip was weakening, most scientists still saw essentialism as a foundation of zoology.

The central role of chance in Darwin's theory also defied the principle of determinism, which holds that nature operates according to knowable laws that dictate outcomes in a manner at least theoretically predictable. The scientist's task lay in identifying these laws. The biologist's version was so-called physicalism, which held that even biological dynamics could be reduced to verifiable physical statements and formulas—that biology, in other words, operated according to laws as consistent and unambiguous as those of Newtonian physics. Darwin offered a law that said while you might reconstruct evolution's past, you could never predict its future.

Even the most basic statement of Darwin's theory, that species change through natural causes, threatened all these principles. But the most radical and novel of his ideas, the theory of natural selection, posed a particularly vexing affront. Even today this concept's brutally mechanistic nature makes it hard to swallow. We balk at its rejection of moral or teleological aim—at the idea that every form of life, including our own, is the result of random chance and opportunism. Darwin's theory of natural selection insists that we exist not because we were meant to but because we happen to, or, to put a slightly more flattering gloss on it, because we and our ancestors happened to receive certain crucial advantages. To accept this goes against every part of our self-conception. The notion is also deeply blasphemous, for in removing God as the shaper of life, it forces the question of whether he even started it. Darwin himself, once a devout Christian but increasingly atheistic as he developed his theory, blanched at these implications. He said that recognizing them was "like confessing a murder."

These conceptual challenges, along with the difficulty of fully describing the mechanism of natural selection without reference to Mendelian genetics (then yet to be developed), made natural selection the last part of Darwin's evolutionary theory to be accepted. While Darwin's argument for evolution by common descent converted virtually all scientists to those views within a decade, the "by means of natural selection" part of his theory took another eight decades to take hold. It's that much more remarkable (and a testament to the power of his argument), then, that Darwin convinced his peers of evolution by common descent, for his theory of natural selection is really his trump card, providing the key missing part—a viable dynamic driving species change—whose absence had crippled previous evolutionary theories. Not until the 1930s, when the so-called "evolutionary synthesis" integrated Mendelian genetics (developed by Gregor Mendel in the 1860s but largely ignored until 1900) into general evolutionary theory, was the theory of natural selection widely accepted among biologists.

In the meantime, rejecting the natural-selection part of Darwin's larger theory spared one from confronting the larger theory's most odious, mechanistic aspect, for it left God a potential role. Many have taken this dodge both in Darwin's time and since, accepting the first definition of "Darwinism" (the idea of evolution and common descent through largely natural means) while still assuming that God somehow directs the evolutionary process, either by manipulating it directly or by having created its laws of operation. An update of this same compromise makes it possible to believe in both God and natural (well, almost natural) selection; you simply figure that God somehow supplies, in untraceable ways, the variations or created their possibility.

Louis Agassiz, however, could hardly take such a straddle. Having preached long and loudly that species were direct, immutable creations of God, he could not allow the notion that all species descended, changing constantly by natural processes, from a common ancestor. Louis saw immediately that he must either destroy Darwin's theory or retract his own. He was not about to retract. Besides, Louis Agassiz seemed genuinely incapable of absorbing Darwin's theory. Though he claimed to have read *Origin* several times, he never wrote or said anything suggesting that he really understood the mechanistic process Darwin described. He was too imbued with the certainties of essentialism, determinism, and creationism to imagine even a God-directed, teleological version of evolution, much less a random, mechanistic one. For him, as for many of his time, the conceptual jump was too great.

Because he failed to absorb Darwin's main arguments, Louis saw Darwin as merely another case of Lamarck warmed over. The debate over this theory, then, would be a rehash of Cuvier versus Geoffroy. And Louis would triumph as decisively as Cuvier had.

Louis probably shouldn't be blamed too harshly for his sclerotic resistance. In addition to carrying particularly heavy versions of his generation's essentialist baggage, he was behorned by a larger dilemma confronting any Western scientist, that of integrating a love of order with the determination to see clearly and think logically. The two passions would seem to complement each other and often do. But the compulsion to parse can lead us to impose a false order that warps our vision and dulls our thinking. Who has not falsely seen the familiar in the strange, the desired in the unwanted? The perching warbler transforms, under increasing light, into a dull leaf; the distant mountains reduce to clouds; the friend in the crowd, turning, becomes a stranger. So an idea offering order can impose one false. Louis's and Cuvier's creationism, *Naturphilosophie*'s archetypal hierarchy, the more general principle of essentialism—any ultimately untestable theory asserting that nature's pattern reflects an ideal order—appeal because they fulfill our yen for order while expressing deeply or widely held beliefs of their eras. We believe the theory because the theory expresses our beliefs. But these idealist theories pose a grave threat to the empiricism that forms the heart of Western science, for they make reality a concept rather than something that can be reliably observed, measured, and known. Rare is the scientist who will confess to idealist thinking. As there are no atheists in foxholes, so there are no idealists (at least, no admitted idealists) in science labs. Louis Agassiz, for instance, would hardly have admitted to being one. He would have argued (and did) that he was an empiricist, insisting he held observation above all. He was deluded, of course. His plan of creation, though supported by his observations, did not really rise from them. Rather, it reflected his notion that the world was created by God and that species were physical expressions of the "thoughts of God." He fit his observations to his vision. He was an idealist masquerading as an empiricist.

4

After Darwin's book came out in late 1859, Louis mounted an all-or-nothing attack on it. He waged his war on two fronts: one among peers, another in the popular press and lecture circuit. On the popular front Louis actually won a draw, at least in the United States, for most Americans chose the straddle mentioned earlier. Even 150 years later, over half of Americans continued to believe that God either created most species as is or somehow directs evolution.[6]

This happy compromise ignores, of course, the philosophical implications that haunted Darwin and overlooks the underlying disagreement about how one should seek answers. Louis's idealist logic and Darwin's empirical method clashed as violently as did their creationist and mechanistic conclusions. For scientists of the era, this argument about method mattered as much as whether we arose from God or monkey. And it was this methodological debate that Louis so decisively lost.

A debate, of course, requires an opponent, and even Darwin couldn't argue effectively from across the Atlantic. He didn't much like arguing anyway, preferring to sway through his writing while friends did the knife work. In England, Thomas Huxley, self-anointed as "Darwin's bulldog," did the bloodiest of it. Huxley won an early and instantly famous debate over Darwinism even though his opponent, the former Oxford debater Archbishop Wilberforce, fired the most memorable salvo of the entire long war: In June 1860, before an excited crowd at Oxford, Wilberforce wrapped up his creationist attack on *Origin* by asking Huxley whether it was through his grand-*father* or grand*mother* that he descended from a monkey. The agnostic Huxley, murmuring to a friend, "The Lord hath delivered him unto my hands," rose, rubbing those hands together, and dismantled the archbishop's argument. He finished by declaring that if given the choice between kinship to a smelly ape or to a man willing to use his intelligence and privilege to twist the truth, he would choose the ape. The packed hall erupted in shouting; one woman reportedly fainted.

Darwin's American advocate was hardly so flashy. The Harvard botanist Asa Gray, it will be recalled, was among those who warmly welcomed Louis Agassiz to America. Far less outgoing than Louis (he preferred doing taxonomy to lecturing about it), Gray, at Harvard since 1842, had won eminence through solid work, lucid writing, and judicious promotion of rigorous science. As charmed as most by Louis's high spirits and dazzling talk, he had accompanied him on his first trip to Philadelphia and Washington in 1846 to introduce him to the country's scientific establishment. He was thrilled when Agassiz joined the Harvard faculty, inviting him to dinner several times to meet new colleagues. Louis would often stay late at these dinners as he and Gray talked deep into the night. Their rapport seemed to promise long allegiance.

The Harvard botanist Asa Gray, among the first to reconcile a devout Christianity with a belief in Darwinian evolution. His conversion turned him from a friend of Louis's to one of his worst enemies.

But the two differed often over the next fifteen years. In the mid-1850s, at a time when the issues of race and slavery repeatedly took the United States to the brink of civil war, Gray was disgusted to see Louis offer scientific views supporting racist arguments. Louis held that different human races, like similar but different animal species, had been created separately—and none too equally. This theory conflicted with both Gray's growing scientific belief in species descent and his Christian belief in humankind's common origin.

Gray also favored a more egalitarian, less authoritarian educational model than Agassiz did, and the two clashed repeatedly over how to shape the growing university. Similarly, Louis favored an elitist, invitation-only structure in scientific organizations, whereas Gray, his geologist friend James Dwight Dana of Yale, and many others preferred a more open, democratic structure based on interest and commitment. And Gray, despite himself, resented that Louis garnered unprecedented attention and funding while he struggled to raise enough money to replace pickets in the botanical garden's fence. Gray, Dana, and others also felt that Louis's pursuit of fame, funding, and lecture opportunities was leading him to practice sloppy science and oversimplify its results. His love of popular lecturing "has greatly injured him," Gray complained at one point, leading him to "tamper with strict veracity for the sake of popular effect."[7] These resentments sharpened in 1858 when Louis sent an article to the *American Journal of Science* expressing support for a book by one of his protégés, Jules Marcou, that harshly attacked the work of Gray's friend Dana (who happened to edit the *Journal*) and other American geologists—and insisted that his letter be printed even though he had not read the book it praised. After consulting Gray, Dana printed Louis's letter along with a rejoinder and a note explaining the whole affair.

All this accrued to quite a pile of bother. But what irked Gray most—more every year—was that the view of species Louis sold so effectively was idealist rather than empirical.

Gray had once held rather idealist views himself, even while professing empiricism. This was a common stance among scientists in the mid-nineteenth century, as a growing commitment to empiricism eroded various idealist assumptions and approaches. The year Agassiz arrived in America, for instance (1846), Gray reviewed a controversial work called *Explanations: A Sequel to "Vestiges of the Natural History of Creation"* that espoused a roughly Lamarckian theory of evolution. (Louis's Lowell Lectures the following winter were partly a response to the same book.) Gray panned *Vestiges,* attacking its shoddy science and concluding that its unproven Lamarckian evolutionary scheme must be rejected because the "unity we perceive in nature" is one to which "sound science has ever delighted to point, as the proof that all is the direct handiwork of a single omniscient Creator." As yet, Gray wrote, those arguing that species arise any other way "are bound to show that natural agencies are competent to produce such results. . . . The burden of proof rests upon them."[8] This could easily have been Louis talking.

For Gray, however, the burden of proof would soon shift—or, more to the point, it would apply as much to speculative religious explanations as to speculative evolutionary theories. During the 1850s Gray grew ever more self-consciously empiricist. He would come to insist that theories correspond first and foremost with observable evidence. Though he was more conscientious about this than most, he was hardly alone. But Gray would only take this push for a more rigorous empiricism so far. If he was among the few to immediately accept the theory of natural selection, he would not admit its ruthlessly mechanistic implications (or those of the larger evolutionary theory). Instead he chose to believe, as would so many after him, not only that God had created life in some manner "lost in the mists of time" but that in some similarly unknowable manner he now directed the selective process. Thus Gray conceded to his devout Christianity, yielding, as he saw it, in an arena beyond the knowable.

Otherwise, however, Gray viewed religious or abstract explanations warily. He trusted instead the literal and demonstrable. In the 1850s, as Agassiz's idealist preachings began to grate, Gray found support for his empiricism in his friendship with several English naturalists, most notably Joseph Hooker, the eminent and well-traveled botanist who would later direct the Royal Botanical Garden at Kew. Gray had met Hooker while visiting England in the late 1830s, and since then the two had pioneered the subdiscipline of plant geography. Like Darwin's and others' close attention to the distribution of animal species, their study of the geographical distribution of plants would reveal much about evolution's dynamics. For now, pre-*Origin*, their efforts were notable for their empirical tenor: a broadening enquiry, ever tied to direct evidence, into why plant species were distributed as they were.

Hooker and the other British scientists Gray corresponded with, all friends of Darwin's, tried to practice the no-nonsense empiricism first articulated by their countryman John Locke a century before and elaborated in the early to mid-1800s by the British philosopher-scientists William Whewell and John Stuart Mill. Gray, besieged by Louis's idealist spinnings as well as by the transcendentalism then being spangled about by Emerson, Thoreau, and their followers, was glad to find such literal-mindedness in scientists so respected and prominent.* By the late 1850s he was ready to let empiricism override not only speculative evolutionary schema such as that of *Vestiges* but creationist elaborations such as Louis's. After all, both made the same sort of unfounded conceptual jump—exciting but ultimately unsupportable—that left one standing on air. As he put it to Hooker in 1858, "[I] sympathize more with & estimate higher the slow induction that leads step by step to sound conclusions so far as they go, than the bolder flights of the genius which so often leads the possessor to mount three pairs of steps only to jump out of the garret window."[9]

The idea that species were God's "direct handiwork"—a conviction Gray had once shared with Louis—was starting to feel like a jump out the window.

---

* Gray found many of the transcendentalists' speculations and poetic expansions unfounded or flatly ridiculous, while they found him a drudge. However, as A. Hunter Dupree notes in his excellent *Asa Gray*, Thoreau, at least, sometimes managed to find in Gray a launch-pad for flights of fancy:

> When Thoreau was struck by a passage in Gray, he read into it a symbolism which changed the matter-of-fact scientific prose beyond recognition. He pondered a statement by Gray that roots "not only spring from the root-end of the primary stem in germination, but also from any subsequent part of the stem under favorable circumstances, that is to say, in darkness and moisture, as when covered by the soil or resting on its surface." It is certain that Gray meant here exactly what he said, but for Thoreau those words meant that "the most clear and ethereal ideas (Antaeus-like) readily ally themselves to the earth, to the primal womb of things."

A. Hunter Dupree, *Asa Gray* (Baltimore: Johns Hopkins University Press, 1978), 222; quoting from *The Journal of Henry D. Thoreau*, eds. B. Torrey and F. H. Allen (Boston, 1949), xi, 208.

5

What brought Gray to ground was a botanical conundrum. As early as the 1840s, he had noted that eastern North America and eastern Asia, especially Japan, had in common many plants found nowhere else—identical or closely similar species growing a world apart. Forty plant genera grew only in these two areas. He noted this oddity in print on several occasions but lacked time to examine it closely.

In 1855, however, a new pen pal revived his interest in the puzzle. Charles Darwin, drawing on their mutual friendship with Joseph Hooker (and having admired a letter that Gray sent to Hooker regarding plant geography), wrote Gray asking for help in solving some plant-species distribution problems he was struggling with. As always, Darwin was humble, solicitous, and subversively Socratic, even while fishing for information he genuinely needed: "As I am no Botanist, it will seem so absurd to you my asking botanical questions, that I may premise that I have for several years been collecting facts on 'variation,' and when I find that any general remark seems to hold amongst animals, I try to test it in Plants."[10] Though in this particular letter Darwin asked about differences among North American alpine plants, his confession to testing ideas on "variation" against Gray's plant data sums up the course of their ensuing correspondence. Their exchanges would greatly strengthen Darwin's theories even as he sold them to Gray.

It wasn't by accident. At the time Hooker reintroduced Darwin and Gray (who had met briefly when Gray toured England in 1838), Hooker was one of just two people to whom Darwin had confessed his theory of evolution. (Charles Lyell was the other.) Hooker and Darwin had corresponded extensively about how anomalies of plant distribution seemed to support Darwin's ideas about species change. Like Darwin's Galápagos finches, plant species on nearby islands often took closely similar forms that suggested descent from common ancestors. Hooker had seen this in the plants Darwin brought back from the Galápagos, and he had noted many similarities in plant communities in the European Alps and the Arctic, as if those two flora had once shared a single habitat and then been separated. Hooker recognized that Gray's North America–Asia conundrum offered a similar puzzle—and that if Darwin's theory helped Gray solve it, it would strengthen the theory and win Darwin an important ally. He set the two men up knowing damn well what he was doing.

For two years, then, Darwin—unassuming, politic, and also knowing damn well—plied Gray with questions about plant-distribution problems in North America and particularly about the America-Asia puzzle, leading Gray to consider more deeply the possible links between species distribution and "variation," or species change. Darwin's intriguing questions, modest suggestions, and requests for clarification helped Gray see much about plant geography that, short of an Agassizian leap of faith in divine creation, seemed explainable only by some mechanism of transmutation.

It was a brilliant strategy, convincing Gray not by rhetoric but by enticing him to reconsider the evidence on his own lab tables. Gray saw that he was being led, and he gathered from Hooker that Darwin was nursing some new evolutionary theory. He recognized that one of his most important tenets, "Like breeds like," was being challenged. Yet he allowed it. For Gray's belief in species fixity stemmed less from religious or essentialist principles than from empirical observation. His thousands of hours classifying plant specimens had convinced him that if species were *not* fixed, if species boundaries could be easily and often crossed, then the order he perceived in his many specimens would have broken down long ago, and he would not find the fairly clear distinctions he saw daily. He believed in species fixity, in short, because it seemed to confirm what he saw. But as a belief based on observation, he held it open to revision. By the late 1850s he had already softened this belief, for he knew Hooker and others were questioning it, and he himself saw growing evidence that species varied so much as to stretch their own boundaries. Many specimens seemed to lie right on species boundaries. The question was what "natural agency," to use the terms with which he'd skewered *Vestiges,* might "be competent to produce such results." Hooker's hints that Darwin was pondering such an agency did not surprise him.

Finally, in July 1857, Darwin fessed up. With a short letter followed by an abstract, he made Gray the third confidant to know of his theory of evolution, including his ideas on natural selection. His letter was typically self-effacing and disarming. He offered his ideas as admittedly blasphemous and doubtless flawed while making clear the key mechanism—the selection and amplification of advantageous traits through greater survival and reproductive rates of the individuals who happened to inherit them—that elevated his above previous transmutation theories. The following summer, Darwin and Alfred Russel Wallace (who had finally scared the cautious Darwin into publishing by writing him of his own, similar theory) published their short papers in the *Journal of the Proceedings of the Linnean Society,* providing a slightly fuller explanation and making his theory a matter of record.

Gray was at first warily receptive to Darwin's theory, then increasingly convinced. The logic seemed sound. Even if Darwin himself worried aloud to Gray (somewhat in the manner of one looking to have an insecurity contradicted) that this theory was "grievously hypothetical," it nevertheless made an argument based on a natural process rather than a supernatural one. But what truly sold Gray, in those months between Darwin's private confession of the theory and his publication of a more fully developed version in the Linnean Society papers and then *Origin,* was the light the theory shed on the botanical puzzle he himself had long been pondering.

How did such a large group of identical or nearly identical species come to exist only in two areas far apart, Japan and North America? Nearby islands, of course, often shared closely similar plant communities, but that was easily explained by assuming that the islands had once been high points on a single landmass that sank. That didn't seem to apply to Asia and North America.

Yet Gray applied something very close to that explanation, solving the puzzle by essentially treating the two great continents as islands formerly joined. Though this seems routine in our post-plate-tectonics era, it was a big leap at the time. In one of the boomerang-like ironies that careened through the contradiction-filled air around Louis Agassiz, Gray connected and disconnected the two continents via Louis's ice age theory. Using a hypothesis Hooker had applied with good results to European alpine flora, Gray proposed that in the warm part of the Tertiary period, a single temperate flora had spread unbroken across the northern reaches of Asia and North America— unbroken, he asserted, because the two continents had then shared a land bridge across the Bering Strait. This band of flora lay well north of what later became Japan and eastern North America. When the next ice age came, however, the cooling climate pushed these plant communities southward, splitting them, as they moved down either side of the Pacific, into separate communities in North America and eastern Asia. Subsequent climate changes, such as the increasing dryness of the American West, then drove the two communities into the more limited areas found by Gray's time.

This explanation was hardly free of speculation. But it was far more empirical than the notion that God arbitrarily placed identical species in two places a world apart. Yet a mystery remained. If these two communities were remnants of a former single community, why were some of the species closely similar but not identical?

Enter Darwin's new theory. In Gray's paper, drafted and refined over late 1858 and early 1859, he accepted and employed, gingerly but quite clearly, Darwin's notion (as Darwin put it in his original letter of confession to Gray) that species "are only strongly defined varieties" that rose from a common ancestor. In the millennia since the two plant populations separated, Gray explained, some of the species had diverged enough to become taxonomically distinct from their cousins across the Pacific.

Gray's Japan paper still stands as a thoughtful, creative, and bold piece of work and a pioneering accomplishment of biogeography. Along with Hooker's papers, it was one of the first to use Darwin's theory in the way it would so often be used later: to explain the anomalies of species distribution. For Gray, the paper confirmed not only the strength of Darwin's theory but the obsolescence of Agassiz's. He realized the Japan paper armed him well to challenge Agassiz, for it contradicted virtually every aspect of Louis's view of species creation and order. It even used Agassiz's own ice age theory (his most solid piece of work, as Gray saw it) against him in a way sure to heighten the contrast between Louis's idealism and Gray's empiricism. For Gray described the ice age not as a sudden holocaust erasing all life so God could start over, but in a more restrained sense, as a gradual natural event that pushed species around rather than wiping them out wholesale.

With *Origin* soon to be published, Gray sensed the time was ripe to dethrone Agassiz and relieve American science of his speculative, idealist vision. Gray had no idea that the Darwinian theory he incorporated into his Japan theory would turn the world upside down. But he saw full well that it might upend Louis.

Gray chose a friendly forum in which to first air his ideas, reading an early version of the paper at a meeting of the Cambridge Scientific Society, a small club of which both he and Agassiz were members, on December 10, 1858. This was a full year before *Origin* appeared, though several months after the Darwin and Wallace papers were read at the Linnean Society in London. Though no transcript of the talk survives, notes from attendees suggest that Gray (like Darwin, a rather cautious revolutionary) presented his ideas on species drift with a delicacy of language similar to that which he used a few months later in the *Memoirs of the American Academy of Arts and Sciences*.[11] In a footnote within that published version of his talk, Gray asserted that Darwin's theory would resolve the "fundamental and most difficult question remaining in natural history" and predicted it would hold "a prominent part in all future investigations into the distribution and probable origin of species." But he described the actual theory of variation and new-species creation in fairly tentative language, writing that "the limits of occasional variation in species . . . are wider than is generally supposed, and . . . derivative forms when segregated may be as constantly reproduced as their originals"—in other words, variations might become new species. Whether the listener would infer those other words (or even read the footnote) was left to chance. As for the Cambridge Society meeting, Gray appears to have drawn on Darwin's speciation theory only enough to help explain his solution to the Japan–North America plant-distribution puzzle.

Gray wrote a friend afterward that Louis took the presentation "very well indeed."[12] In fact, Louis, distracted by museum matters at the time, seemed to miss how large an issue Gray was raising. Gray, however, felt emboldened. He immediately arranged to read the paper before a fuller, more important audience at the American Academy of Arts and Sciences meeting the following month. There, he wrote his friend John Torrey in New York, he would "knock out the underpinning of Agassiz's theories about species and their origin [by] turning Agassiz's own guns [i.e., his ice age theory as well as much of his data on species distribution] against him."[13]

When the meeting came, Gray was indeed bolder. He spoke for more than an hour, laying out his argument and stating explicitly that this view of species distribution, creation, and variability directly contradicted the theory of species distribution and fixity offered by Agassiz—which theory, as Gray put it, "offers no *scientific* explanation of the present distribution of species over the globe; but simply supersedes explanation, by affirming, that as things now are, so they were at the beginning; whereas the facts of the case . . . appear to demand from science something more than a direct reference of the phenomena as they are to the Divine will."[14]

If Louis had missed the directness of Gray's challenge before, he certainly saw it now. Gray stood before a room of peers accusing him of pseudoscience. But Louis was uncharacteristically measured in response. In a half-hour deflection maneuver, he declined to rebut Gray's botanical argument by pleading knowledge mainly of zoology, which knowledge he then drew on to reaffirm his position and deny, without rebutting the evidence just presented, that climate affected species distribution.

Perhaps recognizing that he had not quite risen to the occasion, Louis proposed at the next Academy of Arts and Sciences meeting, two weeks later, that this subject of species origin be pursued in a series of "discussions." His old friend Ben Peirce, possibly hoping to rally the sort of crowd before which Louis usually prevailed, moved that the meetings be open to the general public. (Peirce's and Agassiz's feelings on exclusivity softened when convenient.) The group agreed. Over the months ahead, in a series of three debates, Gray and Agassiz fired the first shots in what would become a loud and long war.

It is one of history's minor oddities that no one saw it that way at the time. The resistance to Darwin's idea was that complete. Everyone saw that Agassiz was being challenged, but they missed that a common, fundamental view of the world was also under fire. The two men debated at academy meetings that February, March, and April. A couple times the debate started from the Japan paper, and once it started from Louis's presentation, yet again, of his "Plan of Creation" lecture. Gray was more explicit and pejorative every time about the difference in views and methods being presented, repeatedly contrasting his view of species distribution and creation to Agassiz's, which he said was so speculative and idealist that it "remove[s] the whole question out of the field of inductive science."[15] Finally, in May, in the cozier forum of a Cambridge Scientific Club meeting held in his own garden house, Gray let the big cat out of the bag. "To see how it would strike a dozen people of varied minds and habits of thought, and partly, I confess, maliciously to vex the soul of Agassiz with views so diametrically opposed to all his pet notions," he explicated Darwin's theory directly, summarizing and reading parts from Darwin's Linnean Society paper and the abstract Darwin had sent him, presenting plainly Darwin's theory of evolution and natural selection and noting once again that this view of species creation directly contradicted Louis's idealist vision.[16]

Well *there,* Gray must have thought; *that* should do it. Yet even now no one seemed to see how huge a door was swinging on the small hinge of these debates. No one seemed to note, for example, the distinction that Darwin's insight about natural selection gave his theory; they instead likened it to Lamarck's. Everyone seemed to regard the debate as a lively but essentially routine academic spat.

The apparent thickheadedness of Gray's Cambridge audiences was almost surely due to the deeply subversive nature of Darwin's thinking. It would take the six hundred pages of *Origin,* with its agile argument wielding a huge weight of evidence, to convince them of evolution and common descent, and decades more before the frighteningly mechanistic natural-selection theory took hold. It would take the inflamed, postpublication shouting of religious rebutters and self-styled Darwinian agnostics to highlight the philosophical and religious differences between the two views. Gray wasn't about to get such work done in a few evenings' repartee with Louis.

Doubtless the attendees were also partly fooled by the debaters' collegiality. A friendly decorum prevailed at these meetings; the two were, after all, neighbors. Gray, despite his directness and his deep, long resentments, was his usual polite self, and Louis, a bit uncertain on this new ground and perhaps not wanting to start a shooting war, remained gracious in response. The gladiatorial atmosphere of the Huxley-Wilberforce face-off never took hold. On the contrary, these meetings in the spring of 1859—before the publication of *Origin,* before the infamous Huxley rejoinder, before America's religionists started feuding with America's scientific rebels and agnostics, before, in short, Darwin's book ignited a popular controversy—witnessed what may have been the last sustained congeniality between two colleagues who had once approached close friendship and now faced each other across an opening abyss. Both still behaved as if their collegiality could span the rift, as if their differences could be raised, explored, summarized, and then set aside like most scientific and philosophical discussions, and that life and work (as Gray probably feared and Agassiz surely hoped) would continue as before.

But if the audience seemed to miss the depth of the chasm dividing the two professors, Gray and Agassiz did not. After the last of the debates, the one held at the garden house where they had once shared long dinners, Agassiz told his colleague, "Gray, we must stop this." Gray would remember the words even twenty years later.

6

A few weeks after that last May meeting, Louis sailed to Europe for a long-planned and much-needed vacation, creating a ceasefire in the debate with Gray. When he returned in late September, things stayed quiet, as he resumed teaching and organizing the new museum.

Almost as soon as the first copies of *Origin* arrived on American shores around Christmas, however, Agassiz could see that this debate would not stop. Darwin's book—engaging and accessible but supported by broad knowledge and compelling detail—was the buzz not only of the scientific world but of wider literary and academic circles, exciting discussion within the same milieu Louis had once effortlessly dominated. It immediately sold well, with a full print run of 1,750 copies selling out in the United States by May 1, a stunning distribution then for a book of science. Several of Agassiz's students read the book in the weeks after its publication, as did others in the close Harvard community. Harvard aesthetics professor Charles Eliot Norton, for instance, wrote a friend that he, the eminent Harvard zoologist Jeffries Wyman, the poet James Lowell (an Agassiz friend), and the historian Henry Torrey met excitedly the day after Christmas and "grew warm" discussing the book, recognizing immediately that "if Darwin is right, Agassiz is wrong."[17]

Louis recognized this too. And now, rested from his trip, invigorated by the enthusiasm of his new students and the possibilities his new museum offered to buttress his case, he took up anew the job of refuting Darwin's folly.

Doing so proved maddeningly difficult. At the January 1860 meeting of the American Academy of Arts and Sciences, Louis reasserted the fixity of species by trying to refute any relationship between Tertiary period seashell fossils and present forms. He was soundly contradicted by William Barton Rogers, a prominent geologist who was then starting the Massachusetts Institute of Technology. Ben Peirce called for another series of discussions, but his friend fared even worse this time around. In early March Louis tried to move the fight from Gray's turf to his own by claiming that "varieties, properly so called, have no existence, at least in the animal kingdom," and at a meeting two weeks later, in a sort of surprise managerial move, he sent a couple of stand-ins—a Harvard philosophy professor defending tenets of essentialism and Louis's old benefactor John Amory Lowell, the textile magnate—to attack Darwin on philosophical and religious grounds. Louis's use of a businessman to forward a scientific debate suggests his growing desperation. (Darwin, on reading a review of *Origin* that Lowell subsequently published, noted, "It is clear [Lowell] is not [a] naturalist.") Yet Louis had method in this madness, for Lowell was a dominant member of the Harvard Corporation, and his active opposition to Darwin carried an implicit warning to Gray about job security. But Gray, ignoring both the zoological bait and the veiled threat, countered the next month by using a wealth of botanical data to show not only that variations existed in nature but that natural selection retained and amplified them.

Meanwhile another debate series had sprung up at the Boston Society of Natural History. Here Louis, rushing from one front to another, found himself again outflanked by the geologist William Rogers. A charismatic lecturer himself, Rogers had transmuted into a sort of American Huxley, repeatedly turning Louis's paleontological and ice age research (as well as his own vast geological and paleontological knowledge) against him. These meetings provided an extra dimension of aggravation and humiliation (not to mention a disturbing sign of things to come) when some of Louis's own students asked provocative questions that fanned the debate.

None of these contretemps were true scientific debates. They were rhetorical battles in which a new argument confronted a wall of stubbornly repeated assertions. Gray pointed this out in a long, lucid, and measured review of *Origin of Species* in the March issue of the *American Journal of Science*. Playing the dispassionate arbiter, he contrasted Darwin's view of species with Agassiz's. Charles Darwin saw facts of nature as "complex facts, to be analyzed and interpreted scientifically" and "view[ed] them in their relations to one another, and endeavor[ed] to explain them . . . through natural causes." Louis Agassiz, on the contrary, treated the facts of nature as "ultimate facts [to be] interpreted theologically" and viewed them "only in their supposed relation to the Divine mind." Darwin's theory of species, despite some flaws Gray perceived, was "a legitimate attempt to extend the domain of natural or physical science." Louis's theory was "theistic to excess."[18] Though the tone was more tactful, the message was as a year before: What Louis Agassiz did could not be called science. Gray would send the same message to an even wider audience in a three-part article on *Origin* in the July, August, and September issues of the *Atlantic Monthly*. This *Atlantic* series extended the debate into the popular realm and, given that the magazine was owned and edited by good friends of Louis, spoke volumes about how far the center of debate had moved in just six months.

Louis, meanwhile, dragged his feet in providing a written critique of *Origin*. He promised to send one to the *American Journal of Science* by early February but did not deliver. This prompted Gray to write Hooker that "Agassiz has *again failed* to provide his promised criticism on Darwin for [the] Jour[nal] after promising it over and over. . . . [He has] failed because [of] the poor stuff—as everybody calls it—he has been pouring out at the Academy. I do not wonder that he hesitates to commit himself to print. I really think his mind has deteriorated within a few years."[19]

When Louis's first printed rebuttal of Darwin finally appeared in the July 1860 *American Journal of Science*, it seemed to confirm that he would rather stubbornly defend an idealist vision than undertake the critical thinking of science. Ostensibly a review of *Origin*, the piece was really an expanded version of a chapter from his own *Contributions to the Natural History of the United States* in which he re-rehashed his plan-of-creation scheme. Here he stated—proudly, as if this proved Darwinism's falsity—that "the arguments presented by Darwin . . . have not made the slightest impression on my mind." Darwin's evolutionary theory was a "scientific mistake, untrue in its facts, unscientific in its method, and mischievous in its tendency."[20]

Yet Louis could not so convince his colleagues. They had read Darwin's book, talked about it extensively, and saw it was no *Vestiges*. While many scientists first received Darwin's theory guardedly, few rejected it outright. They recognized Darwin's empirical basis, respected the voluminous evidence he marshaled, and admired the lucid power of his argument. By trying to dispose wholesale of this engaging new theory, Louis exposed his close-mindedness and a hostility to his discipline's inquisitive, empirical basis. Should someone who so arrogantly closed his mind to a productive idea stand as an icon of American science? More and more colleagues thought not.

Louis, apparently sensing that he was losing the scientific debate, took the fight to other fronts, writing for popular magazines, lecturing, and building the museum, whose collections, he felt sure, would yet prove Darwin wrong. He wrote his own piece for the *Atlantic Monthly*, rebutting Gray and Darwin; gave yet another series of Lowell Lectures on his plan of creation, which he soon published as a book (*Methods of Natural Study*) that went through several printings; gave a variation on that lecture series in New York, which he also quickly published in book form; and then composed a series of a dozen articles for the *Atlantic Monthly* that were *also* turned into a book.[21] Between 1861 and 1866 he gave scores of lectures and published four books and twenty-one articles, almost all in the popular press, asserting his brand of special creationism. Yet even as he fought, he fell. He retained virtually no scientific allies. Most of his Harvard colleagues (as well as the Massachusetts legislature) continued to support the museum, and the scientific community continued to recognize the great value of his taxonomic and curatorial work. But as a theoretician, Louis walked alone. Even he, in writing only for the popular press, recognized that the scientific debate had moved on. His own students were questioning and deserting him. Colleagues grew less deferential. He began suffering political reversals. Members of the Academy of Arts and Sciences, a group that Louis had long dominated, began siding with Gray on political matters, and in 1863 they elected Gray president and William Rogers secretary.

Louis's most searing political defeat came at the 1864 meeting of a new scientific group he had helped found only the year before, the National Academy of Sciences (or NAS—unrelated to the Boston-based Academy of Arts and Sciences). The 1864 NAS meeting took place in New Haven, a location that should have warned Louis of trouble, for New Haven was home to Yale geologist James Dwight Dana, the Gray ally and *American Journal of Science* editor who had been attacked by Jules Marcou with Louis's support. But Louis felt confident, for it was only the year before that he, Peirce, and their closest scientific allies, having had their elitist agenda rebuffed at the Academy of Arts and Sciences, had founded the National Academy of Sciences specifically to emulate the elite, election-only French academies Louis admired. The new academy's elitist function seemed confirmed by its designation as the federal government's official scientific advisor. Membership was limited to fifty and internally elected; since Louis, Peirce, and their allies had handpicked most of the original forty-nine, they figured to control subsequent entries, including the addition of the fiftieth member, which was part of the business for the 1864 meeting.

But the meeting (only the organization's second) brought a stunning reversal. Gray, Dana, and a few allies, using a slippery, last-minute switch of career geologist Dana to the organization's zoology section so he could cast a deciding nominating vote within that section, managed to give the fiftieth spot to Smithsonian Institution director Spencer Baird, a man whom Louis hated because he lent Louis specimens only reluctantly and, worse, had once hired a defecting Agassiz assistant. Louis was livid. Gray had outmaneuvered, outvoted, and embarrassed him in the elitist political structure that he himself had founded. The incident starkly lit his fall from power. On the train back to Boston, he confronted Gray, calling him "no gentleman" and apparently other words less printable, insulting Gray so deeply that the two would not speak again for several years. Back in Cambridge Agassiz complained widely, and rumor spread that he had challenged Gray to a duel (swords, presumably). Had he received such a challenge, Gray, even were he not pacific to begin with, would surely have declined. He had already won.

From this nadir Louis never rose. Fame showed its rough side now, as the scientific world and most of Louis's social circle heard of his humiliating losses to Gray. With Louis's diminished political clout made clear by his failed power plays at both the Academy of Arts and Sciences and the NAS, colleagues and students began to speak openly of his scientific obsolescence. His stock fell particularly low among younger scientists and intellectuals. As his own students deserted him, so the younger intelligentsia in Cambridge and elsewhere, thrilling to the intellectual vitality they found in the discussion of Darwin, began to see in Louis—only five years earlier the prince of American science—an archaic reactionary.

By the fall of 1864, Louis, worn down psychically and physically, decided to take a long vacation the following year in Brazil, where he could visit his old friends the Amazonian fishes. About the time he decided on the trip, John Lowell invited him once again to lecture at the Lowell Institute. At the lectures that winter, Louis, making one last attempt to plough Darwin under before he himself went south, expanded his glacial theory to the Amazon, where he said the zoological and geological record—oh, if only anyone had resources to explore it!—would surely show that even there all life had been wiped out by the last ice age and replaced with new species wholesale, by divine plan rather than evolution.

Nathaniel Thayer, one of Boston's richest men, a longtime supporter of Louis, and an audience member that night, accepted Agassiz's thinly veiled solicitation and offered to fund such a trip. And so in April 1865, as America's Civil War came to a close, Louis sailed off to collect evidence that once and for all would prove Darwin wrong. It was a bizarre trip. Along with three paid scientists, Liz Cary, his old artist Jacques Burkhardt, and for part of the trip a bishop, Louis took along several untrained assistants, including the young William James, who had taken a couple of classes with Agassiz and thought him both fascinating and revolting. Louis had grand plans for this crew. As James noted in a letter home early in the trip, "The Professor has just been expatiating over the map of South America and making projects as if he had Sherman's army at his disposal instead of the 10 novices he really has." James observed that Louis was typically grandiose in other ways as well. When a fellow passenger, a Mr. Billings, offered to lend Agassiz some books, Agassiz asked, "'May I enter your state room and take them when I shall want them, Sir?'

Billings, extending his arm, said genially: 'Sir, all that I have is yours!' To which, Agassiz, far from being overcome, replied shaking a monitory finger at the foolishly generous wight: 'Look out, Sirr, dat I take not your skin!' That expresses very well the man."[22]

Louis and Liz were gone for sixteen months, scattering Thayer's money far and wide. Louis hoped to collect enough species to reveal a pattern that natural selection could not explain and to find geological proof of a cataclysmic ice age. He collected plenty: eighty thousand specimens, so many fish, crustaceans, and mollusks that it took Alex and the museum's minions over a decade to classify them. There were fifty barrels of crayfish alone.

But neither all the fish nor the sparse evidence of glaciation that Louis found proved him out. The geology in the popular account that Liz and Louis wrote (made a best-seller by Agassiz fans and armchair travelers) made scientists shake their heads in wonder. His findings did nothing to refute Darwinism. Yet to the astonishment of many, he professed to believe otherwise. When he returned in August 1866, he immediately began lecturing on the trip's discoveries, incorporating his hurried, rather desperate analysis of Brazilian zoology and geology into his old plan-of-creation spiel. He concluded his talk, titled "Traces of Glaciers Under the Tropics," with the words, "And so that is the end of Darwin."

Twenty years earlier, Louis had wowed everyone—young, old, idealists, empiricists—with an earlier version of this lecture. Much had changed. The impression he now made was captured most bitingly that summer night in 1866 by one of his Cambridge audience, a former student named Chauncey Wright, the brilliant but troubled "philosopher of Cambridge," a friend of William James and a contemporary of Alex's. Wright had once taken a class with Louis, and in 1860, when *Origin* came out, he had been teaching at the Agassiz Girls' School. At that time, having previously taken Louis's professed empiricism to heart, he was so appalled by Louis's reactionary, idealist response to *Origin* that he quit the school faculty. Agassiz's plan-of-creation theory, he had written a friend then, "covers ignorance with a word pretending knowledge and feigning reverence."[23] Now, in the Brazil talk, Wright confronted something worse than ignorance; he saw a calcification of both mind and ego. As he wrote

Charles Eliot Norton, "Agassiz repeated . . . what he has said at every scientific meeting at which I have heard him speak, and he said it with as much animation as if the world were not weary of it. It is a chronic case of public speaking,—a brilliant idea which occurred to him once upon a time, and has been a standing marvel of inspiration ever since."[24]

Alex, of course, was watching.

CHAPTER SIX

Transmutation

I

A LEXANDER AGASSIZ'S response to the controversy over Darwinism offers one of science history's more adept displays of fence sitting. He managed never to take a clear public stand either for or against Darwin's main tenets. But privately and between the lines of his often rather dense technical publications, Alexander revealed a slow but certain conversion to evolution. He always rejected the more speculative flights that sent some Darwin supporters out Gray's garret window. The empiricism he shared with Gray, however, led him to a similar if more private acceptance. It did not happen overnight. But over the decade or so following *Origin*, Alexander embraced some of the most radical elements of Darwin's theory, including those most fundamentally opposed to his father's thinking.

At first, Alexander did not seem to see that a son can't fight his father's battles any more than a father can his son's. In early 1863, while Theo Lyman was still in Europe, Alex wrote asking him to check some fish specimens in London to bolster Louis's arguments against Asa Gray, who was being "uncooperative."[1] He also asked Theo to sniff around Germany to see who was spreading rumors there about Louis's authorship fight with Henry Clark. In defending his father he indulged and took on some of his vindictiveness. Of Christian Hansen, one of first rebels to leave the museum in the early 1860s, Alex wrote to Theo in late 1863:

Alexander Agassiz, circa 1860, the year The Origin of
Species *changed the landscape of science*

I heard today that Hansen tried to cut his throat in Scotland . . . ; his neck being too fat he did not cut half deep
enough to reach any vital part. He has been stiched up and he is
alive and kicking. It seems [a pity] to be so fat that you can not
kill yrself by hanging drowning or cutting your throat. The
only thing left for him to do is to swallow a shell with a long
fuse and then explode it, perhaps he will burst, but perhaps his
fat will save him again.[2]

Clearly Alex, watching his father besieged on the eve of the Salem
secession, does not yet see how avidly Louis cooked his own grief. It
naturally pained him to see his father rail and flail as he found himself rejected by students and forced from the center of American science. That Alex himself suffered Louis's excesses, scrambling to patch

relations, fill vacancies, and defer debtors, only made it harder. Thus the cycles of frustration, anger, and distress, each one ending in a bitter crash after which he would foreswear heroics and pledge to distance himself.

Alexander Agassiz faced a particularly vexing challenge in confronting Darwinism. Even for other scientists, the early, rapid polarization of the dispute between Darwinists and traditionalists made it hard to weigh the scientific issues dispassionately. Absorbing Darwinism demanded difficult choices and the sometimes excruciating rejection of long-held assumptions—a sort of secular exorcism. Even Darwin's prime defenders flinched at this task. Huxley, Lyell, and most other early Darwin allies rejected natural selection, and even Gray, one of the few to accept it, would not acknowledge it as a completely mechanistic force. Yet Alex had to grapple with Darwinism as the son, prime assistant, and housemate of the scientist most famous for opposing it.

In retrospect, Alex separated the personal from the scientific remarkably well. He did this by considering the theory privately, well outside of the ideological battle that was consuming his father, and by rejecting the most extreme and rigid ideas coming from either side. In an important sense he responded to this central intellectual and philosophical conflict of his time much as his acquaintance and sometime dinner companion William James responded to the Civil War: He sought a sort of scientific pragmatism. Pragmatism was the name of the school of philosophy established in the post–Civil War years by James and his colleagues and friends Charles Peirce (Ben's son), Oliver Wendell Holmes, Jr., John Dewey, and others. It was a roughly relativist philosophy that had as a chief tenet a skepticism of all ideology and absolutist thought. James and his philosopher friends (most of them acquaintances of Alex's) had gained this leeriness by witnessing (and in the case of the thrice-wounded Holmes, directly suffering) the butchery of the Civil War, which they saw as partly a clash between fiercely held ideologies—national unity and abolition in the North and slavery and states' rights in the South.

Likewise, Alexander viewed skeptically the more strident expressions of Darwinism and creationism because he had seen the madness made when scientists took theory as dogma.

He sought a place less wearing to stand, one to advance from rather than defend. During the period in which he was venting to Theo about conniving students, he was also cursing the difficulties of living with a righteous idealist. In the same letter in which he imagined detonating the hapless Hansen, for instance, he lamented the departure of another, clearly more valuable student-assistant. A month later he complained of Louis's fury at Asa Gray, of whom "it is dangerous," he wrote, "to speak . . . in father's presence."[3] Over the following months he ceased regularly defending his father and assumed a still-aggravated but more distant point of observation. He railed at the worst personal indignities Louis suffered. But he increasingly saw the damage Louis's imperiousness caused the museum and himself.

> Father I am sorry to say is in no better condition than he was last summer. The boils on his head are as thick as blackberries and keep him in a perfect fever day and night. He will not have a pleasant summer and has thus far not done a thing. He walks into the Laboratory once in the morning and that is all for the day.[4]

It is no coincidence that it was about this time that Alex began thinking more independently about Darwinism. In early 1864 he wrote to Fritz Müller, a German zoologist becoming known as a Darwin champion, expressing what might be called his growing scientific pragmatism. His statements are striking given Louis's presence in the same building.

> Nothing will give me greater pleasure than to answer your questions about Cœlenterata [a phylum of marine invertebrates that both Alex and Müller studied] and Darwin. It is only by discussing these broad questions in the most unprejudiced manner that we may hope to arrive at the truth, and mere dogmatic expressions of opinion ought never to influence us in the least, no matter what the source from which they come, and how great the authority may be. I trust that henceforth in Natural History, workers will not allow themselves to be biased by any weight of authority, either on one side or the other, but will examine the facts and carefully analyze them to see what they

mean. We should not have so many wild theories in our science, did not every one who has studied a subject give generally such disproportionate importance to the particular part which they have examined.

This is the language of one warning of the costs of righteous narrow-mindedness. He then silently refutes his father even while rejecting Darwin:

> With regard to the Darwinian theory, it seems to me to be only bringing up the same arguments as those used by Lamarck, only backed up by greater research and greater knowledge. The same objections which were fatal to the Lamarckian theory . . . will in due time cause the death of [Darwin's] theories; but good his scrutiny has undoubtedly done, as it is always a salutary thing for science to have a skillful skeptic attack its most religiously held dogmas.[5]

Though Alex went on in this letter to mount an embryological argument against Darwin's theory (an argument he would later drop during his correspondence with Müller), his repudiation of Louis's reaction to that theory is clear. What Louis rejected as "unscientific" and "mischievous," Alex receives as a well-informed, constructive argument founded on extensive research and knowledge. While he has not yet accepted Darwin, he has done something for the time more important: He has found a stance distinct from his father's by rejecting the ideologization of science by which Louis rose and fell.

This stance freed Alex intellectually and emotionally to pursue his own path in science. For the time, however, he was starting to feel stuck at the museum. The war increased his restlessness; things went so poorly for the North in 1864 that he began preparing the museum and his own affairs for his resignation so he could enlist. By early 1865 he had things ready for his departure.

That spring, of course, Louis took off for Brazil; and with the war going better, Alex agreed to stay and tend the museum. But his restlessness increased while Louis was gone. Though he no longer faced constant reversal of his organizational efforts, he missed the income Louis usually brought in, especially after a closer, unimpeded look at the accounts unearthed previously undisclosed debts. Desperately needing seven thousand dollars to pay one debt, he secured another by offering as security his father's library and the land on which stood the family house. It was either that, he wrote Theo, "or shut up [the] Museum for the year and pay the thing from income. . . . Things cannot go on as we are now."[6]

2

Soon came an opportunity that not only sprang Alex from the museum but permanently solved the institution's financial problems. In 1865 Alex's uncle, Quincy Shaw, received a visit from a mining surveyor seeking investors for an idle copper mine, the Calumet, that he had found in Upper Michigan. Shaw, familiar with the area from his Oregon Trail trip, promptly visited the site and liked what he saw. When he returned he asked Alex, who had studied mining for his engineering degree, to see if he thought there was some way to extract the copper at reasonable cost. Alex traveled to Michigan to look at the Calumet mine soon after Louis returned in August 1866. What he saw so overwhelmed his usual pessimism that on return he told Shaw he should buy the whole outfit. He then borrowed ten thousand dollars from Theo so he could buy a stake too. Shaw bought a majority share, and Theo, Alex's sisters, and several other family members bought in as well. Shaw hired Alex to get the mine going, and in March 1867, leaving Theo in charge of the museum's finances, Alex traveled by train to Upper Michigan, where Annie, five-year-old George, and infant Max soon joined him.

For the following eighteen months, Alex left the world of science almost completely (though he did find time to write papers on the ducks and beaver dams he saw everywhere in Michigan) and engaged instead the challenge of making a poorly operating mine successful. Working one long week after another for months, learning every detail of the mine's operation, he efficiently solved the mine's two main problems: how to extract the property's diffuse copper from the soil and how to efficiently transport large quantities of copper to market. When he arrived in March, the Calumet mine was running on a skeleton crew and losing money. When he left eighteen months later, it was operating at full crew, expanding its shaft and transportation systems, and producing more copper every month. It began paying dividends in December 1869, and within five years it ranked among the world's most productive mines. During the 1870s and 1880s, still under Alexander's directorship, it would produce half the nation's copper, and it continued to yield large amounts and profits for the next five decades. Alex also made what were then progressive labor innovations, establishing injury and pension funds and building schools, hospitals, and libraries for the several thousand families whose incomes depended on the mines.

While Alex did not return from Michigan rich, he and the other family investors soon knew they would do quite well, and indeed they did. The earliest investors eventually saw returns exceeding 10,000 percent. This bonanza would save Quincy Shaw from financial ruin, for he lost almost all his immense family fortune in a banking collapse in early 1867. But though Shaw began 1870 on the verge of bankruptcy and financial scandal (having borrowed from a family trust fund), he ended it on his way to being obscenely wealthy. Theo Lyman, meanwhile, still blessed monetarily as well as every other way, simply became trebly rich. Alex's sisters also grew flush. And Alex, who had invested more heavily than anyone but Shaw, borrowing from Theo the stunning sum of $110,000 altogether to invest in the early going, eventually became one of the United States' richest citizens, earning many millions from the mine alone. From the mid-1870s on, he would be able to pursue science with a freedom that few have ever known.

When he first returned from Michigan in October 1868, however, he was excited less about his prospects for wealth than about simply returning to science. The museum for once did not seem to need him. Theo had guarded the books well, curbing Louis's worst excesses, and Louis had charmed another $150,000 out of the legislature to expand the building. Alex left well enough alone, taking only a few background duties from Theo and advising on the building expansion but otherwise keeping his distance. He seemed determined to preserve his newly won independence. For the first time, he and Annie rented their own home, a small house near the museum. Mornings she would walk him to his office, where, surrounded by cases and drawers of specimens he and Theo had unpacked years before, he resumed his work.

He concentrated primarily on a project he had tended intermittently for years, an exhaustive account of the great marine phylum echinodermata: the world's starfish, brittle stars, sea urchins, sand dollars, and sea cucumbers. Alex, fascinated by these animals since he'd hunted them as a boy, had studied them seriously since his student days. In the early 1860s he had published several articles and monographs that made him an authority on this much-studied clade. Now he wanted to write the comprehensive taxonomy he had long pondered. Consolidating his existing research over the winter of 1868–1869, he entered the spring of 1869 feeling he had done everything he could from Cambridge and now needed, if the thing was to be complete, to visit several collections in Europe. But though he would soon be rich, he yet lacked the means. Here one of his father's many wealthy friends, James Lawrence (yet another textile millionaire), stepped forward to underwrite the trip, insisting that Alex take Annie and the boys. The money, Lawrence truthfully assured him, would hardly be missed, and the cause was good. Alex accepted.

In September 1869, not quite a year after he had returned from Michigan, Alex and family sailed from Boston for Liverpool. Over the next fourteen months he took what amounted to a scientific grand tour, traveling all over western and central Europe, examining every zoological collection that held echninoderms. He visited London, Belfast, and Paris; Rome, Florence, Bologna, and Venice; Berlin, Hamburg, Bonn, Munich, Heidelberg, Frankfurt, Würzberg, Leipzig, Vienna, Breslau, and Kiel; Copenhagen and Stockholm; doubled back to Switzerland to hike with Annie and show her the train platform where he'd stomped on his violin; and finally returned to Great Britain.

He was widely received as both the son of the famous Louis and, thanks to his own publications and the clear knowledge he showed of his subject, a promising scientist in his own right. His reception gave him a survey not just of museums but of scientific perspectives, from the idealist ruminations of Ernst Haeckel, whom he visited in Jena, to the hard-eyed empiricism of the English. "Haeckel I liked extremely," he wrote Liz Cary, his most frequent correspondent after Theo; "he is, however, of a most enthusiastic disposition and in the Okenistic direction he has taken he is doing himself a great deal of harm. [Oken, who had taught Louis Agassiz as well as Haeckel, was a leader of the *Naturphilosophie* school.] He has left the positive for the speculative, and indulges in fancies which are more like the dreams of Swedenborg than Natural History."[7]

This might have been Asa Gray speaking. And given Alex's Gray-like devotion to empiricism, it's unsurprising that he felt most comfortable among Gray's friends in England. His reception there was particularly warm. Gray had given them good advance notice several years before, writing Darwin that he "expected better things" of Alex than what Louis had become, and since then Alex's own sparse but intelligent correspondence with Darwin himself had confirmed his promise. He spent over a month altogether in London, enjoying himself thoroughly.

"Britain is great," he wrote Theo. "I have been perfectly feasted since I came to London, have seen all the swells . . . and taken a good dose of their claret which is usually very good. Huxley I like particularly."

It neither intimidated Alex nor put him off that most of these men had championed the cause that brought his father low. He met and liked not just Darwin and Huxley but Lyell, Hooker, and Wallace, the cofounder of the theory of natural selection. The man he liked least was Richard Owen, the superintendent of natural history at the British Museum, who gained extra fame as the most prominent British scientist to stiffly resist Darwinism. Owen struck Alex as vain and grandiose.

Darwin, on the other hand, Alex found to be "the most simple and unpretending man I have met and exceedingly cordial," as he told Theo.[8] Alex visited him twice, once soon after arriving and again shortly before he returned to America. Darwin did not often go to town, so Alex and Anna traveled to Down. Alex carried with him a letter of introduction from his father advising Darwin that he would "find Alex more ready to accept your views than I will ever be."[9] So he proved. He and Anna spent the whole day with the Darwins, having what Alex described to Theo as "a very pleasant time" during which the conviviality (or perhaps the claret) apparently went to Alex's head. For it was here at Down that Alex, clearly charmed by Darwin, possibly emboldened by his father's letter, and likely loosened up by almost two months of socializing and study with Darwin's empirical

friends, finally felt it safe to tell someone—Darwin of all people—
that he believed in evolution. So Darwin relates, in a letter written
immediately after Alex's first visit, to Fritz Müller, the German zoologist and evolutionist to whom Alex had written several years before
about Darwin, embryology, and the value of questioning dogma:

> We liked [Alexander] very much. He is a great admirer of yours,
> and he tells me that your correspondence and book first made
> him believe in evolution. This must have been a great blow to
> his father.[10]

It is both stunning and completely in character—revealingly
typical—that amid all available written record the first clear statements of Alex's belief in evolution appear in letters penned by his
father and Charles Darwin. Whence the conversion? Judging from
his confession to Darwin, Alex's swing had come between 1864 and
1867, a period during which he and Müller discussed at length the
embryological evidence for evolution that Müller presented in his
1864 *Für Darwin*. Alex was then studying the embryonic forms of
various classes of echinoderms and finding their close resemblance
suggestive of common descent, much as Gray had with plant specimens. If Darwin's letter is accurate (and he had little reason to lie),
Alex, like Gray, became convinced of evolution when a respected
colleague persuaded him to take a fresh look at the evidence before
his own eyes. It is strange that Alex apparently didn't confess directly
to Müller his apparently Müller-inspired conversion, especially as
Müller had been one of Alex's first friends from the larger world of
science, having thrilled Alex by writing a kind response to one of his
earliest papers on echinoderms. But though Alex's long-running correspondence with Müller includes some of Alex's frankest, most
unguarded letters, none of them refer to this conversion. Alex seems
to have felt it proper to inform the principals in the Darwin-Agassiz
dispute of his beliefs while seeing no reason to tell anyone else. He
probably confided his belief in evolution to Theo and other friends.
And he obviously had to his father, at least by late 1869, apparently
without hard feelings. Now he had confessed the same to Darwin
himself. Yet he kept a public silence ever afterward.

He would hold his cards almost as close in writing the *Revision of the Echini,* which he took up in earnest as soon as he returned home in November 1870. He worked hard on it for two strong years at the museum, in a new, bigger house he and Anna rented, and in summers at the coast. He produced a specialist's tome: meticulous, thorough, detailed, and largely unapproachable. Most of its 762 pages are devoted to defining the anatomical and embryological distinctions of the five classes and many orders, families, and genera into which he categorized the thousands of known species of echinoderm. Like Gray's botanical publications, the *Revision* is an empirical work of the most fundamental sort, drawing heavily on the author's own first-hand observation of specimens. It was almost all description and definition. This 1873 publication was mostly indistinguishable, in other words, from a taxonomic work that Alex or any other smart, punctilious zoologist might have written before Darwin blew things up in 1859.

Yet the *Revision*'s few pages of interpretation embrace one of Darwin's least obvious but most vital and troublesome insights. Of all the ideas Darwin pushed, none was more fundamentally and deeply radical than the notion that species were categories of taxonomic convenience rather than real divisions in nature. Darwin did not simply say that borders between species changed as the species altered; he insisted that the borders were arbitrary boundaries imposed by our own needs, like lines on a map, their artifice proven by evolution. Species, in other words, were quite literally "only strongly defined varieties," as Darwin had put it to Gray, for a species was not a more specific real thing than a variety was, but only a firmer semantic category.

This concept proved hard for many scientists, much less laypeople, to swallow. It infuriated fixed-species creationists like Louis. And it defied long-held assumptions and habits of Western thinking, particularly in science. It contradicted the essentialist and determinist principles then accepted as science's bedrock, for instance, for it ultimately denied that we could know or calculate anything about the biological world, or at least about species, with absolute certainty. It insisted that you practiced biology not with sure laws and categories but with probabilities and flexible definitions. It also defied the "common sense" notion that words named things rather than just our ideas about things. People could buy that one thing could turn into another; it was harder to believe that the one thing was an arbitrary category to start with.

A working taxonomist could accept this idea readily enough, however, for it explained why the occasional specimen lay maddeningly on the border between species: The border did not really exist. It was just an instrument handy to our need to classify.

Alex had run smack into this problem while parsing echinoderms. In 1872 he had written Darwin that

> the number of young I have been compelled to examine has led me to modify my views of the nature of genera, species, and in fact of all subdivisions. I cannot find anything that is *stable* . . . and the gradual passage in Echini of the most widely separated groups leaves in my mind but little doubt that our classification is nothing but the most arbitrary convenient tool.[11]

He could hardly reject more completely his father's definition of the reality of species, genera, families, and orders. But this was just a private letter to Darwin. Would he say as much in public?

He did, if less plainly, in the *Revision of the Echini*. There he made a plea for a more flexible taxonomy that recognized that species boundaries are vague and arbitrary.

> Are we to attempt to define with mathematical accuracy what we mean by a species . . . ? [We might] as well attempt to solve an equation of an infinite number of unknown quantities. . . . The fact is, . . . we can no longer define species as is customary. . . . [Yet] we need not trouble ourselves as to the metaphysical existence of species, genera, etc., or because we have no suitable definition of species applying to all classes of the animal kingdom. . . . It matters only . . . that we should distinctly state the limits we assign to these categories in some way readily understood; and this the individuals or groups of individuals belonging to the different categories will supply.[12]

In other words, it should not cripple us to realize that species are arbitrary categories of *our* thought rather than fixed expressions of God's; we need only have good working definitions that let us usefully classify what we find in the wild.

It's a utilitarian, almost obvious idea, but a necessary one in response to the realization that the world does not exist in objectively real categories. A dog is not a dog; it's a creature matching our ideas about dogness. In recognizing this, Alexander moved from the knowable world of Cuvier and Newton, in which nature and its laws could be cleanly known, to the murkier world of Darwin, in which you must employ, constantly revising, what you recognize are simply the best working definitions and ideas at hand. He had moved, in short, from eighteenth-century essentialism to twentieth-century pragmatism, and thus to the beginning of modernism, with all its doubts and uncertainties.

CHAPTER SEVEN

Selection

*Anna Russell Agassiz, Alexander's wife and
the sister of the wife of his best friend*

A LEXANDER AGASSIZ was not one to dally daily with philosophy. If he dealt with the epistemological issues raised by
Darwin's species view in *Revision of the Echini,* it was only so he could
form a good working response to it. Most zoologists and naturalists,
particularly taxonomists, ultimately reacted the same way. Rather
than being frozen by abstract questions of species essence, they recognized they just needed a consistent functional definition of what
species were.

Having tackled Darwinism's practical implications, Alex forged ahead, dissecting, classifying, analyzing, and writing. *Revision of the Echini* was a huge job that taxed his energies and intellect. Yet the three or four years during which he concentrated on the book were the happiest of his life, partly because he finally had the time and independence simply to work. Touring Europe had reinvigorated his health and scientific enthusiasm, and when he returned he found the museum running so smoothly that he had only to serve as advisor rather than day-to-day manager. The Calumet mine was also "in apple pie order and running as smooth as clockwork."[1]

His only negative distraction was Louis's health. Louis had suffered a small stroke in 1869 before Alex left for Europe, and his strength was returning only gradually. By the time Alex was back, his father was coming to the museum each day for just an hour or two, after which he would go home to rest, sometimes getting more work done there. He was hardly the "steam engine" Alex and Theo had so often marveled at. This worried Alex. But Louis's reduced energy actually proved a bit of a blessing, for a less vigorous Louis made less trouble. He seemed to concentrate more on his main work, that of teaching and his latest investigations, and less on battling Darwin or launching projects that Theo and Alex would have to quell. He was less riotous.

The home Alex and Anna rented, Charles Eliot Norton's mansion known as Shady Hill, was spacious and comfortable, and the growing income from Calumet relieved them of financial worry and (courtesy of hired help) not a few chores. They were free to work and enjoy their children (now out of diapers and the most labor-intensive years) and friends. Summers they spent on the shore, renting a different house each year. Alex, who loved horses, taught the boys to ride during these summers, fitting it in amid more field and book work on *Echini*. The young family spent much of their time with Theo and Mimi. The two couples understood each other thoroughly. The brothers-in-law were almost as close as the sisters, for they had known each other now half their lives. The bonds between the families were further strengthened by the nearness in age of George to Cora, Mimi and Theo's daughter, a much-adored child in whom Theo took immense pleasure.

After a life marked by unexpected setbacks and turmoil, Alex felt a happiness so blooming that he hesitated to trust it. He particularly feared that illness would again strike his family. It was a reasonable fear in that pre-antibiotic time. In the twenty-four years since Alex had moved to the United States, epidemics of cholera, yellow fever, and flu had killed many thousands, and the previous eight years alone had brought lethal outbreaks of typhus, typhoid fever, scarlet fever, and yellow fever. His father's ailments were never far from his mind, and at some level his mother's last illness doubtless stayed near too. Occasionally came close reminders. Early in 1873, while Theo, Mimi, and Cora were traveling in Europe, Mimi, who eleven years before had become dangerously weak after bearing Cora in Florence, fell seriously ill there again, probably with the flu that was then killing many on both sides of the Atlantic. During the lags in transatlantic correspondence, Alex and Anna often feared the worst. When in March they heard that Mimi had pulled clear, Alex felt the relief of someone who had dodged a scripted fate. "Every thing seems so prosperous," he wrote Theo in expressing his great relief, "that I feel as if some of us would have to pay a heavy penalty . . . for all our happiness."[2]

When the penalty came, it struck hard. In July Theo and Mimi were still abroad when Cora took sick. She likely contracted the flu strain that had threatened her mother. Cora, however, did not pull free. After an illness of two weeks, she died at The Hague.

It took the Lymans two months to bring their daughter's body back to Cambridge for burial. Theo, always emotive, was still devastated when they arrived. For weeks he wept at any reminder of his daughter's absence. He had frequently recorded in his diaries and letters acutely observed descriptions of Cora learning and playing and growing—her hopscotch games with new Italian neighbors, comic language miscues with French playmates, her proud mastery of the first German songs she memorized and translated. (Theo recorded in his diary the entire songs, in both languages.) Now, actively prodding his remembrances to keep Cora present, he filled his diary with heartrent expressions of grief. As the months passed, he lamented time's erosion of the pain that was all he had left of his daughter:

The outlines of the painful images are growing less sharp; a sort of perspective begins to invest what once was present. . . . The vivid grief is followed by a state which well may be called "forlorn." To grieve is to live, to be forlorn is a negative existence. "Think of what you have left"—that is the old saying. I indeed have much left—but is life so sweet that we should seek to hold to it when one half is lost? I don't see much chance of dying—my health was never better—and I have no wish to die so long as I can help Mimi.[3]

Theo, who had escaped the Civil War with body and spirit intact, barely survived his daughter's death, and it's clear he barely cared to.

Alex and George, Cora's lifelong playmate, carried Cora's bier to the grave. In the months following, Alex watched in pain as his best friend, long a bright light in his as in many lives, suffered precisely the erasure of happiness Alex had feared. The penalty had been levied.

It soon struck much closer. Some ten weeks after Alex helped Theo and Mimi bury Cora, Louis fell ill. Louis had often been sickly over the previous five years, but he had felt better for months now and had been particularly vigorous since summer, when an innovative natural history course he gave to several dozen public school teachers had provided the thrill, seemingly lost to days past, of sparking inspiration in new followers. He had returned to Cambridge that fall of 1873 full of plans, igniting many burners at once. He even wrote a new rejoinder to Darwin for the *Atlantic Monthly.* He seemed almost back to his old steam-engine self.

Alex and Anna saw all this from close range, for in November, having vacated Shady Hill for the returning Charles Eliot Norton, they had moved back into the Quincy Street house for what was to be a short stay while they looked for another place of their own. On December 5, Alex, Anna, and the boys helped Louis celebrate Liz Cary's birthday with a party that included Alex's sisters, Pauline and Ida, and their husbands, Quincy Shaw and Henry Higginson, as well as several of the Cary family. Spirits flowed and ran high, and Louis even indulged in a forbidden cigar. The following morning, however, Louis complained of feeling "strangely sleepy" soon after getting to the museum, and he returned home and went to bed. When Cary could not rouse him that afternoon, she summoned Alex from the museum. Though Louis would regain consciousness a few times, he could neither rise nor speak. He had suffered a massive stroke. Alex, Liz, and Anna took turns tending him, keeping an increasingly tense and hopeless vigil.

He died after eight days, on Sunday, December 14, 1873. Though Louis Agassiz had lost his intellectual following, he still held a large place in many hearts; the outpouring was extraordinary. Countless elegies and front-page headlines mourned his passing; the Boston papers the next day were rimmed in black. The funeral, held four days later, drew an overflow crowd, as all of Boston and Cambridge seemed to come out. In the foremost rows near Alex, Ida, and Pauline sat not only Charles William Eliot, the president of Harvard, but Henry Wilson, the vice president of the United States.

Missing from the funeral, however, was Anna Russell Agassiz. On the last night of Louis's life, exhausted from tending him, she had taken a bad cold. It had not relented and in fact had grown much worse, with an intense headache and a fever setting in on Monday. Alex, worried almost sick himself, had hardly left the house but to tend to his father's funeral business and then go to the funeral itself. Rushing home from the interment, he found Anna sicker than ever.

By this point he feared she had contracted typhoid fever, the latest outbreak of which was killing many. But a doctor's exam the next day found a different or possibly an additional culprit: Pneumonia had filled her left lung. This was Thursday. For three days, in a struggle that must have seemed nightmarishly familiar to Alex from his mother's Freiburg denouement, Anna lay with labored, rattling breath. Her coughs threw blood. On Sunday the rattle spread to the right lung. A second doctor was summoned, and after conferring, these two doctors, among Boston's finest, prescribed large quantities of brandy. It was a standard contemporary cure-all. But it almost certainly weakened her, depressing her heart, lungs, and immune system—everything that needed to rise to defeat the infection.

The desperately optimistic consensus the next day was that Anna was not much worse. They dared hope that the left lung might clear in time to save her life. But that evening she began to fade and by midnight she was gone. Alex watched her expire, stunned to numbness. His father, he of the long shadow who two decades earlier had left Alex to tend his dying mother, had reached from the grave to claim also his wife.

Part Two

CHAPTER EIGHT

A Still Greater Sorrow

Alexander Agassiz, circa 1875

I WALKED UP and down the library with him till all was ready," Theo Lyman wrote of Alex on Christmas Eve, the day they buried Anna.

> She lay in parlor, hidden in roses and other white flowers. I turned my face to the wall and listened to the service by Dr. Peabody. It was a long way over to Forest Hills—a lovely, sunny day: her grave was . . . decked with branches and flowers. Alex stood at the brink, steadily, and with the tears rolling down his

face, till I whispered to him to go and I would see everything finished.

The next day was only scarcely less grim. The three motherless boys opened their gifts amid likenesses of Annie that Alex had spread around the house, and they somehow bore up as Liz Cary, Theo, and Mimi tried to show some Christmas spirit. Alex was struck dumb. The tears he shed at his wife's grave were the only ones anyone had seen him allow. "[He] can sleep and eat; and can read and write," reported Theo; "but we cannot tell what is going on within."[1]

In the weeks ahead, Alex went to work most days, chipping away at the mountains of unfinished business his father left at the museum. At home on Quincy Street, where he and the boys stayed on with Liz Cary, he occupied himself rearranging bedrooms so as to have the boys' nearer his. For a time he helped Cary with a "life and letters" biography of Louis, but he soon let her take that over; with Louis's piles of unfinished correspondence, projects, and papers to deal with, his life already held too much of his father. He spent much of January responding to the many acquaintances and friends who had sent their condolences on Louis's death. Most of them had written without knowing that Annie had died too. Among these were Ernst Haeckel, the *Naturphilosopher* and Darwin champion whom Alex had befriended in Europe four years before. A few months later, Haeckel would publish a vicious dismissal of Louis's work, calling him a charlatan and a plagiarist, provoking Alex to break off relations permanently. But at this point Alex could still confide in the man with whom he had long corresponded about embryology:

> Your kind note written soon after father's death finds me overwhelmed by a still greater sorrow which has fallen upon me like a thunder-clap out of a clear sky. I had the misfortune a few days after father's death to lose my wife. . . . [Now] all seems of little consequence and I am utterly unable to get reconciled to an existence which is well-nigh intolerable . . . ; at present I can find no incentive for anything and I can only hope that in the course of time my interest in my children and in my work may ultimately reconcile me to a sort of passive life.[2]

While Alexander Agassiz hardly lived a passive life after Louis and Anna died, neither did he ever fully recover from this double blow. Much of the time he pressed forward out of duty, staying home for the boys as long as he could stand it and then, when his grief grew too huge, fleeing, leaving the boys with Cary. His eyes, which during his marriage had lost their boyish wariness to a sure if gruff confidence, took on a more confirmed darkness. "Alex is drawing in, and hiding his grief," wrote Theo, "[but] it tells on him, as you see in his great, sad black eyes, that sometimes wander as if they might see what they sought."[3] This look would remain all his life.

He found the first year nearly unbearable. The restless depression he suffered would today be recognized as mortally dangerous; it was all he could do, he told friends, to sit still, yet if he attempted too much, he collapsed in exhaustion and despair. The Quincy Street house, even the voices of his sons haunted him. In February he escaped, leaving the boys with Cary and going with Theo and Mimi on a six-week, six-thousand-mile trip down the coast to Florida and New Orleans and then up the Mississippi and Ohio to Cincinnati. When they returned, his grief seemed less acute, and for a time he applied himself energetically at the museum, finishing work on some of his father's publications, cleaning up the accounts and operations, proofing the final volume of *Revision of the Echini*.

Then he made a mistake. He tried to run the summer school that Louis had started the year before at Penikese Island, just off the Massachusetts coast. The school was an invigorating thrill for Louis but a stone for Alexander. Theo Lyman, out on the island to teach and help Alex run the place, entered the office one day to find Alex bawling uncontrollably. "It was one of those moments when the load was too heavy," wrote Theo. "He sat in his chamber and cried without control; and seemed like a man who had lost much blood." Theo took him to Brookline to rest. Every morning when Alex woke, Theo reported, "his hands were numb."[4]

Alex's own appraisal was equally blunt. "I was obliged to drop Penikese," he wrote a friend. "It broke me down completely. . . . As long as I am idle I flourish, but the least work unnerves me completely so that I seem to have no control over myself. If matters do not mend I must pack up my traps and go off for a few months for an entire change of scene."[5]

Matters did not mend. The one piece of positive family news was that Mimi Lyman was pregnant. But while Alex was glad for his friends, the solace that the new pregnancy offered them, still grieving after the loss of their daughter, only sharpened his own misery. As Mimi's November due date and the anniversary of Alex's double loss neared, he turned again to the anodyne of travel. This time he would go to the Andes and Lake Titicaca. His ostensible purposes were to examine copper mines, gather artifacts for Harvard's Peabody Museum of Ethnology, and do some zoological collecting. Mostly, however, he would simply try to stay a step ahead of his sorrow.

It worked for the most part, though the early weeks were rough. On the anniversary of Anna's death, having just arrived in Peru and not yet traveling in earnest, he broke down completely, according to his son George in *Letters and Recollections,* penning a "beautiful and pathetic letter" of grief to Liz Cary.* Writing it seemed to bring relief, however, for the next day Alex composed four pages of good travel narrative to Theo Lyman with no mention of heartache. A few days later he set off on his long overland travels.

For several weeks he covered new terrain rapidly enough to divert himself. Though his destination was Titicaca, he was in no hurry to get there, for the whole point was to move. An assistant curator from the museum, S. W. Garman, had come along to help at Titicaca, and Alex now sent him ahead by train—an often vertiginous three-hundred-mile course through the Andes—while he took a more meandering route by horse. Alexander had always loved to ride, and he now rode for most of several weeks, covering up to forty miles a day and getting fit and tough and tired enough to drop straight to sleep each night. Usually he stayed with new friends, for he found that a single letter of introduction (such as those he carried to the managers of the mines he visited, most of them Europeans) would create a running chain of new invitations. He thus generally traveled with good local advice and often a guide provided by his hosts.

Having spent his life in verdant climes, he found the pampas

---

* George did not print or excerpt the letter and seems to have destroyed it, for it is in none of the archives. This was not the only loss to such housecleaning. In Alex's letterbooks—the thin-leaved letterpress volumes in which he recorded copies of all his outgoing correspondence—the four pages spanning December 1873 to early January 1874 are among a dozen or so that someone razored out. In addition, Alex wrote some letters of a more personal nature—there's no way to know how many—without copying them at all.

stark. His letters show a knack for landscape description that surfaces only occasionally in his professional writing:

> What a pretty country this coast range would be were it only green, but you see only here and there a few green bushes; to be sure they say that in spring it is covered with wild flowers, but as in California it lasts but a very short time. Some of the transverse valleys, where a little water still winds its way among the pebbles, are masses of green, and give you an idea of what this country might be with irrigation. There must have been water here in plenty in olden times, for the town of Ovalle and the terminus of the railroad from Coquimbo are placed in the broad bed of an ancient river, and high above the town rise the old terraces over two hundred feet high, through which the former river once cut its way and has now left the huge masses of pebbles and cobble stones which compose the surrounding hills. You do not see, even in the Connecticut Valley, better river terraces than found here, only here they are due to the gradual rising of the whole of the Chile coast, so plainly seen by this sort of formation, and by the old beaches high above the present level which you find all along the coast.[6]

Other areas, such as the Atacama Desert, a great, arid bowl in Chile, were downright surreal. "It is exactly like riding over a dried-up caldron bottom filled with salt," he wrote home, "which is left in huge cakes a couple of feet thick, with horns of salt in all possible shapes sticking out in all directions, through which you wind your way. . . . As you ride along you are nearly suffocated with this salt dust getting into your eyes and ears and mouth." East of the desert, low green hills gave "a very fine panorama" of the mountains cut by deep canyons marking the paths of dead rivers.

"The bleakness of the scene, the utter desolation and waste of the prospect, I cannot describe, [and] not a living thing did I see," he wrote Cary. But while the land's bareness intimidated, it also revealed the geological puzzles of the steep, sharp-crested cordillera. Like others before him, Alexander could not resist the riddles posed by the Andes' exposed history. The raised shorelines and river bottoms fairly shouted of geologic uplift, as did the marine fossils everywhere—

seashells on the shores of mountain lakes, coral embedded in ledges at three thousand feet. It was the most interesting land he'd ever encountered. "I wish," he lamented, "I could have time to remain here to study [it]."[7]

Eventually, having wound over large parts of Peru and Chile, he took a train to Titicaca. The world's highest navigable lake, some 125 miles long and 50 wide (about half the size of Lake Erie), 3,200 miles square, and averaging several hundred feet deep, Titicaca sits in the northern part of the altiplano, a broad, terraced plateau between two of the Andes' tallest ranges. It drains an immense area. Twenty-five rivers flow into it, yet the strong sun and dry wind lift so much water off the surface that the sole river exiting drains only 5 percent as much water as enters the lake. The rest evaporates. The altiplano, still rising, has rearranged itself in tectonic heaves several times just within the last few millennia. Though the lake once spread far wider than it does today, on its bottom rest Incan ruins built only a few thousand years ago, when the topography and climate left them dry.

Alex was interested in these ruins as well as in what life occupied the lake. But when he caught up with Garman, the young curator had discovered only three fish species in weeks of work, bringing the lake's total fish species count to six; as in many other high lakes or polar waters, a few fish species ruled all. Garman fared better with mollusks and crustacea, pleasing his boss, and captured some immense frogs and "an excellent collection" of birds. (He did not collect any local cattle, even though the cattle, descendents of cows brought by the Spaniards, had by now developed some unusual pseudoamphibious habits: In the dry season, finding little on the arid shores, the cows and bulls waded up to their flanks and, mooselike, dunked their heads to pull water weeds.)

Alex, arriving after his weeks of riding horseback and train, checked in with Garman for a couple of days and sent him back out on the lake for more dredging and collecting. Then he set off in the *Yavari,* a small steamer provided by the Peruvian government, to survey the lake and do some dredging of his own. He looked mainly for antiquities and Incan artifacts, a novel use of the dredge that brought him few treasures. He did better bargaining with people for the old things they had in their houses. The straightforward, efficient Agassiz met intense frustration when some object that he spotted in a corner pile or "kicking about in all directions," as he complained to Cary, "much as [in] George and Max's play-room," assumed immense value the instant he showed interest in it. Bargaining maddened him. His cash usually prevailed, of course, and he eventually brought back an impressive trove. In the practice of the day he also dug up a few Indian graves for the mummies and the fishing, hunting, and household implements buried with them.

When not on the boat or traveling the surrounding countryside, he stayed in a railcar that the local mining engineers had outfitted with a tiny kitchen, dining room, and parlor, and in which they granted him one of the five bunks. Here, because he was tired, or because he was at his final planned stop, or perhaps simply because he stopped moving, the gloom caught up with him. Writing Theo to congratulate him on the birth of his son two months before, he despaired of finding the sort of hope that Theo now possessed.

> I wish I could see the youngster and his parents and look in upon your happiness for a moment. You can start life again now with as bright prospects for the future as any one could wish and I hope you and Mimi will have all the happiness you deserve. I find it harder and harder to face my prospects. It is all well enough when hard at work or when I have to make an effort to keep up my spirits as I must do constantly while staying with people who have been so kind to me . . . , but when the necessity of this has passed I am left with nothing to distract me [and] it seems to me as if I could not endure. Time does not make any difference and all I can do is try and distract myself with novelties. As for settling down in any one spot I have not the heart and the prospect of staying proudly at home seems unbearable. I know it is not right to the boys but it is stronger than I am at present and I must keep on the move for a while at least.[8]

He kept on the move for a few more weeks, poking around the towns near Titicaca for more artifacts. By early March he felt it time he got home. He sent Garman away with the zoological and ethnographic collections, then retraced his steps out of the Andes. From Callao he sailed along the coast to Panama, where he visited old friends, then trained across the isthmus and steamed across the Caribbean and up the seacoast to New York. Other than being happy to see his boys, he did not pretend to be glad to return. His past seemed all but obliterated; what remained of it haunted him; and he saw nothing to draw him forward. Yet in fact he had already encountered his future amid the Andes' arid crenulations. It lay in the coral embedded there, and in the trail of a man who had come before him.

CHAPTER NINE

The Pleasure of Gambling

*Darwin in the late 1830s, soon after his return
from the* Beagle *voyage*

I

ALEXANDER HAD been preceded in the Andes by both his
father and Charles Darwin. Louis had visited just two years
before Alex did, taking inland forays from a failed marine-research
trip. His mission, underwritten by his old friend Benjamin Peirce,
who had become director of the U.S. Coast Survey, had rounded
South America in the *Hassler,* an experimental ship designed to
dredge at depths never before reached. Louis hoped the *Hassler*
would pull up early, primitive life-forms that would shed unflatter-
ing light on the theory of evolution. But the boat and its equipment
malfunctioned so often that Louis did little dredging, and the rigors

of the trip taxed his health. He did disembark a few times and rode
high enough into the Andes to find evidence of glaciers there; these,
wrote Liz Cary in the trip's sole publication (an *Atlantic Monthly* article) confirmed Louis's earlier assertions about an ice sheet covering
South America.

Darwin's visit, almost forty years earlier, had been longer and
more productive. The *Beagle,* having spent much of the preceding
few months in dismal weather off Patagonia and Tierra del Fuego,
reached the sunny Chilean port of Valparaiso on July 23, 1834. "After
Tierra del Fuego," wrote Darwin, the dry, clear climate "felt delicious." He was entranced with the sight of the mountains, some as
high as 23,000 feet, dozens of miles away. Securing horses and a
guide, he rode into the foothills. His interest rose with the landscape.
As Alex would later, Darwin found fascinating the uplift suggested by
the steep terrain. "Who can avoid wondering at the force which has
upheaved these mountains, and even more so at the countless ages
which it must have required to have broken through, removed, and
leveled whole masses of them?" he wrote in the *Voyage of the "Beagle."*[1]

In his first trip he headed north along the coast to Quintero "to
see the beds of shells, which stand some yards above the level of the
sea."[2] These were almost certainly the same shells, blanketing seaside terraces several hundred yards high, that Alex would examine
four decades later. To both men these beaches spoke of remarkable,
repeated rises in the land. For Alex, it was these "ancient Sea beaches,"
along with coral he found several thousand feet up in the Andes, that
made him "wish I could have time to remain here to study the uprising of the land; there is a good deal to do and quite interesting
work. . . . I believe however Darwin has already done something in
this line."[3]

Darwin indeed had, for he spent the sort of extended time in the
Andes that Alex didn't allow himself. For much of 1834 and 1835,
while the *Beagle* mapped the coasts of Chile and Peru, Darwin
climbed and rode up peaks and cut across valleys, "geologizing," as
he called it, to his heart's content. These landlocked months in the
Andes contributed as much to his coral reef theory as the Galápagos
visit did to his evolutionary theory. In fact they probably shaped his
scientific approach as much as anything on the voyage. For it was

here, studying uplift, that he began to indulge the broad-scale, speculative theorizing that characterized both his stunning successes, like the theory of evolution, and his embarrassing mistakes, such as at Glen Roy.

The young man who hammered rock in the Andes is unrecognizable as the sedentary, dyspeptic thinker who dominates our popular historical picture of Darwin. He was a healthy, insatiably curious man of twenty-five, younger by more than a decade than Alex was when he rode through the Andes and, during this time of his life, just as rugged, if more innocent. The man who from his mid-thirties on would rarely travel (and then usually only to take a "water cure" or some other palliative for his gastric torments) was at this point strong and lithe, quick to travel amid real dangers posed by bandits, rebels, and deadly weather. While no Thoreau (he was less rowdy and irreverent; indeed, he hated rocking the boat), he was hardly untouched by the age's Romantic vision of wild nature as a transformative place. He took a Wordsworthian pleasure in his rambles. "I cannot tell you how I enjoyed some of these views," he wrote his Cambridge mentor John Henslow. "It is worth coming from England once to feel such intense delight. At an elevation from 10–12000 ft. there is a transparency in the air & a confusion of distances & a sort of stillness which gives the sensation of being in another world."[4] He also found exciting his own growing comfort in these distant heights, so remote and rarefied that even most animals forsook them. "We unsaddled our horses near the spring," he wrote of one excursion he took into the mountains with two cowhands as guides,

> and prepared to pass the night. The setting of the sun was glorious, the valleys being black whilst the snowy peaks of the Andes yet retained a ruby tint. When it was dark, we made a fire beneath a little arbour of bamboos, fried our charqui (or dried slips of beef), took our matte and were quite comfortable. There is an inexpressible charm in thus living in the open air. The evening was so calm and still; the shrill noise of the mountain bizcacha & the faint cry of the goatsucker were only occasionally to be heard. Besides these, few birds or even insects frequent these dry parched up mountains.[5]

Though wilderness was new to him, Darwin was no stranger to the outdoors. He had long been an avid bird hunter and walker. Born in Shrewsbury in 1809, he was the fifth of six children. He lost his mother when he was eight. His father, Robert Darwin, a doctor successful and rich, was a mercurial and sometimes harsh man. Yet he indulged a certain idleness in his youngest boy, whose namesake, the doctor's older brother, had died at twenty, devastating his entire family. The second Charles also had another, more reliably benevolent patriarch in his uncle Josiah Wedgwood, brother to Charles's dead mother and founder of the Wedgwood china dynasty. Josiah lived thirty miles from the Darwins on a huge estate called Maer, where Charles was always welcome. There Charles spent much time hunting, riding, walking, and, in the waning light after a day outdoors, happily conversing with his uncle, aunt, cousins, and their friends.

He especially loved to hunt. Under the tutelage of his uncle, his own older brother, and Maer's gamekeepers, he became a crack shot. He soon outhunted everyone. For weeks each fall he exercised a "zeal . . . so great," he recalled in his charming, disarming *Autobiography,* that "I would place my shooting-boots open by my bedside so as not to lose a half-minute putting them on in the morning."[6] He was obsessed. In off-seasons he refined his upland bird technique by practicing his gun raising before a mirror and shooting out the flames of moving candles with an airgun. In season, he carefully tallied each bird he shot. The seriousness with which he took this head count led two hunting friends to conspire one day to claim, every time he downed a bird, to have fired also, faking a reload of their guns and asking him not to count that last one, as they had shot at the same moment and it might have been one of them who had downed the bird. After some hours, he recalled later (almost fifty years later, actually, and still with some pique), "they told me the joke, but it was no joke to me, for I had shot a large number of birds, but did not know how many, and could not add them to my list, which I used to do by making a knot in a piece of string tied to a button-hole. This my wicked friends had perceived."[7]

Shooting gripped him far more than school did. The man who would later eclipse Louis Agassiz (who, one year younger, was already energetically pursuing his career plan in Germany and Paris) was in his youth a decided underachiever, as distractible as Louis was focused. He had originally planned to follow his father's profession, but when he showed no stomach for it while studying medicine at Edinburgh (witnessing his first surgery sickened him), his father pressed him to enroll at Cambridge so that he could become a country parson. Though Charles did not care for the dogma of the Church of England (he was raised a Unitarian), he went along gamely, for he recognized that otherwise he indeed might, as his father feared, "[turn] into an idle sporting man, which then seemed my probable destination."[8] "How I did enjoy shooting!" he confessed in his *Autobiography*. "But I think that I must have been half-consciously ashamed of my zeal, for I tried to persuade myself that shooting was almost an intellectual employment; it required so much skill to judge where to find most game and to hunt the dogs well."[9]

Cambridge did not immediately reverse this. When he arrived he had to take remedial Greek and Latin, for he found that he had forgotten almost every word he'd supposedly learned in earlier schooling. Almost immediately he fell into a "sporting set . . . [of] dissipated low-minded young men" with whom he "sadly wasted" much time—though apparently not too sadly. "We used often to dine together in the evening," he recalled in the *Autobiography*, "and we sometimes drank too much, with jolly singing and playing at cards afterwards. I know that I ought to feel ashamed of days and evenings thus spent, but as some of my friends were very pleasant, and we were all in the highest spirits, I cannot help looking back to these times with much pleasure.[10]

Such was his later regret about his student indifference. He found boring almost every subject but geometry, so beautiful in its deductions, and chemistry. The one new thing that excited him as much as shooting and cards—the one new thing that engaged this bright young man surrounded by his culture's greatest minds and libraries—was hunting beetles. By his own account, this beetle gathering was "a mere passion for collecting," with no real scientific discipline.[11] It was certainly a passion. Once, having caught a rare beetle in each hand and seeing a third, he popped one of the handheld beetles into his mouth so he could grab the new one. (The one beetle ejected a liquid so foul that he spat it out, losing it and the latest specimen as well.) But he said later that there was no rigor to it; it was mere accumulation, not study. He had no real curiosity about beetles' function in the natural order.

However, chasing beetles did nudge Darwin nearer his final vocation, steering his outdoorsmanship more toward biology. He moved closer yet when he began attending public lectures given by the Reverend John Henslow, the Cambridge professor and leading naturalist who became his primary mentor. Darwin so admired the clarity of Henslow's thinking and the beauty of his illustrations that he began going on the weekly natural history walks Henslow led. Henslow was intrigued by some combination of energy and intelligence in this young underachiever. He took in Darwin much as Cuvier would take in Agassiz a year later. Almost daily they went on long walks during which the lecture-leery but quick-eyed Darwin absorbed a field education in botany, entomology, and geology. Henslow also invited Darwin to weekly gatherings at his home, and frequently to dinner. The two spent so much time together in Darwin's last year at Cambridge that the dons took to calling Darwin "the man who walks with Henslow." Through Henslow, Darwin came to know many of Britain's most prominent scientists, most notably the scientist-philosopher William Whewell, whose empiricist principles were then beginning to exert immense influence on British science, and Charles Lyell, whose work in geology Darwin would soon find so inspiring.

Henslow also introduced Darwin to a work that "stirred up in me a burning zeal to add even the most humble contribution to the noble structure of Natural Science."[12] It was Alexander von Humboldt's 1819 *Personal Narrative,* a six-volume account of his five years exploring South America. Darwin's encounter with this book marked his birth as a serious student and scientist. He read it several times in his last year at Cambridge, relishing this tale of geologizing and collecting in the Andes and the South American rainforest. He fantasized endlessly about taking such a trip. Humboldt profoundly influenced Darwin even as he directly mentored Louis Agassiz 250 miles south in Paris.

Darwin had fantasies but no expectations of following Humboldt. He tried to organize a trip that summer to the Canary Islands, but it fell through for lack of funds and companions. Otherwise he had nothing going. Henslow and Humboldt had fired his enthusiasm for natural science, but the flame was hardly concentrated. As he neared graduation Darwin was still noodling over whether to join the clergy. A quiet country parsonage, he rationalized, would allow him to do the sort of natural history that pastor-naturalist Gilbert White had described in yet another favorite book, *Natural History and Antiquities of Selborne.* Beyond that, he had no agenda other than paying off his school debts and enjoying the opening day of partridge season September 1.

Yet if Darwin lacked the drive of Humboldt's more direct protégé, he shared Louis's luck with mentors. Just before graduating in spring 1831, he was invited by one of Henslow's friends and fellow reverend-professors, Adam Sedgwick, to go geologizing in Wales that August. He accepted and joined Sedgwick after idling away most of the summer. The two walked for miles hunting fossils and mapping strata, having some fair luck and a good time—though they missed the glacial scarring that would leap into view for Darwin a decade later when he had learned of Louis Agassiz's ice age theory. Yet the three weeks of geologizing did not exactly clarify Darwin's calling. When he finished the trip with no other real plans, he could find direction only in the most literal way: "I left Sedgwick and went in a straight line by compass and map across the mountains to Barmouth [where he visited some old Cambridge friends], never following any track unless it coincided with my course. I thus came on some strange wild places, and enjoyed much this manner of traveling." Then he headed home to collect his guns and hunting togs and go to his uncle's estate. It was two days short of September 1. And "at that time I should have thought myself mad to give up the first days of partridge-shooting for geology or any other science."[13]

Yet he would, quite soon. At home he found a letter from Henslow informing him that Henslow had recommended him for a berth as naturalist on the round-the-world voyage of the HMS *Beagle,* a trip projected to take two to three years. To claim the spot he had only to favorably impress the captain, Robert Fitzroy, who at twenty-six was only four years older than Darwin.

Had Darwin never read Humboldt's *Personal Narratives,* he might have blanched at such a lengthy commitment. But coming on the heels of Humboldt and his own aborted Canary Island plans, the invitation inflamed his tropical travel lust. He told his father he would very much like to go.

His father forbade it. He feared the trip would stop forever his son's halting walk toward the clergy. The son, disappointed but nonetheless happy enough to resume his shooting plans, wrote Henslow his regrets the day after receiving the invitation. The next morning he rode to his uncle's, where he told Wedgwood of the vetoed invitation. Uncle Jos was not happy with this turn of events. He immediately wrote Dr. Darwin, answering each of the doctor's objections and appealing his decision, and the next day, doubly determined that his nephew not miss such an opportunity, Wedgwood stopped Charles as he was heading off to the shooting fields, put him in a carriage, and rode with him the thirty miles to Dr. Darwin's house. They arrived to find the doctor already convinced by Wedgwood's letter. After all, he allowed, he had told Charles he would agree to the trip if he could find even one sensible man who thought it a good idea, and he could hardly call Wedgwood otherwise.

Thus Darwin, shoved into an about-face by his uncle, decided to claim the job of naturalist on the *Beagle*. To console his still doubting father, Charles told him that at least aboard the *Beagle* he would not be able to overspend his allowance, as he had so consistently at Cambridge, "unless I was deuced clever."

His father responded, "But they tell me you are very clever."[14]

2

The *Beagle* trip made Darwin, forming his mind and giving him the material for most of his major works. He later called the journey (which took five years rather than two) "by far the most important event in my life. . . . I owe to the voyage [my] first real training or education" as well as the "habit of energetic industry and . . . concentrated attention."[15] He began the trip an easily distracted idler and finished it a hard worker and penetrating theorist.

His wistful recollections of the journey also suggest that he later saw this period as the time he was most completely alive—still physically adventurous even as he first experienced the exaltation of deep intellectual engagement. His physical and mental exertions were linked more seamlessly than they ever would be again, for his field-work sparked an ongoing interplay of observation and abstraction. "Everything about which I thought or read," he said of that time, "was made to bear directly on what I had seen or was likely to see."[16] This sentence describes precisely the loop of thought, observation, speculation, and reshaped thought that marks Darwin's mature method. The method puts thought first—ideation inspiring exami-nation rather than vice versa—and weighs reasonable conjecture ("what I . . . was likely to see") as heavily as actual observation ("what I had seen"). Every outing both shaped and was shaped by the theo-retical framework taking shape in his head.

Darwin was introduced to this approach early in the *Beagle* voy-age by another book that changed his life and thinking, Charles Lyell's *Principles of Geology*. Reading the freshly published first vol-ume (of an eventual three) in his first days at sea, he thrilled to find an intellectual world opening in his head even as a new, corresponding physical world opened beyond the ship's rail. "The *Principles*," Dar-win would write a decade later, "altered the whole tone of one's mind and thence when seeing a thing never seen by Lyell, one yet saw it partially through his eyes." The influence was so great, said Darwin, that "I always feel as if my books came half out of Lyell's brain."[17]

This first volume of the *Principles* was a gift from Captain Fitzroy. Fitzroy later regretted it intensely. The captain was so conservative that he had almost rejected Darwin for the naturalist post when he heard he was a Whig. He was also an evangelical Christian, and he was so appalled when Darwin published his evolutionary theory in 1859 that he became a vociferous and prominent critic. The tension from maintaining this public opposition to his old friend helped drive him mad; in 1865 he killed himself by slitting his throat.

Darwin probably sensed that Lyell's *Principles* was seditious. Henslow, while recommending the book to him as interesting, had warned him not to believe it. Darwin not only believed but reveled in it. "The very first place which I examined," he wrote in the *Voyage of the "Beagle,"* "namely St. Jago in the Cape de Verde islands, showed me clearly the wonderful superiority of Lyell's manner of treating geology."[18]

It wasn't only Lyell's geology that Darwin considered superior; he loved Lyell's imaginative approach to making sense of nature. Lyell

rejected the prevailing catastrophist explanations of the earth's features as well as the contemporary inductivist prohibitions against
speculation. He insisted, in short, on both sticking to the facts and
using them as springboards for bold conjecture. In doing so he at
once confirmed and pushed ahead of the empirical tenets of his fellow British scientists, alarming some while thrilling others.

Lyell's break from catastrophist theory was sharp and explicit,
and it liberated geology as thoroughly as Darwin's evolutionary theory later liberated biology. Doubtless that explains some of its attraction to the young Darwin. The catastrophist geology taught during
Darwin's college days left him cold, for despite its visions of flying
rock, lava, water, and ice, catastrophist geology offered a static view
of nature. It saw the earth as essentially nondynamic, with a stable
order occasionally disrupted by huge, presumably divine catclysms—
global floods, immense volcanic eruptions, disturbances from passing comets—that had shaped its crust. The outbursts were exciting.
But as the order was God's, the forces driving these spasms needed
little further explanation.

Lyell rejected that as no science at all. He insisted on explaining
geologic history not by reference to divine act but by means of natural causes presently in effect. This uniformitarianism, as Whewell
would later term it, was really both a geologic theory and a wider scientific principle. *Principles'* main geologic argument was that the
earth's features were formed over long periods by forces still in operation; it followed that one should explain geological phenomena by
referring to causes demonstrably at work. As geology, this uniformitarianism, or gradualism, would eventually be considered overkill; a
twentieth-century "actualism" would reconcile it with a more natural catastrophism to allow for occasional events we've never directly
witnessed but for which ample evidence exists, such as tectonic col-
lisions, ice ages, and meteor strikes. As a working principle, however, Lyell's uniformitarianism cleared the way for science's advance
in profound and badly needed ways. For while the insistence that
every theory use verifiable existing causes sometimes left science
short of explanations for complicated or elusive phenomena, it fos-
tered more certain progress by preventing science from accepting
idealist or catastrophist explanations. It forced empiricism. It was
not enough to say that an apple falls because God tossed it down;

you had to define and calibrate the natural force that makes the apple drop. You were required, in the schoolteacher's term, to show your work. Of course, much of the most lasting science had always been done in this manner. But the indulgence of catastrophism allowed such empirical thinking to be set aside, and science to stagnate, whenever a natural cause proved too elusive or threatening. Uniformitarianism meant *always* seeking a natural explanation—even if it meant not finding one.

Lyell did not invent uniformitarianism. The British geologist James Hutton had first proposed it in his 1795 *Theory of the Earth.* But neither Hutton's leaden prose nor a clearer 1802 explication by his friend John Playfair could unseat the catastrophist geology then being elaborated by Cuvier. Lyell had better luck. Cuvier died soon after Lyell's first volume came out, for one thing. More important, in the quarter century since Hutton and Playfair, British science had grown increasingly confident in its empiricist principles. Finally, Lyell simply made a better case for uniformitarianism than Hutton had, demonstrating repeatedly over three volumes how it was not just possible but necessary, as his book's subtitle put it, to "explain the former changes of the Earth's surface by reference to causes now in operation."

Principles similarly pressed another Lyell innovation: It rejected inductivist taboos regarding speculation. This innovation posed more of a challenge to many of his British colleagues than did his uniformitarianism, for at the time, a cautious, gradual method of theory building was de rigueur among British scientists. This strict inductive model—the insistence on moving slowly and carefully from the specific to the general—had originated in 1620 with Francis Bacon, who forged it to liberate science from the bonds of church, state, and errors of logic. Bacon outlined an elaborate process of inductive inference to replace the deductive approach that had been established by Aristotle two thousand years earlier. Aristotle's deductive model called for juxtaposing two or more known truths to reach a third, as in the classic syllogism "Gods are immortal; humans are mortal; therefore, humans are not gods."* Aristotelian deduction worked

---

* As Aristotle put it, "A deduction is speech . . . in which, certain things having been supposed, something different from those supposed results of necessity because of their being so." Aristotle's *Prior Analytics* 1.2, 24b18–20.

splendidly as long as you used sound premises. But it begged error and abuse. Obviously you could err if you used a false premise—if, say, you had somehow overlooked some mortal gods—for one false premise could produce many others that would in turn produce yet more mistakes. The method's susceptibility to abuse had proven even more serious: If someone could dictate which premises were to be considered true, the syllogistic method generated stasis. Thus astronomy was inhibited (to put it mildly) by the Catholic church's insistence that the earth was the center of the universe, and geology and biology had long been hampered by Christian dicta about the earth's age and humanity's origin. You would only get so far in astronomy, for example, if you had to use as a premise "The universe orbits the earth."

To free science from these dangers, Bacon offered his slow, incremental inductivism. Here was a way to peg theory to observable fact. It's no coincidence that he worked in the wake of Martin Luther, who in the early 1500s had launched Protestantism by insisting that religious truth lay not in the church's authority but in the evidence of Scripture. Bacon, also hoping to supplant authority with evidence, tried to design a scientific method that left nothing to leaps of faith, unsupported assertion, or unfounded supposition. Rather than work from untested premises or move from a few observations to an "illicit and hasty generalization," the scientist would use observed particulars to slowly build a pyramid of "gradual generalizations" leading to broader theories or laws.

Bacon's method quickly won great standing in Britain. By the early 1800s it had been bolstered by the empiricist philosophies of Locke and Hume and the accomplishments, held to be reached in Baconian fashion, of Kepler, Newton, and other scientific giants. The tension between British inductivism and Germany's idealist *Naturphilosophie* only deepened British allegiance to Bacon's method. By the time of Lyell and Darwin, inductivism had become the rule of the day in the British scientific establishment; to deny you practiced it was to risk your credibility.

In 1830, however, the Englishman John Herschel, a respected member of the British scientific establishment because of his careful mathematics and astronomy, argued in his *Preliminary Discourse on the Study of Natural Philosophy* that too strict an inductivism need-lessly hampered progress. In a lucid discussion of how scientific the-ories are formed and tested, Herschel held that it mattered little how you came up with a hypothesis—it could be an educated infer-ence, a wild guess, or a dream—as long as you tested it rigorously against observation. We shouldn't hold a theory's creation to the same standards as its proof. Since a hypothesis was just a provisional explanation that required testing to become a legitimate theory, why should its genesis be relevant? Why couldn't you leap to the top of the pyramid and then build the understructure, revising as needed? If a child joked that the sun was at the center of the solar system, wasn't this as useful a hypothesis (assuming you tested it against observation afterward) as a conjecture based on years of telescope work? The real test of either lay in measured observation; origin hardly mattered.

Herschel's proposal stirred a long, uneasy controversy, for he had articulated a fundamental tension in the accelerating push toward empiricism. Did a primacy of the observable require that knowledge move from the particular to the general? Everyone agreed that a the-ory must not merely fit a few facts but stand in accord with virtually all available relevant observations and experiments. But must it rise directly from observations and experiment? Or need it merely agree with them once conceived? This debate would run for another century, expressed as much in people's work as in their talk. Both Darwin and Alex Agassiz would find themselves enmeshed in its labyrinthine difficulties.

Most of the published response came soon after Herschel's *Pre-liminary Discourse* appeared in 1830. The eminent empiricist William Whewell, for instance, objected sharply in his review, insisting that while scientists must use inference to form a hypothesis, those infer-ences should be incremental and rise from sober consideration of sig-nificant evidence. They could not be large deductions or flights of imagination. The path from fact to theory must be one of many steps, not a jump over a gap that you fill in later.

As Whewell was a man of immense intelligence, accomplish-ment, and influence, his review, as well as his arguments in con-versation in London and at Oxford and Cambridge, did much to discourage acceptance of his friend Herschel's argument. A decade after Herschel published his *Preliminary Discourse,* Whewell authoritatively elaborated his inductivist caution in his monumental, two-volume *Philosophy of the Inductive Sciences* of 1840, which built on his equally weighty *History of the Inductive Sciences* of three years before. In the *History* Whewell had described how key scientific advances had been made; in the *Philosophy* he drew on that history to update and elaborate Bacon's inductive method. He wrote—and at Henslow's and other Cambridge gatherings, talked—all during the 1830s and 1840s on these ideas, which were given extra credibility by his brilliance, his voluminous reading, and his experience in mathematics, mineralogy, and tides.

Coming atop almost two centuries of inductivist tradition, Whewell's deeply learned advocacy won the day and even the century. Throughout the 1800s, his neo-Baconian approach remained the standard prescription for inductive method, especially among the British. Scientists might privately admit that they sometimes yanked ideas from the blue. But publicly they sided with Whewell rather than Herschel. Thus in his *Autobiography* Darwin, though he named Herschel's book (along with Humboldt's) as one of the two that most influenced him, would claim that in forming his evolutionary theory he worked on "true Baconian principles."[19]

Lyell preferred Herschel's model. In *Principles* he put it to work with unprecedented boldness, freely jumping to hypotheses about the earth's crust and openly justifying the need to speculate. In a way he was simply making virtue of necessity, as replacing catastrophism's miracles with natural forces sometimes required conjecture. But he did so unapologetically. He was happy to value observations not merely as facts to be accumulated incrementally but as the basis for imaginative conjecture. Once he had leapt to a new idea, he would amass robust evidence to support his position. But he was not shy about having leapt to get there.

Lyell was also willing to argue through relevant analogy as well as direct evidence, another Herschellian idea that defied Bacon. This greater use of speculation and analogy made many of his colleagues queasy. Yet he used this method so productively and backed his assertions with so many observations that even those wary of his speculation agreed that he had greatly advanced geology.

For the young Darwin, as for many others, the effect was breathtaking. Lyell changed geology from an enumerative task to a quest engaging eyes, legs, intellect, and imagination; one saw both the earth and the possibilities of science in a new light. Geologizing before and after reading Lyell was something like the difference between simply hunting beetles and studying them with their evolutionary arc in mind. To be a pre-Darwinian beetle collector, as Darwin had been, was to gather bugs and fit them, unquestioning, in a stable, divinely designed system. Like finding and piecing together the lenses of a stained-glass window, it gave a certain pleasure but ultimately only confirmed a prescribed order. In that sense, as Darwin wrote Henslow early in the *Beagle* voyage, "in collecting, I cannot go wrong."[20] Yet for Darwin, such work created no excitement beyond the hunt. He cared less for completing a prescribed vision than for sketching a new one. Thus *thinking* about beetle collecting bored him, as did geology before Lyell.

Geology after Lyell was another story. Nothing, said Darwin, now matched the pleasure of hammering rock and pondering its meaning. "The pleasure of the first day's partridge shooting or first day's hunting," he wrote his sister from Tierra del Fuego, "cannot be compared to finding a fine group of fossil bones, which tell their story of former times with almost a living tongue."[21] Geology had eclipsed even shooting. Looking over his time geologizing in South America, he wrote in his *Autobiography*,

> I can now perceive how my love of science gradually preponderated over every other taste. During the first two years my old passion for shooting survived in nearly full force, and I shot myself all the birds and animals for my collection; but gradually I gave up my gun more and more, and finally altogether, to my servant, as shooting interfered with my work, more especially with making out the geological structure of a country. I discovered, though unconsciously and insensibly, that the pleasure of observing and reasoning was a much higher one than that of skill and sport.[22]

It comes as a jolt, reading *Voyage* and Darwin's letters from the trip, to realize that history's most famous biologist began his career

far more entranced with geology. His zoological and botanical collecting on the *Beagle* trip, he said later, were at the time valuable
mainly for sharpening his powers of observation; only when he was
back in England did he see the evolutionary patterns in his zoological data. During the trip, he still saw zoology as just collecting. In
contrast, "the investigation of the geology of all the places visited . . . was far more important, as reasoning here comes into
play."[23]

His *Beagle* field notes show clearly his enthusiasms: He took just
four hundred pages on zoological topics and some fourteen hundred
on geology. Of the five books he wrote soon after he returned, the
three most technical and scientifically substantive concerned geology, as did a portion of a fourth. In 1839, meeting part of his obligation to the voyage, he wrote a section of the official account, the
*Narrative of the Surveying Voyages of Her Majesty's Ships "Adventure"
and "Beagle,"* and also published the *Journal of Researches into the
Natural History and Geology of the Countries Visited During the Voyage
Round the World of H.M.S. "Beagle,"* which soon became a best-seller
known as *The Voyage of the "Beagle."* Much of *Voyage* concerned geology, and his next three books focused on it exclusively: his coral reef
book in 1842, a volume on volcanic islands in 1844, and one on the
geology of South America in 1846.[24] Nothing excited him as much as
geology did. Nothing so engaged his suddenly curious mind. The
task of discerning the earth's evolution gave a thrill, he wrote a
cousin, "like the pleasure of gambling."[25]

3

Darwin's delight in geology peaked in the Andes, where he found his
investigations so enthralling, he wrote his sister, that he "could hardly
sleep at night for thinking over my days' work."[26] Through much
of 1834 and most of 1835, he took long horseback expeditions all
over the still-rising Cordillera and its flanking ranges. Ignoring the
ocean almost completely and leaving most zoological collecting to
his assistant, he paused in his travels only when he had to reboard
the *Beagle* to sail up the coast or, twice, when gastrointestinal torments laid him out. (Though these illnesses were apparently gen-

uine, probably due to intestinal parasites, they seem to have planted the mental seed for the psychosomatic gastric distresses of his later life.)

Roaming the Andes in clear light, he found they beautifully demonstrated Lyell's long, incremental view of the earth's construction. "The stratification in all the mountains is beautifully distinct and from a variety in the colour can be seen at great distances," he wrote Henslow; they lay like the page edges of a book. "I cannot imagine any part of the world presenting a more extraordinary scene of the breaking up of the crust of the globe."[27]

He had not been there long before he witnessed this breaking up directly. On February 20, 1835, he was camping in the dense forest of southern Chile when a massive earthquake struck. Though Darwin was some twenty miles from the epicenter, the quake rearranged his visceral sense of the earth as thoroughly as Lyell had rearranged his theoretical conception of it: "An earthquake like this at once destroys the oldest associations; the world, the very emblem of all that is solid, moves beneath our feet like a crust over a fluid; a second of time conveys to the mind a strange idea of insecurity, which hours of reflection would never create."[28] He told Henslow that the sensation underfoot was "like that of skating over very thin ice; that is distinct undulations were perceptible."[29] The unsettling feeling was reinforced when he visited Concepción, a port city of several thousand people that stood (briefly) at the quake's center. He found the town "nothing more than piles and lines of bricks, tiles, and timbers," he wrote his sister Caroline. "It is the most awful spectacle I ever beheld," he went on. "The force of the shock must have been immense. The ground is traversed by rents, the solid rocks are shivered, [the cathedral's] solid buttresses 6–10 feet thick are broken in to fragments like so much biscuit."[30] Seventy villages in the nearby countryside were similarly destroyed. Only the animals seemed to have sensed it coming. Gulls were seen heading inland two hours before the quake, and Concepción's dogs, which typically howled "as if hearing military music" during low-grade tremors common in the area, quietly left about an hour before the shock; they were standing on the surrounding hills when the quake hit and came slinking back afterward. The earth's undulations threw cattle and horses to the ground, from which they rose "exceedingly terrified, running about as if mad, with their tails in the air."[31] Cows on one steep slope rolled into the sea. Trees slammed against one another. Jets of lava burst from the water near the beach.

After the earth stopped moving, huge swells appeared on the Pacific horizon; a quarter hour later, waves twenty-five feet tall slammed ashore and smashed several hundred feet inland, dumping schooners into the middle of town and carrying away anything that floated. Afterward "the coast was strewed over with timber and furniture as if a thousand great ships had been wrecked. Besides chairs, tables, bookshelves &c &c in great numbers, there were several roofs of cottages almost entire, Store houses had been burst open, and in all parts great bags of cotton, Yerba [maté], and other valuable merchandise were scattered about."[32] It was one of the most violent quakes ever to strike South America.

Though several hundred people died in Concepción, the quake would have killed many more had it struck at night. Thousands survived because they were working outdoors or, if indoors, had "the *constant* habit," as Darwin noted, "of running out of their houses *instantly* on perceiving the *first* trembling. . . . The inhabitants scarcely passed their thresholds before the houses fell in." The English consul, for instance, scrambled outside at the first motion; he had just reached the courtyard

> when one side of his house came thundering down; he retained
> presence of mind to remember that if he once got on the top of
> that part which had already fallen, he should be safe; not being
> able, from the motion of the ground, to stand on his legs he
> crawled up on his hands & knees; no sooner had he ascended
> this little eminence, than the other side of the house fell in; the
> great beams sweeping close in front of his head.[33]

For the rest of his life, Darwin often called this earthquake the most fascinating spectacle he'd ever seen and said that he considered earthquakes "one of the greatest phenomena to which this world is subject."[34] Their possible cause intrigued him. Humboldt, in the six-volume work Darwin read so many times, had offered that quakes were caused by the same subterranean pressures that drove volcanoes and argued that they helped lift the Andes. Lyell had expanded on this quake-volcano connection in the first volume of *Principles,* speculating that quakes were essentially repressed volcanoes—would-be eruptions that couldn't escape and so lifted the earth instead. Now Darwin, privileged to be on hand at a major quake, was thrilled to see that much of the land had indeed risen. The bay around Concepción jumped three feet, as shown by the rim of mollusks, barnacles, and other sea-edge life now a yard up out of the water. The island of Santa María, thirty miles offshore, rumbled upward eight feet. Other spots along the coast rose up to a dozen feet. Darwin was giddy. Having come to ponder what built the Andes, he had seen them grow several feet. He also talked to locals who told of harbor shores that over the previous two decades had risen four feet in unnoticeable increments (as evidenced by the rise of dock anchors and other things they knew were formerly at the surface); it seemed that along with moving in jumps of a few feet, the earth also rose steadily and less violently, en masse, at rates almost too slow to measure.

In the weeks after the earthquake, wandering the barren heights and canyons of the Andes, Darwin found yet more evidence of such gradual elevation. Canyon walls showed layers tilted upward by some uprising force. The "strata of the highest pinnacles," he wrote his sister Caroline, were "tossed about like the crust of a broken pie." These upsurges had clearly occurred in stages, not the one-rip, mountain-building spasms the catastrophists proposed. He found seashells and coral at numerous heights—at shoreline; at elevations of a few dozen, a few score, and a few hundred feet; at thirteen hundred and three thousand feet; and finally, at twelve thousand feet. Only a series of rises over time could explain this.

Consolidating bits from Lyell, Humboldt, and a few others, Darwin formed a theory of mountain building that saw volcanoes and earthquakes as part of a dynamic that could either slowly lift land, rend it, or suddenly raise it several feet. Driving these movements was a layer of molten rock, varying in thickness and pressure, beneath the earth's crust. Lyell, Humboldt, and many others had written of cavities of such molten or gaseous material underlying volcanic regions, but Darwin was one of the first to propose that a layer of such material wrapped the entire globe and that it was either more active or closer to the surface in some areas than in others. In a theory that anticipated plate tectonics, he proposed that most or all of South America floated atop this layer of molten rock and lava, the pressure from which gradually raised most of the continent through long periods and occasionally caused volcanoes or earthquakes or pushed the range sharply up via "angular displacement" caused by the injection of lava beneath.

Finally, if he was to believe what he saw, the land did not merely rise; it often dropped. Amid the volcanically formed layers of the Andes he found layers of sedimentary rock—earth laid down through millennia of deposition and compression. Some of these layers held marine fossils, making it clear they had formed underwater. The most spectacular find, which he stumbled across at around seven thousand feet, was a grove of large, pale, smooth, ancient trees preserved in sandstone holding seashells; clearly the trees had grown hundreds of years on land, then ridden a subsiding landmass down below sea level, where eons' worth of sediment—now sandstone—accumulated around them before the Andes rose again to lift them high. This was only one of many arresting finds. By the time Darwin was done, he had found evidence of two or three cycles of uplift and subsidence that had carried South America several thousand feet above sea level and at least two thousand feet below.

The earth's crust, then, bobbed up and down almost constantly. The relation any expanse of crust bore to sea level depended on timing, the pressures beneath it, and, no doubt, some factors that no one yet understood. Like Lyell before him, Darwin stressed that, given the difficulty of knowing what happened underground, any theory regarding earthquakes, elevation, or subsidence entailed speculation. Yet some things seemed clear. It seemed obvious, for instance, that some areas tended to move more up than down, or vice versa, which is why the Andes' up-and-down cycles left them ever higher. The same would apply to sunken areas. Lyell had speculated that falling land or seafloors subsided when underlying cavities collapsed after their pressurized lava, steam, or gas escaped or condensed. But Darwin, happily insomnious with his vision of South America rising on swelling magma, regarded this notion of collapsed lakes as small thinking. The crust's movements might be slow, but they were large.

And as Lyell had suggested, a rise in one place tended to be balanced by a drop somewhere else. If the molten layer beneath the crust could lift whole continents, then perhaps the floors of entire oceans were also dropping en masse.

Which invited a question: How did all these rising and subsiding forces operate in the huge bowl of water to his west? What did one make of the vast basin of the Pacific and its coralline archipelagoes?

4

Even as he was composing his Chile notes, Darwin was turning his mind west. The *Beagle,* having finished its laborious survey of the South American coast, was making ready to sail. Examining charts of the route ahead, Darwin contemplated the oddity that is the Pacific: a broad pan, immensely deep, with arcs and ovals and doglegs of coral isles rising, as he put it, from its "profoundest parts." Several of these archipelagoes—the Galápagos, the Tuamotus, French Polynesia, the Fijis, and the Friendlys—lay along the *Beagle*'s route. In the sixty years since Captain James Cook had mapped them, these islands had commanded much interest among geologists and naturalists. They were intrigued by the great depths from which they rose; their volcanic nature; their ordered but irregular arrangements, like pearl necklaces tossed to the floor; and the islands' distinctive annularity.

Someone excited sleepless by geology wasn't likely to resist such shapes. Darwin's Andean wanderings and ruminations had whetted what would prove an insatiable appetite for discovering patterns spanning space and time. These ringed islands presented precisely such a pattern.

The puzzle seemed ripe for solution. Though coral islands and reefs had intrigued Europe's scientists and public for almost a century (an interest greatly boosted by the descriptions Cook brought back of the South Pacific archipelagoes in the 1770s), no one had plausibly explained how they came to be. They were initially appreciated mainly for the sheer wonder of their existence, apparently climbing from the sea's depths to create new landscapes. In the eighteenth-century fascination with the idea of a Great Chain of Being, corals held a special place for seeming to bridge the gap between plant and animal, and, after Jean-André Peyssonnel showed them to be animals in 1753, for creating with their calcified skeletons the huge structures that joined the organic and the inorganic worlds as well as sea and land. In the early nineteenth century, some saw in coral reefs a welcome antidote to the erosion that, according to Huttonian geology, was erasing humankind's terrestrial platform. "Whatever destroying tendencies . . . exist on the earth," wrote one prominent geologist in 1818, "these renovating powers compensate for them."[35]

Such speculations rose naturally when geology was so young, the reefs so many, and scientific visits to them so few and brief. Naturalists on the Cook and other expeditions of the late 1700s, however, began to fill in the blanks. They established that the reefs were formed by the accumulating skeletons of huge colonies of tiny, tube-shaped animals known as coral polyps. These polyps, which would later be found to be hard-bodied cousins of sea anemones, were also variously referred to as insects, "molluscus worms," or even "animalcules." They seemed to live only in warm tropical waters, generally no further than twenty-five or thirty degrees from the equator. The polyps apparently built their great works extremely slowly. No one who lived in coral regions described discernible growth, and while nineteenth-century European visitors who compared the reefs to descriptions and charts from the previous century discovered that some reef areas had apparently been torn up by storms, they could not find measurable expansion. At first it was thought that the reefs might build themselves up from sea bottom as deep as several hundred or even several thousand feet. But by 1820 scientists knew that corals grew only in water no more than one hundred or two hundred feet deep.

These observations presented two critical mysteries. One was how shallow-water animals came to grow on platforms that rose from the Pacific's greatest depths. Did they just happen to find these plateaus, or did they somehow build them? The other puzzle was the distinctive annularity of reefs surrounding islands, of many coral islands themselves, and even of the vast coral atolls, or groups of smaller islands, that were strung around the Pacific. The reefs encircling islands followed their contours, often ringing them with a calm lagoon between reef and shore. Other reefs surrounded lagoons only, with no island in the lagoon's center. And the Pacific's many atolls tended to be ringlike or looplike themselves. With so many reefs and atolls taking circular and ovoid forms, it seemed unlikely that reefs just happened to grow on convenient platforms. Some dynamic relationship between the reefs and their foundations seemed to shape them.

The first coral reef theories, offered in the late 1700s and early 1800s, gave fairly simplistic or teleological answers to these questions. For instance, J. R. Forster, the naturalist on Cook's second voyage in the mid-1770s, proposed that corals simply knew they needed to build a circular structure to give themselves a sheltered environment. Another early theory, that of the naturalist and vulcanist Christian Leopold von Buch (1774–1853), had coral reefs growing on the rims of "elevation craters" that had formed when huge, gaseous blisters (quite distinct from volcanoes) raised the sea bottom and then popped and collapsed. This theory, which ignored the fact that every major known reef lay in a volcanic area, was a strange one coming from Buch, for he was a noted vulcanist, having firmly established, early in the 1800s, that lava formed new rock. Buch's discovery of the volcanic nature of rock greatly advanced uniformitarianism, for catastrophist theory had maintained that all the earth's rocks and land had long before precipitated from a primordial ocean. Yet this pioneering vulcanist overlooked the seemingly obvious connection between coral reefs and volcanoes. A few other reef scientists, citing what seemed plain in Caribbean and Atlantic reefs, which emerged from shallower depths, offered that most reef platforms consist of sediment deposited by current.

The first theory to get wide acceptance was that of Johann Eschscholtz, who visited the Marshall Islands on an 1815–1818 Russian voyage led by Otto von Kotzebue. Eschscholtz hypothesized that corals, responding to the influx of oxygen and food as they rise on existing platforms, slowly create a bulwark that grows faster on its sea-facing side. Reefs grow from the center outward, in other words. This, he said, creates a tendency toward annularity that, along with the shape of the platforms they grow on, accounts for typical reef forms. Though Eschscholtz overextended this idea to unlikely deeps because the depth limit of coral growth wasn't established until just after he offered his theory, his hypothesis seemed to cover many reef forms and helped to explain lagoons.

Eschscholtz experienced mixed luck with this theory. While his reef-building model exerted immense influence, it was incorrectly attributed for seventy-five years (fifty years beyond Eschscholtz's death) to his colleague on Kotzebue's voyage, a poet-naturalist named Adelbert von Chamisso. In any event, the Chamisso-Eschscholtz hypothesis, especially its assertion that coral reefs grow faster to seaward, shaped thinking about reefs for a century, generating further theories.

Foremost among these other theories, and the one that came closest to enjoying a consensus in the early 1800s, was what might be called an elevated-volcano theory. This held that most of the world's coral reefs grew on volcanic mountaintops that had risen close to the sea's surface, presumably lifted by mountain-building forces similar to those on land, and then expired, leaving only the round ring of the volcano's mouth. The round shape of many islands and atolls supported this idea, as did the existence of old coral on some islands jutting well out of the water. For how would those corals have reached terrestrial mountaintops if the mountains hadn't been pushed from below?

This raised-volcano hypothesis, as it happens, was the one backed by Lyell and presented in *Principles of Geology* as the most authoritative explanation. This theory held weaknesses too, however, and Darwin, pondering the charts in Chile, found them damning. Yes, he recognized, many isles had risen well above the surface, suggesting elevation. But the charts showed that those taller islands were vastly outnumbered by the thousands of coral isles and atolls, including archipelagoes hundreds of miles long, that barely cleared the water. The above-water portions of these low structures were clearly created by coral debris and sand being tossed atop subsurface reefs. Were we to accept that the foundations of all these isles had conveniently risen to within a couple hundred feet of waterline and then stopped growing so that coral could complete the trip? Hardly. As he put it in the *Voyage of the "Beagle,"*

It is [highly] improbable that the elevatory forces should have uplifted throughout . . . vast areas, innumerable great rocky banks within 20 to 30 fathoms . . . of the surface of the sea, and not one single point above that level; for where on the whole surface of the globe can we find a single chain of mountains, even a few hundred miles in length, with their many summits rising within a few feet of a given level, and not one pinnacle above it?[36]

Besides, he noted, the vast spans of many atolls, some of them rough circles dozens of miles in diameter, others oblongs thirty miles by six, or fifty by twenty, could hardly mark the rims of volcanoes, for where had there ever been volcanic craters so large or oddly shaped?

He didn't care either for the second-most popular hypothesis then around, which was that reef platforms accumulated through sedimentation. "It is improbable in the highest degree," he noted, "that broad, lofty, isolated steep-sided banks of sediment, arranged in groups and lines hundreds of leagues in length, could have been deposited in the central and profoundest parts of the Pacific and Indian Oceans, at an immense distance from any continent, and where the water is perfectly limpid.[37]

But what *could* explain these huge chains and rings of coral? Some of these island groups stretched hundreds of miles. At least one pair of Pacific archipelagoes, the Low and the Radack, together had hundreds of low coral isles spread along a line over four thousand miles long, and a similar formation fifteen hundred miles long curved across the Indian Ocean. All of these isles grew atop shallow platforms that fell away steeply to immense depths. What could have created such long curves and circles of shallow platforms rising from deep water?

Darwin, having for weeks mulled over the image of South America rising next to a falling Pacific, saw what now seemed to him obvious: The Pacific's coral islands did not form on *rising* mountains; they formed on islands and the high points of large landmasses— possibly even continents—that were slowly sinking.

The thought, he said later, came to him in a flash while he was still on the coast poring over charts. Indeed, his notes and correspondence show that he first saw the Pacific reefs not so much as something to be explained but as evidence of a Pacific subsidence that balanced the rise of the Andes. In his *Autobiography* (not too many pages before claiming that he developed his evolutionary theory through "strict Baconian methods"), he confesses of the coral reef theory that "no other work of mine was begun in so deductive a spirit as this, for the whole theory was thought out on the west coast of South America, before I had seen a true coral reef."[38]

This was enough to make a Baconian inductivist quake. Yet Darwin could hardly reject his notion of falling islands, for it seemed to explain everything about reefs. In particular, the man who would later study variations in finch beaks found it especially compelling that this idea explained why coral islands, reefs, and atolls appeared in ringlike or looping forms. The different reef and atoll shapes reflected different stages in the subsidence of the islands on which they took root.

Take a volcanic island, proposed Darwin. Corals would naturally form on the shallows surrounding it. At first this reef, which he called a "fringing reef," would be thin and lie directly against the island's shores. But if the island slowly dropped, these corals growing in its surrounding shallows would slowly grow upward, ever thickening but never breaking the surface, to provide a platform for yet more coral. The fringing reef would thicken and broaden, reaching further out to sea.

The fringing reef would soon change, however. If, as Chamisso held, corals grow more quickly toward the open ocean than toward protected water, the reef would grow faster toward the sea than it would toward the sinking island, and as the shore sank, a lagoon would form between the reef and the land. The fringing reef would now be a barrier reef—that is, a reef with a lagoon or channel between it and the land it grew around. As time took the island further down, the reef would continue to thicken to stay near the surface, and it would continue to grow outward toward the sea. Eventually the island would sink beneath the water. Then the barrier reef would become an atoll—a ring of coral matching the former outlines of the island but now surrounding only a calm lagoon. In the meantime or soon after, the waves might throw enough coral debris and sand atop the reefs to create some of the narrow, strip-shaped islands so common to the Pacific's coral archipelagoes.

To Darwin, this theory not only explained all three types of reefs—fringing, barrier, and atoll—it seemed to be the only theory that satisfactorily explained barrier reefs and atolls at all. Fringing reefs could be explained simply by the fact that corals grew in shallow

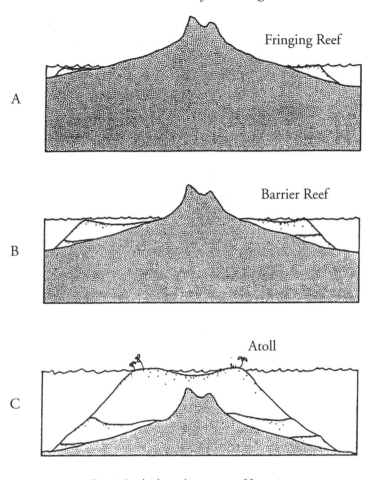

*Darwin's subsidence theory saw reef formation as
a continuous process that transformed the fringing
reef surrounding a slowly sinking island (A) to first
a barrier reef separated from the island by a lagoon (B)
and finally a ring-shaped atoll (C).*

water. But barrier and atoll reefs required some other theory, and no other theory accounted for both of them. Even if you bought that circular atolls had grown on submerged volcanic rims, that idea didn't cover barrier reefs or more oddly shaped or huge atolls, and it asked you to believe that in some areas, thousands of these dead volcanoes came within one hundred fathoms of the surface while none reached above. The other explanations either ignored common reef forms and features or asked you to believe the unbelievable. It was absurd to assert that thousands of mountains all came close to the surface without breaking it; only subsidence could explain these strings of low islands. And only subsidence could plausibly explain barrier reefs and atolls. The logical link was so strong, Darwin thought, that the barrier reefs and atolls in turn provided evidence of subsidence.

This was all from the west coast of South America. When he hopscotched across the Pacific and finally visited atolls and barrier reefs in Tahiti and at the Indian Ocean's Cocos (or Keeling) Islands, the sight of the formations—particularly the Tahitian island of Moorea, which sat surrounded by its lagoon and barrier reef like an engraving by its mat and frame, as he put it—confirmed for Darwin the accuracy of his vision. "I glad we have visited these islands," he wrote in his diary, for the coral reefs "rank high amongst the wonderful objects in the world. . . . [They are] a wonder which does not at first strike the eye of the body, but, after reflection, the eye of reason."[39] As lovely as the reefs were in aesthetic terms (and Darwin keenly appreciated their beauty), they provided for him the even deeper thrill of embodying a deep, time-based pattern apparent only to the imaginative intellect.

This subsidence theory was an audacious idea for a twenty-six-year-old. Conceptually ambitious and blatantly deductive, it begged trouble from all quarters. While challenging the coral-formation theory favored by the new leader of British geology, Lyell, it also aggressively pushed Lyell's controversial gradualism and speculative method into new territory. As the *Beagle* rounded Africa and made for England in early 1836, Darwin worried how the senior colleagues he admired, particularly Henslow and Lyell, would receive his theory.

He was elated when, on his return in fall 1836, the scientists most important to him, starting with Lyell, found it as thrilling as he did. When he told Lyell of the theory at a lunch at Lyell's house soon after returning, his host became so excited he leapt around the room shouting and laughing, and he immediately dropped his own idea that reefs grew atop mountains that had risen. Darwin's idea, he agreed, was far more powerful and beautifully concise. Reefs were not caps atop mountains that had fallen short. They were, as Lyell put it in a letter to Herschel, "the last efforts of drowning continents to lift their heads above water."[40]

Lyell immediately arranged to have Darwin read an abstract of the theory at the Geological Society. He warned Darwin that others might not share his own excitement. "Do not flatter yourself that you will be believed till you are growing bald like me, with hard work and vexation at the incredulity of the world."[41] Yet to Darwin's delight, he was believed almost immediately. The positive reception began as soon as he read his paper before the Geological Society, in May 1837. Herschel liked it and Whewell did too, despite its non-Baconian birth, for the thing worked. Darwin soon won over a wider circle with his presentation of the theory in *Voyage* in 1839 and more fully in the 1842 *Structure and Distribution of Coral Reefs.* Meanwhile, Lyell incorporated Darwin's subsidence theory into his 1840 edition of *Principles,* making it the textbook explanation. Pacific investigations in the 1840s by the British researcher J. B. Jukes and a young James Dwight Dana seemed to confirm the theory. Jukes, having looked extensively at Pacific reefs, said Darwin's explanation "rises beyond a mere hypothesis into the true theory of coral-reefs."[42]

Doubters lurked. Some geologists found it difficult to envisage the tectonic movements of which Darwin said subsidence was part. One reviewer called the idea of such movements "bold and startling ... even to the most hardy of our geologists."[43] Another scientific reviewer hoped "to find the boldness of [Darwin's] theories a little modified; and . . . resting upon a more solid foundation than the supposed undulations of subterranean fluid."[44] A few people considered these objections quite damning. John Cluines-Ross, the owner of Cocos Islands, where Darwin saw the atolls that confirmed for him his theory, called it "palaver" and dismissed it out of hand.

These arguments worried Darwin only slightly, for he recognized that they came from people who simply didn't buy the Herschel-Lyell need to speculate. They were fair objections regarding rightly debatable conceptual issues. Of more concern was the way the existing empirical evidence often contradicted his theory and offered it little direct support. As skeptics noted, most of the coral isles studied so far showed much evidence of elevation and no sign of subsidence. Explorers had found corals and other marine fossils atop the taller islands, for instance, but no corresponding terrestrial fossils or structures beneath the surface. And though many (including Darwin) had observed contemporary elevation in action, no one had observed ongoing subsidence. Darwin's defense—that the recent elevations were cycles amid an overall pattern of marine subsidence, the evidence for which had not been observed because it was hidden underwater—couldn't be backed by anything tangible.

Even more troubling to Darwin was that in the world's expanding catalog of examined strata, no one had discovered any deep thickness of continuous coral. Geologists had found many thick layers of marine sandstone and sedimentary limestone above ground; why no great thicknesses of coral? When he and Lyell couldn't resolve this one despite extensive discussion, Darwin had to admit it was a "weighty and perplexing" objection.

These and other objections, however, scarcely slowed the theory's acceptance. By 1850 Darwin's theory, backed by Lyell and his own expanding base of supporters, became the single-most widely accepted theory of coral reef formation. Meanwhile he moved on from it and other geology to work on barnacles and, quietly in the background, his transmutation theory. Even as he did so, the reef theory consolidated its hold. By the time he wrote his *Autobiography*, in 1876, he could accurately say of *The Structure and Distribution of Coral Reefs* that it was "thought highly of by scientific men, and the theory therein given is, I think, now well established."[45] He still got a kick out of its simple power and success; he said it gave him more pleasure than any other theory he'd ever come up with.

For good reason. It's hard to overstate how vital Darwin's coral reef theory was in developing his career and thinking. It paved the way, conceptually and methodologically, for everything to come, particularly his transmutation theory.[46] The likenesses startle. Like the transmutation theory, the coral reef theory described how small, virtually unnoticeable changes could create differences of essential type in seemingly immutable forms—and in doing so, account for broad patterns of development and difference.

Thematically, formally, and even psychologically, then, Darwin's coral reef theory served almost as direct progenitor of his species theory. As perhaps nothing else could have, it prepared him for the conceptually similar but more difficult work on evolution and natural selection. He seems to have needed this dry run—a theoretical foray into the relatively tame territory of rocks and reefs—before pursuing a similar argument on the more perilous species question. He barely thought about the species issue, in fact, until he had finished developing his coral concept. Though the raw zoological data and specimens he collected on the *Beagle* proved key to his evolution work, they did so only later. His expedition notebooks contain no real contemplation of evolution or variation until he was in Australia, well after his Galápagos visit, when he had just finished recording in his notebook, on the sail from Tahiti to Sydney, the first full abstract of his reef theory. In Australia, with the abstract sketched out, he made a few brief notes on species variation, then resumed expanding his reef abstract on the Indian Ocean leg. Returning to London six months later, he told and wrote not of species variation but of coral reef variation. It was only the following summer that Darwin, who always started a new, subject-specific notebook when he began thinking in earnest on some problem, dedicated his first notebook to "transmutation of species." That was in July 1837, a few weeks after he successfully presented his coral reef paper to the Geological Society and began drafting its full explication in *The Structure and Distribution of Coral Reefs*. The one theory seemed almost to spring from the other.

The coral reef theory's subsequent success doubtless helped sustain Darwin during the two decades that he agonized over his transmutation theory. But as he surely recognized (and probably would have liked to forget), another early theory of his also shared the reef theory's conceptual hallmarks: Glen Roy. His botched explanation of that valley's parallel roads, published two years after his initial coral reef presentation, also sought to solve a geologic mystery by proposing a series of changes over long periods. It too sprang from a vision of rising and falling landmasses. Yet in the decade after he published it, his Glen Roy theory fell to Louis Agassiz and became Darwin's most painful humiliation. ("Eheu! Eheu!") If the success of his reef theory buoyed him in his evolution work, the Glen Roy debacle served as a sober warning. Indeed, that reversal gave him ample reason to doubt his coral reef theory. He had erred at Glen Roy both by overlooking contradictory evidence (the streams that he missed but Agassiz found) and by downplaying the lack of direct confirming evidence, such as the missing marine fossils, as a type of evidence that was simply unlikely to be found. In his coral reef theory he chose to overlook the common signs of elevation and dismiss the absence of direct evidence of subsidence. Might these errors prove as fatal as those he made at Glen Roy? Darwin seemed to set aside such questions as the decades passed. But they were right there for anyone else to pick up.

CHAPTER TEN

To Light: Murray's Reefs

Sir John Murray, age forty, in 1881.
His notions about coral reef genesis
would set Alexander on a long search for a more
comprehensive alternative to Darwin's.

I

"I DREAD THE MOMENT when I shall reach home," Alexander Agassiz wrote a friend from Lake Titicaca in spring of 1875, "or rather my house, for no place can henceforth be a home to me."[1] He indeed found his faith in hearth tested. In August, just four months after he returned from Chile, his sister Ida and her husband Henry Higginson lost their six-year-old daughter, Cecile, to meningitis. Alex and son George carried the bier to the grave. The following May, Mimi, in whose company Alex had taken such comfort in the first year or two after Annie's death, lost a child in her eighth month of pregnancy. A week later Theo's brother Fred lost both his wife and child in childbirth. The family started to fear, always, a new tragedy lurking. "That little boy of mine!" Theo wrote of the still healthy son that Mimi had given birth to two Novembers previous. "He may fade in a night; but then too, he may live to close my eyes. Let us hope for the good, ever ready to be resigned to evil."[2]

This hail of loss, begun by the deaths of his father and wife in December 1873, marked Alexander Agassiz the rest of his life. Through his remaining years he alternated through a series of wanderings and returns driven on the one hand by the desire to escape and to accrue knowledge (for he was a sort of empiricist magpie, compelled to gather facts) and, on the other, a deep ambivalence about the prospects of home. The home he returned to from Chile— a new summer mansion he had built across Narragansett Bay from Newport, Rhode Island—was itself an escape, letting him vacate Cambridge every summer to live in the salt air and do his research. After that first winter back in Cambridge in 1875–1876, he usually went elsewhere in the cold months as well, traveling almost every year to some warm place, sometimes down the coast to Florida or the Caribbean, sometimes to the globe's farthest points. While he grew more comfortable at his home in Newport, he would never again live extensively in Cambridge, and his winter range expanded as he aged. By his last decades he traveled less to indulge his restlessness than to work, and he traveled then particularly to solve the mystery of coral reefs.

2

He took his first trip with any real purpose at the end of 1876, to Scotland. Since returning from the Andes he had spent most of his time close to home, tidying things at museum and mine and trying to work through his sorrow even as the three new deaths in the family deepened it. Sandwiched between those losses, his own more personal loss, marked by the ghosts of his wife and father waiting every December, had made that first winter back in Cambridge intolerable. When he received an invitation from Scotland to help sort the specimens from the just completed voyage of the *Challenger*, he jumped at the chance.

The *Challenger* voyage, a three-and-a-half-year, round-the-world oceanographic expedition, did for oceanography what James Cook's voyages had done for navigation a century before: It established the first reliable, comprehensive baseline of worldwide oceanographic data. The first long marine expedition devoted exclusively to science, the *Challenger* essentially founded oceanography as a discipline.

The expedition's main focus was the exploration, via sounding line and dredge, of the deep sea, an area so unknown, yet suddenly considered so crucial to knowledge of the planet, that the trip inspired the kind of interest that the first manned spaceflights evoked a century later. Only twenty years before the *Challenger's* voyage, scientists had been in agreement that virtually nothing lived deeper than three or four hundred fathoms, despite a few starfish pulled up from deep-water soundings. In 1860, however, a telegraph cable laid one thousand fathoms deep in the Mediterranean three years earlier and now pulled to the surface for repairs came up encrusted with more than a dozen kinds of bottom-dwelling animals. This erased the well-entrenched notion of a lifeless deep.

Darwin's just published theory of evolution, meanwhile, held that evolution proceeded rapidly in fast-changing environments and slowly amid stasis. If this was true, the presumably static deep might include unchanged species—"living fossils"—from the evolutionary past. This notion was encouraged when deep-sea dredging in the 1860s (deep for the time, anyway: up to two thousand fathoms) found a few crinoids (primitive cousins of starfish) and other simple animals closely resembling known fossils. And Thomas Huxley (an able working biologist when not writing or debating) had found in some specimen bottles from these same early deep-sea expeditions a mysterious, protoplasmic goo—a "primordial ooze" or "living slime"—that he proposed might be both the base of the ocean food chain and the bottom rung of the evolutionary ladder. He called it *Bathybius haecklii* after his Darwinist compatriot Ernst Haeckel. Discovering more about *Bathybius* and other deep-sea forms was a major goal of the *Challenger* as it set sail in December 1872.

Setting off with 144 miles of sounding rope, a large onboard lab, and nine scientists, the 238-foot *Challenger* sailed amid great expectations. Scientists and the popular press alike followed its reports closely. Led by renowned zoologist Wyville Thomson and his second, John Murray, the expedition did not disappoint. Even while under way, the *Challenger* answered crucial questions about the life and topography (or bathymetry, as it is known) of the ocean bottom. It found and named the Mid-Atlantic Ridge running the full length of that ocean, confirmed the Pacific's astonishing depths and charted some of its contours, and verified that even the deepest parts reachable—over five miles down—held life. To Huxley's disappointment, however, the voyage showed that this life did *not* include *Bathybius*. One day, when one of the *Challenger* scientists poured a large quantity of alcohol into a bottle containing deep-sea ooze and the mixture almost instantly produced something remarkably like the mysterious *Bathybius*, they realized that Huxley's ancient slime was simply a new goo produced by the reaction between alcohol and the quite ordinary ooze made up of planktonic skeletons. The stuff in Huxley's tubes had apparently been formed more slowly by traces of alcohol left after washing. Thomson immediately wrote Huxley, breaking the news with remarkable tact, and Huxley promptly sent the letter to be published in *Nature* along with a graceful and funny letter confessing his error.

Yet if it lacked *Bathybius,* the *Challenger* returned to Britain in July 1876 with plenty: Having traveled 68,930 miles (averaging just over a walking pace), the boat brought home more than 13,000 kinds of animals and plants, including more than 4,000 new species; 1,441 water samples; and hundreds of seafloor deposits. All of these needed to be tagged, packed, and distributed to the specialists for description and examination.

Thus the call to Alexander Agassiz. Thomson, who shared Alex's fascination with echinoderms, had met Alex in 1869, when Alex traveled to Great Britain, and again in 1873, when Agassiz had visited the *Challenger* in Halifax, after the ship had completed a loop in the first, Atlantic stage of its journey. Impressed at both meetings, and further impressed in the meantime by *Revision of the Echini,* Thomson knew that Alex had experience organizing and handling large collections and coordinating their examination and the publication of findings. He also knew that Alex, as de facto director of the Museum of Comparative Zoology, was owed favors from many specialists on both continents. He now asked Alex to come help sort and distribute the *Challenger* haul.

Alex happily obliged. Having followed the trip in the journals and through direct correspondence with Thomson and Murray, he recognized the *Challenger* voyage as a milestone in the study of the ocean.* To a discipline long on questions but short on hard data, the *Challenger* results gave a badly needed boost.

Thomson, the leader of several short but groundbreaking expeditions in the 1860s, had already been a prominent figure in ocean studies when he started the *Challenger* project in 1872, and Murray, five years Alex's junior, had gained similar status by helping lead the *Challenger* expedition. Murray had actually been a last-minute addition to the voyage, taking the place of someone who had fallen sick. But he had come into his own on the trip and was now Thomson's second on shore as well. The two decades of sorting, study, and reporting that lay ahead would make him known as a founder of oceanography.

Murray and Alex hit it off immediately. Murray had already met and worked with much of the crème of European science, unpacking boxes with everyone from Haeckel to Huxley, but he held a special regard for Alexander's ability to find a no-nonsense way through the thicket of theories and ideologies that marked the times. When Alex had visited the *Challenger* in Nova Scotia the summer of 1873, many of the ship's younger scientists, enthusiastic Darwinists, had expected him to share his father's antievolutionism, and Murray had admired the matter-of-fact way in which Alexander made known his acceptance of a measured evolutionism without either fashioning himself a Darwinist or casting a bad light on his father. At a time when the polarized debate over evolution made it hard to find real independence of thought, Murray recognized the strength this required of Alex.

Now he saw this strength tested, even three years after the deaths of Louis and Anna.

"When he arrived in Edinburgh," Murray later recalled, "I referred to the death of his wife, but he held up his hands and said, 'I can not bear it.' His expression was such that the subject was never again mentioned."

---

* The full *Challenger* report, which took nineteen years to publish and occupied fifty volumes, proved not only astonishingly comprehensive but quite durable. For decades, new findings tended to supplement rather than revise its findings, and much of the data was still being used and cited even at the end of the twentieth century.

Alex did not socialize much during his two months in Edinburgh. He declined all invitations even during the holidays, and he never traveled down to London to renew his many acquaintanceships there. He proved a tireless and ceaselessly curious workmate for Murray. The two worked almost every daylight hour, unpacking, sorting, and repacking thousands of specimens of starfish, urchins, and sea stars for Alex to take home and thousands of specimens of other taxa to ship to other specialists. As they worked, Murray told Alex of the weird mix of exhaustion, boredom, unexpected pleasure, and sudden agonies that, typical of the era's expeditions, had made up the *Challenger* tour. On many days the shipboard routine stretched out interminably and noisily: The dredge often took hours to reach the bottom, and everyone would then wait even longer for the miles of rope to be drawn in as the steam engines thumped and the winch screamed. If the equipment survived (one trawl reached deck with its main beam snapped by the submarine pressure, the wood so compressed the knots stood out a quarter inch), it might hold some new wonder or virtually nothing. The first samples from great depth contained only worms.

But the scientific crew brightened, at least at first, as they found more than four thousand new species. Of those, more than three thousand were radiolarians—microscopic, single-celled plankton that secrete exoskeletons of silica shaped like tiny vases, starbursts, or burrs from which they extend pseudopods to snag even tinier plankton to eat. It was Murray who realized that the beautiful, glasslike skeletons of these animals, drifting down by the billions, compose much of the "ooze" that covers the deep-ocean floor. Occasionally the dredge fetched something that at least approached the antiquity the crew had hoped to find common. One day they sieved from the muck a dead—but recently dead—*spirula*, a small squid identical to fossilized forms. They also found shark's teeth millions of years old encased in globules of manganese; astonishing variations in temperature even at great depths; bits of metal Thomson recognized as meteor fragments; a surprising biological diversity in the extreme deep and dark; and, on a more mundane level, that the Galápagos tortoises they had captured had eaten the crew's pineapples. They shot the Straits of Magellan in a howling, ecstatic seventeen-knot run. They picked their way among pack ice and icebergs on the

Antarctic Circle, walked long curves of lovely beach in Tahiti, and brought souvenirs and syphilis home from the scores of harbors they visited.

The trip strained patience and health. Of the 243 people who sailed (214 sailors, 20 officers, and a scientific crew of 9), 61 deserted and 10 died. The first was sailor William Stokes, killed by a block and tackle fired across deck by a snapped dredging cable; he was lowered the next day into four miles of water. Several more succumbed to various accidents, two more to drownings, two to suicide, one to food poisoning, and one, the voyage's last fatality, to erysipelas, a purulent skin infection that kills rarely but painfully. Chief scientist Thomson returned exhausted. He would live only another five years.

Murray, however, had recovered both health and enthusiasm in the six months since the ship's return. Alex, in his subdued way, shared Murray's excitement about the information and specimens the ship had collected. Alex had seen how vital fieldwork and collections were to terrestrial earth science; only work like the *Challenger*'s could provide the same crucial piles of information about the ocean and answer basic questions about how its life was distributed, how its currents flowed, and how its bottom formed and shaped. He felt certain that these questions of environment, geology, and zoology would often be linked. How could they not be? Such issues always entwined on land, where geology not only told the story of former life but set limitations for present forms. In the Andes, for instance, the rising terrain exposed yesterday's fossils and, as in the high, almost sterile waters of Titicaca, dictated what might live today. The ocean could hardly be otherwise.

Alex took particular interest in Murray's discovery that planktonic debris (the skeletons of radiolarians and other minuscule floaters) formed a thick blanket over much of the deep seabed. Thomson, half hoping to find *Bathybius* or something else fantastic, had initially resisted this pedestrian explanation of ooze. Alex admired Murray for his independence in proving the less glamorous answer, against the resistance of his boss and mentor, by painstaking microscopic examination (never fun, worse at sea) of ooze and near-surface plankton to find conclusive similarities.* This was Alex's kind

---

* Murray's interest in seafloor muck also led to his discovery that in some areas the ooze was mostly volcanic debris and—a new find—metallic clumps shed from meteors.

of science: Damn the theories and authorities; work closely and heed the specimen.

Now Murray told Alex of another implication of all that plankton: Plankton floated in such numbers and fell so thickly, he believed, that they, not Darwin's slowly sinking mountains, provided the platforms on which coral reefs grew. It seemed far-fetched that tiny animals could build these platforms. But Murray was not suggesting that dead plankton piled up thousands of fathoms thick to bring deep bottom near the surface. Rather, they accumulated atop existing mounds or ridges that already reached to within a few hundred fathoms of the surface and eventually raised them to coral-friendly heights. Only banks at these modest depths—up to five hundred or perhaps a thousand fathoms—gained significant height this way, for only at those depths did the rain of skeletal debris outpace the corrosion that the tiny skeletons faced on their descent. At depths beyond one thousand fathoms, the carbonic acid in seawater dissolved most of the tiny skeletons before they could reach bottom and hide from its solvent action; this Murray and Thomson had concluded from the scarcity of surface-plankton debris at such depths. But at shallower depths, especially between one hundred and eight hundred fathoms or so, the minute skeletons of surface plankton fell faster than seawater could destroy them. Over millions of years, they piled high enough to give corals a foothold.

Two *Challenger* discoveries had convinced Murray of this. The first, revealed by the expedition's hundreds of soundings, was the existence of scores of mounds and ridges that came to within one thousand fathoms of the surface. The second was the incredible density of plankton that Murray found in tropical waters. To gauge this density he towed, in four separate samplings, a twelve-inch-diameter sieve through a half mile of water at a depth of a few fathoms, then boiled the trapped plankton in a caustic solution. This left only the animals' skeletons. He weighed these remains. Then, extrapolating from his half-mile-long, square-foot-wide tows, he figured the total mass of planktonic skeletal material that would occupy a volume of water a mile square and one hundred fathoms deep. It worked out to over sixteen tons.

As most plankton live only days or weeks, this ever-replicating sixteen tons would send a steady rain of skeletons to the bottom, slowing adding to any mounds within a thousand fathoms of the surface. Mollusks, brittlestars, starfish, anemones, and other mid-depth bottom dwellers would stabilize the mound as it grew. Some mounds might also be lifted by seismic forces, speeding their rise. When a mound or ridge reached within one hundred fathoms of the surface, corals would take over and bring the mound to just beneath the surface. Once at the surface, the bank would begin to expand sideways, especially to windward, because coral is nourished by current-borne plankton. The surf would break off coral that would tumble seaward, creating an ever-thickening talus slope on which the reef could further expand. As the reef grew seaward on this thickening talus slope, the surface corals behind the leading edge—those left unwashed by incoming seas as the reef expanded outward—would die. These dead inner corals would eventually dissolve, creating behind the breakwater a lagoon, which, cut off from a new food supply, would deepen over the years from further solution. Thus the reef would form either an expanding ring—that is, an atoll—or, if the reef had formed around a volcanic island, a barrier reef that would expand ever outward. This combination of planktonic accumulation, solution of inner corals, and outward expansion atop the talus slope could account for the barrier reefs and atolls that Darwin had claimed as proof of subsidence.

Alex liked this idea immediately. He had long had trouble fitting Darwin's theory either to his own limited coral reef experience or to the observations he had read about. Certainly Darwin's model did not seem to explain the reefs Alex had seen with his father two decades before in Florida. Those reefs were thin veneers rising from broad, shallow slopes that stretched out all around. Louis had noted this at the time in his reports, though mutedly, for not only was this before his feud with Darwin, but Darwin himself had conceded in 1842 that most of the Caribbean reefs, which lay in broad banks in shallow water, were probably exceptions to his subsidence theory.

To Alex and Murray, however, it seemed that most of the reefs that other researchers had examined since that time also appeared to be exceptions, casting doubt on the rule. The main support for Darwin, meanwhile, seemed to come from the work of James Dwight Dana (the same Dana who had given Louis so much trouble in the 1860s), who in a Pacific expedition just after Darwin's had found

Darwin's theory confirmed by his own extensive examination of the Fijis and briefer looks at many other Pacific archipelagoes. Dana admitted he was convinced more by the reef forms than by any direct evidence of subsidence, but then again, subsidence tended to bury its direct evidence. Alex knew Dana to be a good geologist—the most renowned in the United States, in fact. But he felt that Dana's confirmation of Darwin's theory, based mostly on indirect evidence hurriedly observed, hardly proved that Darwin's theory explained most of the world's reefs.

To the extent that Alex had thought about it, then (and up to now he had not thought about it very much), coral reef research since the 1840s suggested that Darwin had oversimplified and overreached. A more flexible theory—or perhaps a package of explanations—was needed to account for the world's reefs and atolls. Alexander knew that other scientists more familiar with the problem, including leading researchers in America, Britain, and the Continent, felt the same unease with Darwin's model. Yet, unable to suggest an alternative (and cognizant of Darwin's ever-growing reputation), no one had seriously challenged it. Though it had been weakened, Darwin's theory remained the most accepted and comprehensive explanation.

Murray, however, now appeared to offer one far superior. Like Darwin's theory, his explained how every variety of reef could be formed, but without requiring the seemingly unproveable subsidence that Darwin called on. All Murray's key processes were easily observed. And his theory rose not from speculation deduced from broad concepts about huge movements but from measured, repeated observations. It was, in other words, more scientific.

The two young oceanographers, quite conscious, as they unpacked the *Challenger*'s goods, of being part of a new, more rigorous oceanographic discipline, discussed Murray's idea at length. The more they talked, the more Alex liked it. By the time he left to return to Cambridge, in February 1877, he had not only tentatively adopted this new hypothesis; he had decided to take up the job of testing and verifying it.

"I never really accepted the theories of Darwin," he wrote Murray on returning home. "It was all too mighty simple."[3]

CHAPTER ELEVEN

A Question of Science

I

FOR THE FIRST TIME since Anna's death, Alexander felt something other than duty drawing him forward. "I can't tell you what a pleasant time I have had in Edinburgh," he wrote Wyville Thomson toward the end of his visit. "It is really the first time since the death of my father and my wife that I have felt in the least as if there were anything to live for, and I hope you have put me on the track to get into harness again."[1]

For a man who lived mainly for work (and disinclined to reflection), this was a startling declaration of rebirth. What he had found to live for were not the echinoderms he had brought back to Cambridge, though he did dutifully classify those over the next few years. What Alex had found were the reefs. In the mystery of their genesis glimmered something alluring enough to tug him free of the past.

Hindsight, of course, makes it easy to see how Alexander Agassiz, finally moving forward to pursue coral reefs, set out on a path back into his own history. For all the light, adventure, and new terrain reefs promised, they held for Alex treacherous ground full of holes and old snags. In letters and the dozens of monographs he would publish about reefs, he usually projected an air of unprejudiced scientific interest, and when he grew passionate in print, as he did in a few notable spots, the proximate cause was always an issue of science—the reading of strata, the interpretation of a pattern of soundings, a colleague's rush to theory. He clearly liked to feel that he was approaching the question from a disinterested place and that when he got mad, he did so on principle.

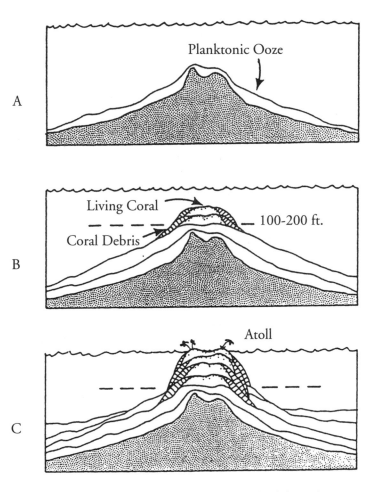

John Murray's coral reef theory. Murray speculated that reef foundations were formed when a high submarine mound (A) accumulated enough planktonic debris (B) to reach coral-friendly depths, allowing coral to grow upward into an atoll (C).

Yet the reef question carried immense emotional implications for Alexander—too great, perhaps, to be admissible. It inevitably engaged not just his ferocious beliefs about how to do science but his mixed emotions, buried but still strong, about the entwined fates and legacies of Darwin and his own father. This was perhaps unavoidable, so entangled were the two men's scientific philosophies and personal histories. For Alex, the great clash between idealism and empiricism—the central conflict within his time's science and culture—was unavoidably enmeshed with family history.

It wasn't enough, for instance, that in taking up coral reefs Alex, like his father, committed to both an evidentiary and a philosophical battle with Darwin (albeit this time with Darwin taking the more speculative stand). He also took on many of his father's most formidable personal rivals. The most significant was James Dwight Dana, who as a young naturalist on the Wilkes expedition (an American-sponsored scientific voyage that circled the globe from 1838 to 1842) had collected so much evidence to bolster Darwin's reef theory. This was the same Dana who had helped Asa Gray evict Louis from his throne in the 1860s, embarrassing Louis in the *American Journal of Science* in 1862 when Louis tried to defend the Desor book that he hadn't read, and it was the same Dana who had switched voting groups at the 1864 National Academy of Sciences meeting to help Asa Gray elect the hated Spencer Baird. Alexander had then called Dana "contemptible" and arrogant and referred to him as "his majesty." By 1876 Alex, disciplined at ignoring his feelings about his father's tormentors, had been on cordial terms with Dana for several years. But he surely hadn't forgotten his earlier conclusions about him; he was too much a grump for that. When Alexander took up the coral reef question, Dana was in his sixties and still going strong; he would hold his Yale professorship until 1890 and publish until his death in 1895. Alexander might have preferred to forget Dana. Taking up the coral reef question made that impossible.

And Dana could not be easily dismissed, for his claim to authority in coral reefs (unlike Darwin's) was founded on extensive fieldwork. On the Wilkes expedition Dana had seen reefs and atolls in Tahiti, Samoa, and the Tuamotus and classified them into the same three types that Darwin did (fringing, barrier, and atoll) even before he read an early report of Darwin's theory, which he did at an 1839 stopover in Sydney. The theory "threw a flood of light over the subject," he said later, and for the rest of the trip, particularly during a three-month stay in the Fijis, he collected evidence and observations that he concluded "afford striking illustrations of [Darwin's] views, establishing the theory on a firm base of evidence, and exhibiting its complete correspondence with observation."[2] He even added a key support Darwin had overlooked, arguing that the bays and fjords that Darwin had thought were carved by waves and currents were actually "embayed valleys," gorges that had been eroded in typical river-valley fashion while above the surface and then became bays and fjords as the islands sank. Though this was still indirect evidence, consistent with subsidence but hardly definitive of it, Dana's work provided Darwin's theory with the strongest indication yet that these islands were subsiding. Darwin, who had wrung his hands over his belief that in subsidence he had "a movement the tendency of which is to conceal the parts affected," expressed great delight.[3] "I write from exuberance of vanity," he wrote Lyell after reading Dana's 1849 coral report. *"I am astonished at my own accuracy!"*[4]

His excitement was well founded. In the decades that followed, Dana played a badly needed Dr. Watson to Darwin's Sherlock Holmes. While Darwin had been theorizing in his study, Dana had been seeing more coral formations than any other scientist. Dana actually made a strange ally for Darwin, just as he had for Gray, for he rejected the theory of evolution and was unashamed to see in coral reefs an expression of God's glory, even as they also confirmed Lyell's slow uniformitarianism. For some, Dana's eloquent description of reefs—geologically uniformitarian but biologically creationist—was like Louis's plan of creation or the notion of a God-steered evolution: It provided an exciting and apparently safe way to embrace modern science while clinging to the notion that we are all God's creatures. Here was a slow-working, transforming dynamic designed ultimately to serve humans. The lovely coral trees and shrubs, Dana wrote, "stand and wave unhurt in the agitated waters," supporting millions of polyps that "cover the branches, like so many flowers, spreading their tinted petals in the genial sunshine, and quiet seas, but withdrawing when the clouds betoken a storm," and so surviving to slowly build the reef. "Finally, the coral becomes subservient to a still higher purpose than the support of polyps and nullipores" when the debris raises them above water to form an isle on which "the coral polyps, now yielding place to the flowers and groves of the land, . . . fulfill their end in promoting the comfort and happiness of man."[5]

This startlingly Agassizian prose is from Dana's 1846 expedition report on zoophytes. He maintained this higher-calling thesis (though in less purple form) in his major works on corals, the 1853 *On Corals and Coral Islands* and its 1872 update, *Corals and Coral Islands*. Yet if Dana's teleology conflicted with Darwin's mechanistic materialism, his thick strands of fact provided crucial stays to the lean spire of Darwin's theory, saving it from many a blow that might otherwise have tipped it. Because of Dana, anyone challenging Darwin's theory had not only to offer another conceptual framework but to counter or reinterpret Dana's evidence. Though Murray and Agassiz disagreed with Dana's conclusions, they recognized *Corals and Coral Islands* as a formidable obstacle. By their lights it was—unlike Darwin's coral reef book—sound work and fair play.

2

Alex did not think fair, however, another publication of the time. In 1876, a few months after returning from Edinburgh, he received a stunningly venomous attack launched on his dead father by Ernst Haeckel in *Ziele und Wege* (*Goals and Paths*), a long essay about the era's great changes in developmental biology. Haeckel was the lively embryologist and *Naturphilosopher* Alex had met on his 1870 European trip and "liked extremely" despite their philosophical differences. He had sent an especially kind note of sympathy after Louis's death, drawing from Alex one of his most heartfelt expressions of devastation and hopelessness. The two had since shared a sporadic but warm correspondence. They seemed to have the kind of friendship that is especially valued because some vital connection transcends seemingly larger, more obvious differences.

Now came to Alex, not long after a friendly letter from Haeckel on other matters, a long essay on the recent history of biology containing an attack on Louis that stands out sharply even amid science's long history of collegial muggings. Written with the energy, wit, and bite for which Haeckel was famous (and which Alex had found so charming), the document is a rant against idealist resistance to Darwinism. Given the subject, and that Haeckel and Louis had traded spirited critiques in journals over the years, it wasn't surprising that Haeckel would spend some time countering Louis's creationism. But his remarkable assault—several sharp, contemptuous jabs scattered through the first seventy-five pages and then a murderous eight-page flurry toward the end—is not simply an insulting counterargument. It is a calculated effort at character assassination. Haeckel acknowledges as much, asserting that destroying Louis Agassiz's reputation was "advisable" because creationist opponents of evolutionary theory still regaled him as a "pious natural scientist" and "crowned him with a halo." Haeckel proposed to examine the halo with a spectroscope.

The potshots Haeckel begins with, calling Louis's plan-of-creation theory "amusing nonsense," are fairly standard. Then, however, he sets to in earnest and pounds Louis mercilessly page after page. He restates as established fact the charges of plagiarism that had been leveled at Louis over the years by some of his collaborators, saying that Louis did virtually none of the work he was most celebrated for but either exploited his stable of students and assistants or stole outright from other independent workers. Louis, he tells us,

> began his well-conceived and highly successful system of robbery not in the United States but in Switzerland, and with his emigration to North America (1846) merely continued it to a greater degree. Many influential scientific theories that usually carry his name were not set out by him but stolen from their actual authors, given a superficial polishing, and brought to bear by him. Thus the famous ice age theory was set out not by Agassiz but by Charpentier and Karl Schimper, the glacier theory by Forbes, etc.

He goes on to say that it is already well known in Europe and in North America

> that Louis Agassiz owes his prominent place as America's foremost natural scientist for the most part not to the scientific worth of his own works but to the extraordinary skill with which he could use the work of others, the rare entrepreneurial knack with which he could liquefy great sums of money for his ends, and the remarkable talent for organization with which he created the most magnificent collections, museums, and insti-

tutes. Louis Agassiz was the most ingenious and energetic rack-
eteer in the entire domain of natural history.[6]

Then, resuming at least somewhat his historical agenda, Haeckel
asserts that Louis's prominence was a problem not only because it
was falsely built but because it encouraged reactionary creationist
opposition to Darwinism. As the creationists' champion, lauded as
"the greatest natural scientist of his time" who knew how to "bring
natural science into the nicest harmony with the . . . Bible," Louis
continued to harm science.

"The consequence of this charlatanry is not to be underestimated," writes Haeckel. "But I, at least, see clearly the hoof of
Mephisto peeking out from under the black robes of the priest in
which the sly Agassiz, with his theatrical decorum and talent for
ornament, knew to wrap himself."

Nothing burns like malevolent exaggeration. Alex immediately
wrote Haeckel calling him a "calumnious slanderer," saying he
wished he'd never met him, and declaring their relationship finished.[7] A few days later, when he responded to a letter his uncle
Alexander Braun had written him objecting to Haeckel's attack, he
said he was aching to beat Haeckel senseless:

> I must say I was stung to the quick when I saw Haeckel's Ziele
> und Wege. I did not think it possible for a man like Haeckel to
> use the weapons of a Vogt.* This is more astonishing to me as
> to the very day of issuing that I was receiving the most friendly
> letters from Haeckel! When the *Anthropologie* [a previous
> Haeckel essay that attacked Louis less viciously] was published,
> I remonstrated with Haeckel (in lettres) about his treatment of
> father and hoped he would not push his discussion [to] degen-
> erate into personalities. He wrote me subsequently, but made
> no reference to this and because he wished it closed that way,
> you can imagine my astonishment at receiving from *him* the
> Ziele und Wege, an advance copy at that! I wrote him a letter
> such as I have never written a mortal being and should I ever
> meet him my only answer can be the horsewhip.

---

* Vogt was one of the Neuchâtel "scientific factory" assistants who spoke ill of Louis after
he left.

Still, Alex shows in this same letter to Braun the sort of restraint—a sensible determination to stay out of such fights—that he had learned a decade before when his father was having his worst fights with Gray and Dana.

> I was very glad . . . to hear again directly from you and especially about the conviction of feeling regarding the article of Haeckel and his attacks on father. . . . But I hope that you will not pursue this fight any further. What is the use of it? Have we not better things to do than to be constantly firing off fireworks, which after all do not convince and will hardly silence opponents?[8]

This is the same letter in which Alex tells his uncle (like Haeckel, an idealist *Naturphilosopher* and an evolutionist) that he leans toward evolution "in the general sense," but that he has so adroitly sat the fence that he is "claimed equally by the extreme evolutionists and the most ardent Cuvierian, so that I must have expressed myself much like the Delphian oracles to suit all parties so well."

In its opaque way, this letter is one of the most revealing Alex ever chose to preserve. He still loves his uncle Braun, brother to his mother, and feels compelled to clarify for him not only his own position on evolution but why he chose, in the long, bloody brawl between Louis and Darwin, creationists and evolutionists, idealists and empiricists, not only to abandon Louis's corner but to sit in the darkest, most remote rows of the hall. He urges Braun to take the same sort of back-row seat and keep his head down. Better, he says, to avoid "the present mania for extremes," for "I know . . . that those who have kept cool and continued to work quietly during this time of transition will find themselves someday just so much ahead of their metaphysical opponents."

It's good advice. But coming atop Alex's description of fence sitting regarding evolution, his plea for silence regarding Haeckel speaks volumes about his determination not just to stay clear of distracting peripheral spats but to take a position on central matters that is so inscrutable, so consciously limited to the factual, and so stridently avoidant of the emphatic that he could not possibly be spattered in the sort of blood match his father fought. All his life he tried to stay clear of any arena that smelled of either evolution or metaphysics. He was determined not to be dragged into such a thing.

The problem with avoiding the arena, of course, is that it denies you the chance to swing the horsewhip. Alexander never saw Haeckel again, so he never had to confront the opportunity to thrash him. After his Edinburgh visit, however, he did have the coral reef question, which offered a more appropriate way to rebut both the Darwinist zealots like Haeckel and the imaginative excesses of Darwin's method. Facts would trump speculation, rigorous work the flights of philosophers and theorists. And so only six months after advising Braun to step back, seemingly unaware of what he was doing—thinking he was going back to the office—Alexander Agassiz rose from his seat and stepped into the arena. He would be there an awfully long time.

CHAPTER TWELVE

Accrual

I

AT FIRST IT appeared it might be easy, if you can call easy a
decade that included several expensive and grueling sea journeys and some scientific tug-of-war. But within a few years of
Alexander's pledge to Murray to "investigate coral reefs," he, Murray,
and others accumulated enough evidence to confidently believe they
were displacing Darwin's theory with another one more multifaceted
and accurate.

The first step was the paper that Murray read before the Royal
Society of Edinburgh and then published in its proceedings as well as
in *Nature* (then a more popular and less technical science journal
than it is today) in 1880.[1] "The Structure and Origin of Coral Reefs
and Islands" offered a well-documented argument that Darwin's
"simple and beautiful theory," though "universally accepted," was
wrong. After describing Darwin's subsidence theory in fair-minded
and admirably concise language, Murray observed that in the time
since its rapid acceptance, most investigators had "experienced great
difficulty in applying Darwin's theory" to the coral isles and atolls
they actually encountered. He then stated that his goal was "to
show . . . there are other agencies at work [besides subsidence] . . .
by which submarine elevations can be built up from very great
depths so as to form a foundation for coral reefs [and] that all the
chief features of coral reefs and islands can be accounted for without

calling in the aid of great and general subsidences." In short, Darwin's theory was not accurate or even necessary, for a better one was at hand.

He then presented a quantified elaboration of what he had told Alex in Edinburgh: that in every ocean throughout the world, the *Challenger* and other post-*Beagle* cruises had found numerous mountain ranges and other banks that rose to within one thousand fathoms of the surface; that in the tropics, planktonic skeletons fell steadily and heavily enough on these mid-depth platforms to raise them to coral-friendly depths; and that the formation of these accrued slopes, along with the advance of the thickening talus slope on the reef's outer edge and the solvent action of seawater in the lagoon behind, could explain every feature of every type of reef, fringing, barrier, and atoll. The "submerged banks" on which reefs form, he said, "are continually in the process of formation in the tropical regions . . . , and it is in a high degree probable that the majority of atolls are seated on banks formed in this manner."[2]

With his own alternative theory presented, Murray then described one archipelago after another that researchers had found to contradict Darwin's theory. This catalog included Tahiti, where Darwin had his mountaintop epiphany; the Maldives, a vast Indian Ocean atoll that Darwin did not visit but that he considered a particularly strong argument for subsidence; and the Fijis, which Dana had claimed was an almost ideal illustration of Darwin's principles. Murray pointed out that the heart of Darwin's theory, the idea that most reefs form on sinking volcanoes, conflicted with the long, well-known association of volcanoes with elevation. Murray didn't know it, but his doubts about this contradiction had been shared by Lyell—who, having died in 1875, was now spared having to decide whether to respond to Murray's expression of them. "There has always seemed to me a difficulty," Lyell once confessed to his journal in 1856, "in reconciling two facts in Darwin's theory of volcanic and Coral areas—namely that Volcanoes are the upheaving power and yet, that nearly all the islands in the middle of great oceans are volcanic."[3]

Murray was more direct. "Throughout the volcanic islands of the great ocean basins," he wrote, "the evidence of recent elevations

Yale geologist James Dwight Dana, whose voluminous
observations on Pacific reefs supplied the main
evidentiary support for Darwin's reef theory

are everywhere conspicuous," while evidence of subsidence was rare. It was true, he admitted, that signs of subsidence tended to be hidden or ambiguous. But that didn't mean they could be assumed, and they in fact needn't be looked for. Given tectonic elevation and planktonic sedimentation—causes that are "proximate, relatively well known and continuous"—"it is not necessary to call in subsidence to explain any of the characteristic features of barrier reefs or atolls."

It was a good argument, delivered cleanly and with an occasional touché. It did not immediately win over Darwin's advocates, but this didn't bother Murray or Agassiz. For it gave the many public doubters of Darwin's theory an alternative to gather around, and these scientists, who included several of the world's most experienced coral reef observers, immediately began developing and elaborating Murray's idea. Secret doubters and undecideds likewise gained an alternative, and many scientists who had not already made up their minds, as well as some who had previously accepted Darwin's theory, now decided to remain neutral and wait for more research. Murray and Agassiz saw this as a significant victory. Almost every serious coral reef researcher since Dana had found reason to doubt the subsidence theory. More data would only strengthen Murray's hand.

2

That Darwin himself remained unconverted surprised no one. Yet Murray's theory got his attention and, if you wanted to read him that way, opened some doubt in his mind. Alex discovered this not long after Murray's paper came out, when he sounded out Darwin with a letter from off the tip of Florida. He wrote from the U.S. steamer *Blake,* tanned, tired, and with several volumes of new reef data freshly recorded from the last of three research cruises off Florida and the Caribbean that he took from 1877 to 1881. While these were general, comprehensive oceanographic expeditions, with extensive bathymetric soundings and zoological collecting, they mark the beginning of Alexander's serious coral reef work. Seven years later he would publish the results of those cruises in the two-volume *Three Cruises of the "Blake,"* a thick and sometimes dense report that nonetheless contained enough evocative passages and illustrations to sell well. (Apparently there was still demand for natural history works by an Agassiz, even sans metaphysics.) In *Three Cruises* he would argue that the foundation underlying the Florida reefs, along with the entire peninsula and its vast surrounding shoals, was created by deposition of not just planktonic debris but the remains of huge numbers of animals brought there by the Gulf Stream. Atop these banks, which had been formed long ago and had scarcely moved up or down since, the coral merely formed a thin veneer. "This explanation," as he would put it in *Three Cruises,* "tested as it has been by penetrating the thickness of the beds underlying the coral reefs, seems a more natural one . . . than that of . . . subsidence."

By the time he wrote *Three Cruises,* Alex had enough confidence in Murray's theory to cite Florida as a first proof that deposition could work globally. "If . . . we have succeeded in showing that great submarine plateaux have gradually been built up in the Gulf of Mexico and the Caribbean by the decay of animal life," he wrote, then "we shall find no difficulty in accounting for the formation of great piles of sediment on the floors of the Pacific and Indian Oceans, provided these banks lie in the track of a great oceanic current." For now, however, writing Darwin from the *Blake*, Alex stuck to local specifics:

TORTUGAS, 16 APRIL 1881

It is very natural you should be in my mind, as I am in the midst of corals. . . . The Tortugas being the very last of the Florida reefs [to be researched] I find much that has not been noticed before and helps to explain, somewhat differently from what was done by Father, the formation of the reefs. . . . Everything . . . tends to show that the immense plateau which forms the base upon which the Peninsula of Florida is formed, was built up by the débris of animal remains,—Mollusks, Corals, Echinoderms, etc. (after it had originally reached a certain depth in the ocean), until it reached the proper height for corals to flourish.[4]

This was hardly news to Darwin. He had acknowledged in the 1872 edition of *The Structure and Distribution of Coral Reefs* that the banks around Florida and in the Caribbean "clearly show that their origin must be chiefly attributed to the accumulation of sediment."[5] He saw the region as an exception to his theory.

Alex's letter, then, might have drawn a blunt rejoinder pointing out Darwin's prior caveat on Florida and noting that Alex's Florida findings didn't really speak to the larger subsidence argument. It might have drawn such a rejoinder, that is, were Darwin a different sort of polemic. Instead, Darwin responded with a rebuttal that was simultaneously concession, counterargument, and invitation. It's an extraordinary letter, classic Darwin in its graciousness, its mixture of spirited assertion and humble consideration, and its noncommittal commitment to open-mindedness. Even while defending his view and questioning Murray's, he allows doubt about his own theory— and flatters Alex that he, perhaps more than anyone, has the resources to settle the issue.

5 MAY 1881, DOWN

It was very good of you to write to me from Tortugas, as I always feel much interested in what you are about, and in reading your many discoveries. It is a surprising fact that the peninsula of Florida should have remained at the same level for the immense period requisite for the accumulation of so vast a pile of debris.

You will have seen Mr. Murray's views on the formation of atolls and barrier reefs. Before publishing my book, I thought long over the same view, but only as far as ordinary marine organisms are concerned, for at that time little was known of the multitude of minute oceanic organisms.

With his "only as far as . . ." he admits that his theory had not considered the rain of planktonic debris Murray had found. Yet he goes on to disallow Murray's idea anyway, at least for the time. "I rejected [Murray's] view," he wrote, "as from the few dredgings made in the *Beagle* in the S. Temperate regions, I concluded that shells, the smaller corals, etc., etc., decayed and were dissolved when not protected by the deposition of sediment; and sediment could not accumulate in the ocean open."

He then casts doubt on Murray's central mechanism—but immediately pulls his punch:

I have expressly said that a bank at the proper depth would give rise to an atoll, which could not be distinguished from one formed during subsidence. I can, however, hardly believe in the former presence of as many banks (there having been no subsidence) as there are atolls in the great oceans, within a reasonable depth, on which minute oceanic organisms could have accumulated to the thickness of many hundred feet. . . . Lastly, I cannot understand Mr. Murray, who admits that small calcareous organisms [such as planktonic debris that supposedly build up the banks] are dissolved by the carbonic acid in [sea] water at great depths, and that coral reefs, etc., etc., are likewise dissolved near the surface, but that this does not occur at intermediate depths, where he believes that the minute oceanic organisms accumulate until the bank reaches within the reef-building depth. But I suppose I must have misunderstood him.

We see what Alex is up against: a mind agile, determined, and gracious. He could hardly be more dangerous. Darwin is like the wizened martial arts teacher, warmhearted but deadly, who humbly compliments your efforts even as he deflects your every blow and occasionally delivers, from nowhere, a smack upside the head. Darwin's graciousness is genuine. But it's also a serious weapon meant to disarm. When he says in a kindly tone that he finds a fact surprising or an idea's meaning elusive, it's never clear whether we should consider the stupid thing to be him or the fact or idea—until we realize that since it's Charles Darwin speaking, chances favor the latter. He shows too the smoothness of the passive-aggressive dinner host who raises a contentious subject just long enough to score a point, then forestalls response by sweeping the subject away as too odious. He even manages to wield the same phrase as sword and shield in a single paragraph: "I cannot understand Mr. Murray [in his insistence that shells dissolve in shallow and deep water but not at medium depths]," he says to open the attack that he ends with the disarming "But I suppose I must have misunderstood him." It all seems calculated (or, more to the point, spun with unconscious ease) to destroy Murray's argument while launching a preemptive strike of politesse to prevent counterattack.

But then, just when he has genially painted Murray's theory as an unworkable stretch and left Alex almost no equally gracious way to differ strongly, Darwin, in another combination of directness and obliquity, suggests that he might have got everything wrong after all and so perhaps an adjudicator is needed—and that Alex, with his expertise, knowledge, and money, is best qualified to serve:

> Pray forgive me for troubling you at such a length, but it has occurred to me that you might be disposed to give, after your wide experience, your judgment. If I am wrong, the sooner I am knocked on the head and annihilated so much the better. . . .
> I wish that some doubly rich millionaire would take it into his

head to have borings made in some of the Pacific and Indian atolls, and bring home cores for slicing from a depth of 500 or 600 feet.[6]

This makes a strange call to action. It recalls the dance with which Darwin led Gray along in their extended and oblique correspondence about plant distribution before confessing his evolution theory. Was he doing the same here with Alex, only inviting him to prove him wrong? One can't quite call his request for Alex's clarifying opinion a challenge; the tone is too gracious. Yet his astonishing mix of antagonistic counterargument, seemingly modest half-admissions of thin evidence and poor thinking, and flattery amounts to a dare. The wish for a "doubly rich millionaire" is a particularly deft touch; Darwin knew well that Alex was trebly rich. The final, irresistible goad is the suggestion that a few hard facts might settle the whole issue. The deductive theorist is cooking a meal the aroma of which the inductivist investigator can scarcely resist.

Darwin wrote Alex this letter on May 5, 1881. When Alex found it on returning to Cambridge from Florida two weeks later, he wrote back immediately. His response matches Darwin step for step in a dance of half-concession, correction, and counterproposal. He begins by confessing that he thinks Murray might be overplaying the planktonic-debris factor; to him it seems more likely that planktonic debris are joined by the skeletons of mollusks, starfish, echinoderms, crustacea, and other bottom dwellers to build more solid, current-resistant banks than Murray proposed. As to the question of shells and planktonic skeletons dissolving at different rates at different depths, Alex, mirroring Darwin nicely in his disarming false modesty, says he wouldn't really know about *that*, but in *his* experience (which he needn't trumpet, since Darwin has just acknowledged it as wider than his own) calcareous skeletons actually stay "fairly well preserved after death" once they've reached bottom. He finishes this polite opining by saying that he still sides with Murray, with some caveats, and agreeing amiably that more facts are indeed the key to settling the matter: "Your objection that there is not a great probability of finding in the Pacific as many banks as there are atolls is . . . one which seems to me can only be met by showing in subsequent surveys that these atolls are themselves only slightly raised patches upon large banks. . . . This is a problem . . . which I have had in view for a long time and hope to solve one of these days.[7]

Eleven months later, on April 19, 1882, before the two could continue this correspondence, Darwin died. He was seventy-three. His death, and the convivial tone of his brief exchange with Alexander on coral reefs, leaves us to wonder whether these two men, who seemed to share an extra mutual regard for having found in each other an unexpected warmth and open-mindedness during Darwin's feud with Louis two decades earlier, might have advanced the coral reef debate along more constructive lines than it ended up following.

Such speculation is moot, of course. One might just as readily have predicted that Darwin's exit would allow a more objective, less personality-laden consideration of coral reef genesis. But that hardly proved the case either.

3

For three years, health problems, other travels, the demands of running the museum, and the composition of *Three Cruises of the "Blake"* (five hundred pages thick with illustrations) prevented Alex from reaching the Pacific. In December 1884, however, he sailed to Hawaii (then still called the Sandwich Islands) and spent two months looking for signs of elevation and subsidence. He saw "[everything] there was to be seen in the way of coral reefs" on Oahu and much on Maui and Hawaii as well, and he exhaustively reviewed previous reports. Dana and others who had been there before him had done most of the sounding work, so he was free to move quickly between places to examine the physical structure of the corals. Without a boat himself this time, he usually hired fishermen to take him over the reefs in their outrigger canoes so he could peer down on the coral. At other times he borrowed a boat and rowed himself out over the reefs. He talked to well drillers and copied their bore records to see what strata they punched through when looking for water. Everything he found confirmed his feeling that Hawaii, his first Pacific reef area, fit Murray's model of an advancing reef atop an accrued bank better than it fit Darwin's subsidence theory.

When he got back he wrote Dana, whom he had also written before the trip. In both letters Alex steers clear of any sharp differences.

> You will be interested to hear that while at Sandwich Islands I followed in your tracks and explored the area pretty thoroughly [and discovered] some interesting points. . . . I must now look up carefully all you have done . . . and shall then take the first opportunity of publishing a short paper on the reefs of the Sandwich Islands. What a delightful place these islands are. It seems a . . . paradise, especially as called up on a raw specimen of a New England spring day.[8]

It's the tone of someone seeking the camaraderie of two old friends who disagree about something they love. Alex would respond much differently when he read Dana's next reef paper a few months later.

Meanwhile he had reason to take heart in the increasing number of researchers who said that their field observations in the Pacific didn't agree with Darwin. Such objections had actually begun decades earlier. Louis Agassiz, as mentioned before, had found in 1851 that the Florida reefs didn't appear to be the result of subsidence. The German geologist J. J. Rein had concluded the same about the Bermudas in the 1860s, and Alexander himself had corroborated these views and expanded them to the Bahamas in his *Blake* cruises. Carl Semper's 1860s examination of the Palau Islands (now called the Pelews, part of the Carolines) had found them incompatible with the subsidence theory. And Henry Forbes, visiting the Indian Ocean's Cocos atoll in 1879, saw neither signs of subsidence nor any necessity to call on it to explain this atoll that Darwin had found so confirming.

These pre-Murray refutations, having no theory of their own to reinforce, had received little attention. Once Murray published his theory, however, refutations got more play, though most appeared in the proceedings of the Murray-friendly Royal Society of Edinburgh rather than in *Nature*. H. B. Guppy, cruising the Solomon Islands in HMS *Lark* in 1882–1884, concluded that subsidence played no role in creating this large archipelago just east of Papau New Guinea; rather, the Solomons' barrier isles and atolls formed roughly as Murray suggested, starting atop banks or in the shallows around volcanic islands and then extending outward on talus while erosion and solution formed lagoons behind. Gilbert Bourne, an Oxford professor and later director-general of the General Survey of Great Britain, closely investigated the Chagos Islands in the Indian Ocean and decided that though "Darwin [working from charts] considered that the Great Chagos bank afforded particularly good evidence of the truth of the subsidence theory . . . [a] more intimate knowledge of the Great Chagos Bank . . . shows this view to be untenable."[9]

Alex, meanwhile, was slow to publish his own results about either the *Blake* or the Hawaii trip. He had the usual distractions of mine, museum, and other work, but it also seems he was hesitant to enter a fray in which he might be quickly identified as a leader. It was a strange time. The mounting evidence and number of opponents against the subsidence theory made it a good moment to lead a charge. But having seen his father fare poorly from them, Alex viewed tussles between men rather than ideas as a destructive distraction rather than as how science should be done. He felt strongly that if an idea was solid enough, it would win out. And as evidence against Darwin's theory piled higher in the 1880s, he had reason to believe that its weight would tilt the scales without him. The cause already had two worthy champions: Murray, who held unequaled prominence as an oceanographer, and Archibald Geikie, the director-general of the General Survey of Great Britain. In 1883 Geikie had greatly bolstered Murray's theory by publishing a long review article in *Nature* that summarized the breadth of evidence contrary to Darwin's theory.

Alex thus left most of the publishing to others, communicating his own findings either slowly or in letters. He wrote Dana and Murray with similar frequency and congeniality. He sought to keep his end of it a collegial tug of ideas and (more to the point, since he always valued evidence above abstractions) evidence. He seemed to assume that both men would recognize the implications of the mounting evidence against Darwin's theory.

He got a dose of reality in the fall of 1885, when he read a new thirty-eight-page paper from Dana, "Origin of Coral Reefs and Islands." Alex had just written Dana another in that year's series of friendly-rivalry letters, ending it with a comradely confession: "It has been one of my dreams," Alex told Dana, "to make an expedition with modern methods to the great coral areas of the Pacific and with Calumet's financial success I hope I now may secure a vessel to go solve what I look upon as one of the most interesting problems in geology, the array of Pacific Islands and the whole subject of coral reefs."

In his paper, however, Dana made it clear that he considered the problem already solved. In a tone that sometimes drifted toward sarcasm, he vigorously rebutted the new attacks on Darwin's theory and specifically refuted Murray's argument. He also claimed the empirical high ground, asserting that with the importance that Murray and his supporters gave to field experience (and Darwin's lack thereof), and "knowing that we are all for the truth and right theory, [I have] reason to believe that those who have been led to object to Darwin's conclusions will be pleased to have their objections reviewed by one who has a personal knowledge of many of the facts."[10] Dana was flashing the trump card he still held as the single most widely experienced reef observer.

Alex was both miffed and strangely heartened. He found it encouraging that Dana felt a need to refute Murray's theory. And Dana's rebuttal could be read in places as a retreat. Dana here withdrew, for instance, the notion of a vast, continent-size area sinking, allowing that the area of subsidence might not prove as extensive as suspected before. But he also said that even if he and Darwin were wrong about an entire continent's sinking, that exaggeration did not detract from the value of the central thesis: Subsidence could just as well occur more locally or within certain regions or arcs.

Yet if he showed some signs of moderation, Dana clearly didn't intend to surrender: He spent twenty-two of his thirty-eight pages countering every one of the objections cited by Geikie in his long, damaging review of two years before. He also threw new, painful darts at Murray's work, reinterpreting *Challenger* soundings to support Darwin's theory instead of Murray's. And he finished by declaring Murray's and others' theories "incompetent" and stating that "the hypotheses of objectors to Darwin's theory are alike weak. . . . Darwin's theory therefore remains as the theory that accounts for the origin of coral reefs and islands."[11]

Alex was taken aback. The margins of his copy of Dana's paper are filled with annoyed rejoinders like "not at all," "why so?," "why not?," "facts not so," "[Darwin] never saw them," "oh no such thing," "*bad* chart," "what has that to do with coral?," and, regarding Darwin's reliance on charts to interpret the structure of entire archipelagoes, the crucial "danger of leaps." The paper cooled his attitude toward Dana. It instantly put an end to the letters Alex had been writing him about the beauty of the Pacific islands and the interesting problems that remained.

Yet still he hesitated to enter the fray. He was at that point writing up his Hawaii report and struggling with even more revisions to *Three Cruises.* He also continued to tend the museum and mine and had started, at his big summer place in Newport, a small summer research institute for advanced students from the Museum of Comparative Zoology and elsewhere.

The Newport house, in fact, had become a great pleasure to him, and by this time it held a draw that almost outweighed his ambivalence about home, his aversion to New England winters, and, at times, his desire to pursue the coral reef question. The house—a mansion, really, with more than two dozen rooms—was built on a point of land that gave great views as well as easy access to both Narragansett Bay and the open Atlantic. Alex had started spending summers there in 1875, working in a special room outfitted as a lab, and in 1877 he had constructed a research laboratory in an entirely separate building. The place even had microscope tables that rested, each via its own brick pier, directly on the granite ledge beneath the lab so that footsteps wouldn't vibrate the instruments. Seawater, pumped into live tanks by a windmill on the point, was oxygenated with compressed air to allow the keeping of live specimens. He soon added another wing for his own private offices and lab. Every summer a dozen or so students came (some of them yearly for almost two decades) to pursue largely independent study there—a sort of precursor of the summer research programs that would later be established at Woods Hole.[12]

Here, during summers in the 1870s, 1880s, and 1890s, Alex happily studied yet more echinoderm embryology as well as such matters as how flounders change their colors to match whatever surface lies beneath them. It was a comfortable return to small questions. He stayed out of the students' hair for the most part, concentrating on the satisfaction of doing his own work undistracted by anything other than afternoon horseback rides with his sons. By the 1880s the comfort of this routine had eased the intense restlessness he'd felt in the mid-1870s. His health also weighed heavily in his consideration of how avidly to pursue the reef question. He was in his forties now, and a combination of leg problems and what were diagnosed as circulatory ailments combined with his susceptibility to seasickness to forbid sea journeys much of the time. (A particularly harsh bout of seasickness can quickly convince almost anyone that death is near; because Agassiz's doctors had told him he risked precisely that, his sufferings were that much more distressing. He was as seasick on his trip to Hawaii as he'd ever been.) At other times—twice during the 1880s—his health was too fragile in winter to do more than travel overland to Florida (where he stayed ashore) or the American West. Most other winters during this period he traveled mainly on land, boarding boats only to cross the sea rather than study it. He journeyed to Egypt and North Africa, Mexico, India, Europe, and Japan. These visits of escape began to seem not merely distractions, as they had been in the late 1870s, but pleasurable goals. Fond of roughing it but with the money to rest or travel in luxury when he desired, he enjoyed these trips tremendously. He loved, for instance, trying to figure out the geology of the Sahara, and he made a rigorous hobby of hunting for artifacts and photographing ancient architecture.*

Next to this, the risks and discomforts of further journeys on the Pacific were daunting. As the 1880s wore on and he passed fifty, it increasingly seemed sensible not only to let others wield the pen against Darwin's theory but to let younger men do the field research as well. Some already were. In the 1880s alone, researchers such as Guppy and Bourne were rapidly adding new archipelagoes to the list of those that defied Darwin's theory. Alex had reason to believe that such fieldwork would eventually win the day.

By the nature of it, of course, it was hard to know how decisively the coral reef issue was moving his way. A multifaceted, locality-

---

* His gathering of artifacts greatly enriched the collections of Harvard's Peabody Museum. By 1890 he had seen and photographed almost all known ancient sites in North and South America, for example, and from his pictures constructed a theory, remarkably similar to that held by twenty-first-century anthropologists, about the migration of the first Americans from the far northwest southward all the way to the west coast of South America, where the hunters-turned-farmers turned hunters again.

specific, conditional explanation like his would not be suddenly hailed far and wide but would gain credibility only gradually. It would not set in with the sudden power of an epiphany, for unlike an epiphany it was not simplistic. For Alex, this was almost the whole point. Later he would come to favor a particular model of reef building. But for now his explanation was so conditional that it was almost an antitheory: He was pushing the idea that no single theory could cover all or even most coral reefs, that instead the origins of each reef system must be considered separately. Such an explanation could win out only in suitably subtle fashion, one reef system at a time.

As he worked up his Hawaii notes in the mid-1880s, precisely this seemed to be happening. The reports of Bourne, Guppy, Rein, and others were pebbles that would raise the theory high enough to obscure Darwin's simple, shimmering idea. Let Dana be stubborn. He was only one man. Most scientists without entrenched interests were feeling that Darwin had overreached. Alex had reason to believe that as more reef data accrued, a more multifaceted model would win. It would take some time, but it was happening. And that was all right. That was how science worked.

Then came a row that made it clear that all such thinking was fantasy.

CHAPTER THIRTEEN

"A Conspiracy of Silence"

I

IN 1847, when Alex was twelve and collecting beetles and nursing his mother in Freiburg and Darwin was thirty-eight and studying barnacles, George John Douglas Campbell, twenty-four, inherited the title he would thereafter prefer, the eighth Duke of Argyll. Campbell also inherited a castle and 170,000 Highland acres. The land included some of the United Kingdom's most intriguing geology. The Duke, intelligent and energetic, was soon spending considerable time studying it. Inspired to a gentleman's life of science, he joined the Royal Society of London in 1851 (the same year as Huxley), and for the rest of his life he fit an amateur scientific career around distinguished service as a politician and diplomat. Appointed to several cabinets and as secretary of state for India, he was active in the Royal Society of Edinburgh, Murray's home group, to which he was once elected president. He was a familiar figure amid both the London scientific establishment of Buckland, Lyell, and Darwin and the Scottish scientific community that included Thomson and Murray.

The Duke was proud to be a high figure in the world's dominant power, and while he held liberal (if not exactly egalitarian) sentiments in governmental matters, he was conservative as a scientist. A catastrophist, he wanted no part of the Lyellian uniformitarianism that emerged in the 1830s, and he despised Darwin's theory of evolution and the seemingly atheistic positivist philosophies it epitomized.

He did not espouse the special creationism of Louis Agassiz, but he believed that since God created the world, the study of nature should at least implicitly be the study of God's work. To reduce nature's phenomena to arbitrary processes, to deny its workings any sense of purpose, and to sever facts from values was to cast God away from both the world and humankind.

George John Douglas Campbell, the eighth Duke of Argyll, in an 1869 cartoon. Campbell's entry into the coral reef debate a decade later brought it a prominence no one had expected.

These attitudes were not uncommon among Victorians. Indeed, their prevalence was what made Darwinism so controversial. But the Duke articulated them with uncommon energy and skill, writing often and eloquently on science, education, religion, and philosophy. He clashed constantly with Thomas Huxley. If Huxley was Darwin's bulldog, the Duke was the terrier who plagued Darwin by forever popping out of hedges to yap and snap. Huxley and the Duke first tangled in the early 1860s, and their dogfights ran clear into the 1890s. Huxley's side won the war, of course, but his scraps with the Duke cut scars that ached for at least another generation. As late as 1918, Leonard Huxley, Thomas's son, called the Duke (safely dead by then) "a polemical upholder of ideas left stranded by the progress of science."[1] And indeed the Duke looms in his period like a Churchill, an imposing, proudly archaic figure who fought with a frightening arsenal of rhetorical weapons and no apparent fear. His prose—just shy of florid, exquisitely structured and paced, embellished with metaphor, understatement, and backhanded malice—exudes the elegant malevolence of swordplay. He had a particular knack for raising bloodlust while seeming to appeal only to the highest sensibilities. In the late 1880s, he played the role of antagonist in a controversy that tied the coral reef problem to the most contentious figures and ideas in science.

The coral reef controversy of the late 1880s emerged from an essay by a Duke ally, W. S. Lilly, who in November 1886 published "Materialism and Morality" in the prominent literary magazine the *Fortnightly Review.* Lilly, expressing earthily what the Duke had oft suggested, alleged that the positivism practiced by Thomas Huxley and others "reeks of the brothel, the latrine and the torture trough." Huxley returned fire the next month. Lamenting that "the proprieties do not permit me to make [my response] so emphatic as I could desire," he refuted Lilly's positions. Two months later he opened a broader counterattack with a withering critique of the ideas of catastrophe and miracle titled "Scientific and Pseudo-scientific Realism."

Enter the Duke, who responded to Huxley's essay with one calling Darwinism a "muddy torrent of bad physics and worse metaphysics" and complaining (in the sort of language guaranteed to fire the agnostic Huxley) of "the fumes of worship and of incense raised before the fetish of a Phrase ['natural selection']." Darwinian idolatry, the Duke said, was suppressing the scientific world in a "Reign of Terror," and "it is high time indeed that some revolt should be raised."

Huxley responded by trying to kick the Duke's own high rhetoric from beneath him. "Can it be," he asked, "that a guillotine is to be erected in the courtyard of Burlington House for the benefit of all anti-Darwinian Fellows of the Royal Society?"[2]

The Duke had in mind no literal guillotine, of course. But after a few weeks, obviously having worked at it a bit, he revealed the instrument by which he hoped to decapitate Darwinist theory and idolatry. If evidence was everything, then he would offer a specific example of a sound, empirically based theory that Darwinists had unfairly repressed: John Murray's coral reef theory.

2

For an attack, the Duke's "Conspiracy of Silence" essay, as it came to be known, opened kindly. The Duke, writing now in another leading literary magazine, *The Nineteenth Century,* began with a glowing portrait of a *Beagle*-era Darwin who had "a mind singularly candid and unprejudiced—fixing upon nature a gaze keen, penetrating, and curious, but yet cautious, reflective and almost reverent." He spends a good two pages painting a Darwin anyone could love—curious, humane, impartial, and graciously, lucidly eloquent. The Duke then takes another ten pages to describe, apparently admiringly, Darwin's theory of coral reef formation. This glowing, even moving account, written as by an advocate, ends with the Duke's acknowledging that the theory was not only ingenious, showing deep thought and a thorough knowledge of almost all that was known on the subject, but beautiful:

> There was an attractive grandeur in the conception of a great continent sinking slowly, slowly, into the vast bed of the Southern Ocean, having all its hills and pinnacles gradually covered by coral reefs as in succession they sank down to the proper depth, until at last only its pinnacles remained as the basis of atolls, and these remained, like buoys upon a wreck, only to mark where some mountain peak had been finally submerged. . . . It was a magnificent generalisation. . . . I have heard eminent men declare that, if he had done nothing else, [Darwin's] solution of the great problem of the coral islands of the Pacific would have sufficed to place [him] on the unsubmergeable peaks of science, crowned with an immortal name.

He's setting Darwin up, of course, raising him high so he can drop him far. The attack comes after fifteen pages.

And now comes the great lesson. After an interval of more than five-and-thirty years the voyage of the 'Beagle' has been followed by the voyage of the 'Challenger,' furnished with all the newest appliances of science, and manned by a scientific staff more than competent to turn them to the best account. And what is one of the many results which have been added to our knowledge of nature—to our estimate of the true character and history of the globe we live on? It is that Darwin's theory is a dream. It is not only unsound, but it is in many respects directly the reverse of truth. With all his conscientiousness, with all his caution, with all his powers of observation, Darwin in this matter fell into errors as profound as the abysses of the Pacific.

The Duke's beef is not, he says, with the late Darwin, who had tried to solve an enormous puzzle with the best information at hand (albeit with a bit too much imagination). His beef is with Darwin's followers, who defend his views even when it means ignoring growing mounds of contrary evidence. Recent findings confuting Darwin's coral reef theory, he says, show that

all the acclamations with which it was received were as the shouts of an ignorant mob. . . . Can it be possible that Darwin was wrong? Must we indeed give up all that we have been accepting and teaching for more than a generation? Reluctantly, almost sulkily, and with a grudging silence as far as public discussion is concerned, the ugly possibility has been contemplated as too disagreeable to be much talked about. The evidence, old and new, has been weighed and weighed again, and the obviously inclining balance has been looked at askance many times. But despite all averted looks I apprehend that it has settled to its place forever, and Darwin's theory of the coral islands must be relegated to the category of those many hypotheses which have indeed helped science for a time by promoting and provoking further investigation, but which in themselves have now finally "kicked the beam."

And what had exposed this error? It was the reef theory of John Murray,

> supported with such a weight of facts and such close texture of reasoning that no serious reply has ever been attempted. . . . Here was a generalisation as magnificent as that of Darwin's theory. It might not present a conception so imposing as that of a whole continent gradually subsiding. . . . But . . . the new explanation was more like the analogies of nature—more closely correlated with the wealth of her resources, with those curious reciprocities of service which all her agencies render to each other, and which indicate so strongly the ultimate unity of her designs.

Thanks, however, to the "curious power which is sometimes exercised on behalf of certain accepted opinions, or of some reputed Prophet, in establishing a sort of Reign of Terror in their own behalf," Murray's new theory had produced only "slow and sulky acquiescence, rather than that joy which every true votary of science ought to feel in the discovery of a new truth and—not less—in the exposure of a long-accepted error." The whole affair showed, said the Duke, that solid science was being held hostage by those who considered Darwin's theories sacrosanct.

As a final slap at Huxley and his fellow travelers, the Duke dredged up the decade-old *Bathybius* debacle. This great mistake regarding the "mother slime" with the "fine new Greek name" had caught on, the Duke alleged, only because Darwin's theory of evolution made the idea of *Bathybius* so attractive that it "ran like wildfire through the popular literature of science." The farce ended only when the *Challenger* crew, with Murray playing a prominent role, discovered that the primordial ooze was just a lab artifact. "This was bathos indeed," punned the Duke, "a case in which a ridiculous error and a ridiculous credulity were the direct results of theoretical preconceptions."

It's rare that an argument so lively and caustic—so much plain fun—carries such lyrical grace. The lyricism wasn't just dressing. To begin with, it protected the Duke from the charge that he was blind to the beauty of elegant theory; the man gushed about ideas the way

Louis Agassiz gushed about creatures. This style, and particularly the lovely account of Darwin's theory, also co-opted Darwin as an ally against his own supporters. By describing Darwin's ingenious attempt so sympathetically and eloquently—all the while praising his renowned open-mindedness—the Duke sharpens his assault on the close-minded idolaters who would ignore new evidence.

In part, the Duke was making a wider argument that would be an accepted truism a century later: that science, being a social as well as an intellectual enterprise, is prone to errors of idolatry, pride, cowardice, and politics. A scientific orthodoxy (at least that of Darwinism) could legitimize bad theories the way governments legitimized bad laws.

This infuriated the empiricists who championed Darwin. The Duke was calling them atheistic churchmen and closet idealists, pseudoempiricists who would adore a theory because it reflected an ideal order not in nature (much less God) but in the theory itself. In love with elegant thought, elated at being free of the restraints of religion, they worshipped not thoughts of God but those of man—and particularly of the man named Darwin.

3

Huxley responded with polite acidity and some deft stratagems of his own. He declared that given the difficulties of studying something so complicated as reef formation, he (who had spent three years among reefs) doubted there were ten people in the world fit to weigh the merits of Darwin's and Murray's theories. (Presumably the Duke, who'd never been to the tropics, wasn't among them.) Then, turning to the Duke's charges of idolatry and censorship, he hammered at the weak spots in the Duke's argument.

"The Duke," Huxley declared, "commits himself to a greater number of statements that are demonstrably incorrect . . . than I have ever seen gathered together in so small a space." Huxley actually counted off the major errors (seven) and answered them in order. He noted, for instance, that when the Duke said that no one had attempted a serious response to Murray's theory (incorrect statement number one), he overlooked Dana's extended and highly specific rebuttal of 1885; that the "ignorant mob" that received the theory (error number four) apparently included Dana and other widely renowned men of science; and, most damningly, that far from being ignored or suppressed (falsehood number six), Murray had published his theory in two major journals, Geikie had elaborated it in his 1883 *Nature* review article, and several recent geology textbooks discussed it. Huxley also rebutted in detail the Duke's accusation (inaccuracy number seven) that Murray had been improperly discouraged from publishing his theory in the first place.

Huxley wasn't the only one fuming. Many in the British scientific world had felt attacked, and some of them joined the fight. As the discussion moved from the monthly *Nineteenth Century* to the letters page of *Nature* (where "weekly publication," as historian Susan Schlee put it, "allowed for a quicker and more satisfying exchange of insults"[3]), the barrage leveled at the Duke provided one of the livelier strings of letters that *Nature* had yet run. John Judd, a prominent geologist and supporter of Darwin's theory, cited the several textbooks and articles that had discussed Murray's theory and quipped, "If [Murray's treatment] be a 'conspiracy of silence,' where, alas! can the geological speculator seek for fame?"[4] University of London geology professor and immediate past president of the Geological Society Thomas Bonney, who would soon emerge as a major defender of Darwin's theory despite his lack of coral reef experience, confessed he was "old-fashioned enough to resent being called a knave more than being called a fool" and said the Duke's charges of repression suggested that he was either "strangely oblivious of, or, among the cares of a statesman, has failed to keep himself *au courant* with, the literature of geology." (Several combatants voiced this pseudosympathetic lament that the Duke's political duties must have left him behind; Bonney was the only one to season it with French.) When the Duke wrote a letter offering a second example of suppression, accusing the Darwinian establishment of stifling a paper Guppy had offered the Royal Society, Huxley quipped that "as fast as old misrepresentations are refuted, new ones are evolved out of the inexhaustible inaccuracy of his Grace's imagination."[5]

This pithy fight about knavery quickly made the coral reef problem one of the most prominent and explicitly controversial in science. It also created, amid the sword work, the most thorough discussion yet of the arguments for and against the two theories.

Many who had not yet read Darwin's and Murray's theories now did, and virtually every scientist who had actually seen a reef chimed in. Murray was invited to present his theory (updated with additional data) to the Royal Society of London, and this updated account ran in *Nature* in early 1888, as did pretty much anything else Murray wanted to say on the subject.

The more substantive parts of the debate covered several key issues. One was Murray's idea that lagoons formed not through subsidence but through solution of coral by seawater. Any reef-genesis theory had to explain how lagoons were created, and many of his peers considered Murray's notion of lagoon formation the weakest part of his reef theory; quite a few, including some who favored Murray's general theory, doubted that seawater dissolved corals fast enough to create lagoons. Others, echoing the objection Darwin had written to Alex, pointed out that if seawater *did* dissolve calcium-based material quickly enough to create deep lagoons, the same solvent power should prevent the banks from piling high enough to provide coral foundations in the first place. Some who supported Murray's larger theory about planktonic accumulation suggested other mechanisms that could account for lagoon formation. Captain William Wharton of the Royal Navy, for instance, an accomplished marine scientist who would soon become a rear admiral and hydrographer, reiterated the Eschscholtz-Chamisso observation that since corals grew most rapidly to seaward, a Murrayesque reef—one mounting on a sediment-formed bank—would naturally create a lagoon behind the faster-rising seaward edge or perimeter. Corals growing on island banks would thus form bowl-shaped atolls, and a shoreline bank could give rise to a barrier reef. If a rising reef took such a form, even modest destruction of the reef interior by solution, perhaps combined with the erosive power of current and tide, might produce even deep lagoons. Wharton's lagoon-formation thesis was seconded by Oxford geologist Gilbert Bourne, whose long examination of the Chagos and other banks in the Indian Ocean led him to "conclusions nearly identical" to Wharton's and quite opposite Darwin's. "The true cause of the atoll and barrier lagoons," wrote Bourne, "lies in the peculiarly favorable conditions for coral growth present on the steep external slopes of the reef."[6]

Wharton, who wrote carefully and tactfully, clearly not wanting a scrap, also stressed how little was known about the bathygraphy of most coral areas. Of the 173 larger islands in the Tuamotus, Ellice (now Tuvalu), Gilbert, Marshall, and Caroline Islands, for instance, only four had been even partially sounded. Data so sketchy hardly justified grand generalizations.

How to pull all this together? Guppy, hoping to twist the various antisubsidence threads into a cord, noted that among those who accepted Murray's account of reef foundations, the differences concerning the creation of lagoons were academic and likely solvable; they need not sink the theory. It might be, he suggested, that

> in our present state of knowledge it will be wisest to combine in one view the several agencies enumerated by [Murray, Semper, Agassiz, and others] as producing the different forms of coral reefs. On the outer side of a reef we have the directing influence of the currents, the increased food-supply, the action of the breakers, &c. In the interior of a reef we have the repressive influence of sand and sediment, the boring of the numerous organisms that find a home on each coral block, the solvent agency of the carbonic acid in the sea-water, and the tidal scour. These are real agencies, and we only differ as to the relative importance we attach to each.[7]

4

Alex must have given a shout of assent when he read Guppy's plea. He too was becoming convinced that reefs were built by numerous forces that combined in different ways at different locations. He didn't say so in *Nature*'s letters column, for that wasn't his type of forum (though he was quick to tell Murray he was glad to see *him* speak up there). Yet the debate sparked by the Duke's provocations did draw a response from Alex. The Duke flap happened to erupt just as Alex was finishing his long-gestated *Blake* report and his shorter monograph on the 1885 Hawaiian trip. His earlier papers on Florida and the Bermudas had largely avoided broad theoretical statements. Now he finally got explicit.

In *Three Cruises of the "Blake,"* Alex offered for the first time, briefly but plainly, an argument, similar in essence to the Duke's coral reef comments but more measured, that the evidence against Darwin's theory had reached critical mass. After making the case that the Florida and other nearby reefs formed atop sedimentary banks, he went on to say that

> the evidence gathered by Murray, Semper, and myself, partly in districts which Darwin has already examined . . . tends to prove that we must look to many other causes than those of elevation and subsidence for a satisfactory explanation of coral-reef formation. . . . If . . . we have succeeded in showing that great submarine plateaux have gradually been built up in the Gulf of Mexico and the Caribbean by the decay of animal life, we shall find no difficulty in accounting for the formation of great piles of sediment on the floors of the Pacific and Indian Oceans.[8]

Little else in *Three Cruises* hints at which theory should prevail. Alex reserved his longer say for his Hawaii monograph, a more logical place to address Darwin's theory and one that may have felt safer, since *Three Cruises* was meant to be a popular book, while the Hawaii paper appeared in the *Bulletin of the Museum of Comparative Zoology*. He opened with what amounted to a long review article—half of the forty-four-page paper, in fact. This is itself revealing, for the scientific-review article is usually an explicit attempt to shape (or reshape) the conclusions drawn from a body of work. Alexander clearly hoped to do just that: to show that the total body of reef research compelled replacement of Darwin's theory with one less simple.

He began by rebutting some of the arguments leveled against Murray in the *Nature* exchange. He reserved a particularly curt dismissal for the mathematical arguments of T. Mellard Reade, a dry-footed mathematician who had called Murray's overall theory "far-fetched" and who was especially critical of the lagoon-solution thesis. Such "investigators who know little of coral reefs from their own observations," Alexander said pointedly, "have ignored or flatly denied facts which can hardly be dealt with in so summary a fashion." Alex countered Reade's objections with evidence from reef observers such as Jukes and himself as well as other lab experimenters.

Yet while Agassiz answered those objections to Murray's lagoon-solution thesis, he also took pains to express his own reservations

about his friend's model, saying "it is pressing the theory too
far . . . to consider [solution by carbonic acid] the principal cause of
the formation of lagoons."[9] It was more likely, he said, that lagoons
were formed, as Guppy had suggested, through a combination of
forces. He also agreed with another Guppy assertion, that the "new"
accrual theory was itself built upon one of the earliest reef theories
based on actual observation:

> Chamisso* seventy years ago advanced the view that an atoll
> owes its form to the growth of corals at the margin [of a subma-
> rine bank] and to the repressive influence of the reef debris in
> the interior; but this view gave no satisfactory explanation of
> the foundation of such a coral reef [that is, how the submarine
> bank formed], and Darwin was driven to his theory of subsi-
> dence. The great defect in the way of Chamisso was, however,
> removed by Murray, who supplied the foundation of an atoll
> without employing subsidence, and investigation in the Florida
> Sea (Agassiz) and in the Western Pacific (Guppy) have con-
> firmed his conclusions.

The confirming evidence, he emphasized, had come from a much
longer list of researchers than just Guppy and himself. The harsh
fact, he noted, was that only those who originally bought Darwin's
theory still supported it, while all subsequent investigators had found
that the evidence argued against it. To Alex, this alone was reason to
set aside Darwin's theory.

> With the exception of Dana, Jukes, and others who published
> their results on coral reefs soon after Darwin's theory took the
> scientific world by storm, not a single recent original investiga-
> tor of coral reefs has been able to accept [Darwin's] explanation
> as applicable to the special district which he himself exam-
> ined. . . . The great mass of observations since the promulga-
> tion of Darwin's theory is on the side of the more recent
> explanation of the formation of coral reefs, while the older the-

---

* Alexander here unknowingly repeats the historical misattribution of Eschscholtz's idea
to Chamisso.

ory rests upon an hypothesis of which it is under most circumstances extremely difficult to obtain any proof whatsoever.[10]

He then took a dozen pages to detail the evidence against Darwin and for an accrual theory as it had emerged in journeys that not only covered most of the world's tropical coral reef areas but that together outweighed what Darwin and Dana had seen. There had been Louis Agassiz, J. J. Rein, and himself in the Atlantic and Caribbean, and Forbes, Semper, Guppy, and Bourne "in the very regions explored by Darwin" (the Pacific).[11] In each case he explained how the researcher's key findings refuted both Darwin's generalizations and his theory's applicability in the explored region. Finally, he described how his own Hawaiian findings, particularly the borings that showed only thin layers of coral, contradicted Darwin's generalities and Dana's assertion that Hawaii was formed through subsidence.

Alex's long catalog of evidence expressed well his basic contention and his belief in how science worked. As observation piled atop observation to raise the pile of evidence higher, the conclusions became obvious. This was science working properly: not through intuitive leaps and study of maps but through eyes-on observation and the tireless accumulation of reliable information.

That was his evidentiary argument. He also articulated an explicitly methodological argument: Darwin's theory, he insisted, was both circular and speculative in its reasoning, and as such had to be rejected as a matter of principle, especially in the face of a more empirically based and better-documented accrual theory. Science was about evidence, not beautiful ideas. We cannot buy a theory that is its own proof. Yet that is what Darwin and Dana asked. "Darwin and Dana have assumed a possibility as a fact, and, the theory once given, have attempted to prove the subsidence instead of bringing the subsidence of coral reefs as a proof of the theory."[12] Committed to using an unprovable subsidence to explain reefs, they had resorted to using the reefs themselves to prove the premise: *What makes reefs possible? Subsiding land. How do we know the land subsides? Because there are reefs.* No certain knowledge—no known fact, no proven process, no unambiguous observable evidence—held this circle together. It rested on strength of reason—a sort of faith in the logic.

Such speculations occurred when you jumped to conclusions too soon. This was clearly true of Darwin, Alex argued, who, "it should be remembered, examined only the Great Chagos Bank, and based his speculations on the observations he made on this single group."[13] But it was also true of Dana, despite all his field experience. In his Hawaii report, having worked some of Dana's tracks, Alex took a first shot at rebutting him directly, and his attempt illustrates what a vexing problem Dana presented to him. Alex tried to deal with Dana both by emphasizing Dana's differences with Darwin—using him to damn Darwin, in other words—and by dismissing Dana's agreements with Darwin as observational mistakes made under the sway of Darwin's theory. He discarded Dana's speculations about the timing and extent of subsidence as "immaterial" next to the question of whether reefs require subsidence at all. He acknowledged that reefs doubtless did sometimes form atop subsiding areas but argued that if they formed on stable or rising areas as well, then the subsidence theory was not the sweeping, complete explanation it was said to be. Likewise the theory was wrong, or essentially useless as science, if subsidence could not be proven.

And this, he said, was precisely the case. Certainly Darwin hadn't proven subsidence, for he had seen only a few reefs. Neither had the many who based their conclusions on charts. And neither had Dana, who despite his vast field experience had few soundings to document his assertions and so had to rely instead, even in the face of considerable evidence of elevation, on topographical features such as his famous drowned-valley fjords to "prove" subsidence. It was, he concluded, "a most unsafe method of reasoning."[14]

5

As he was writing these words, Alex was again beginning to feel that his side was winning. The row over the "conspiracy of silence" had made quite a stink, but the ensuing debate revealed where the weight of evidence lay. In April, as he was composing his Hawaii paper, he wrote Semper, "After all that has of late been written against the theory of subsidence I do not believe we shall hear much again of Darwin's theory."[15]

This confidence faded, however, as the Duke of Argyll controversy continued into 1889 without seeming to convince any prominent subsidence advocates or fence sitters. Then came a double blow that knocked Alex's hopes into sand. Late 1889 and early 1890 brought new editions of Darwin's and Dana's coral reef books, the reception of which showed that while the balance may have tilted away from Darwin, his theory still held substantial ground. Both books staunchly maintained, as Dana stated at the end of a new section in his book dismissing Agassiz's and other objections, that "Darwin's theory . . . remains as the theory that accounts for the origin of atolls and barrier islands."[16] The landlubber Thomas Bonney, meanwhile, concluded likewise in a literature review appended to the new Darwin edition, saying it was "premature to regard the [Darwin] theory . . . as conclusively disproved."[17]

These prominent entrenchments from either side of the Atlantic, representing the two men still seen (though in Alex's opinion with little reason) as the world's leading coral reef authorities, seemed to epitomize the staying power of the Darwin theory. It was hard to say which was more exasperating. Here you had Bonney—a man whom Darwin's son, Francis, had chosen as editor of the new edition despite a complete lack of reef experience, and who only three years before, in his first letter to *Nature* on the Duke of Argyll flap, had said that he felt qualified only to comment on the "literary" aspects of the coral reef controversy—presuming to pass judgment on phenomena and structures he had never seen. Bonney was backed by another British geologist with no field experience in coral reefs, John Judd (the series editor for the new geological editions Francis Darwin brought out in 1889), who in a preface opined that "while . . . Darwin was betrayed into some grave errors, yet the main foundations of his argument have not been seriously impaired by the new facts observed in the deep-sea researches, or by the severe criticism to which his theory has been subjected during the last ten years."[18]

Dana, meanwhile (seventy-seven by then), seemed willing to go to any length to deny the significance of the evidence against the theory he'd fallen in love with a half century before. In response to Guppy's damning observation that in the Solomons "the coral reef rock forms a comparatively thin layer" over several hundred feet of elevated sedimentary limestone—extremely strong evidence that subsidence played no role in forming this prominent atoll—Dana said the Solomons "only prove that in coral-reef seas corals will grow over any basis of rock that may offer where the water is right in depth and other circumstances favor. They are not evidence against the subsidence theory, but simply local examples under the general principle just stated." This had to have sparked a howl from Alex, for to him it was the very fact that "corals will grow over any basis of rock that . . . depth and other circumstances favor" that both negated and obviated the subsidence theory. Yet here was Dana insisting that this particular instance (a major archipelago) was not merely an exception to the rule of subsidence but that this exception somehow proved the rule. Apparently the rule of subsidence was one that no number of exceptions could disprove.

The whole thing was getting to be too much. It especially irked Alex that scientists would accept on faith such a huge, nearly Pacific-wide movement to explain something that occurred in so many locations and circumstances. To Alex, pointing to a huge, unproveable subsidence as a cause improved only slightly on pointing to God's hand.

"It is remarkable," he wrote in his Hawaii paper, "that Darwin, who is so strongly opposed to all cataclysmic explanations, should in the case of the coral reefs cling to a theory which is based upon the disappearance of a Pacific continent, and be apparently so unwilling to recognize the agency of more natural and far simpler causes." Darwin's coral theory was indeed beautiful. Unfortunately, it defied both the mass of evidence and the principles of empirical practice. Alex could fathom its stubborn persistence only by recognizing in it what Lyell had once seen in Louis's plan of creation—that for many people, the idea was so lovely that they could not help but want to believe it.

The stubbornness of Darwin's theory seemed to prove the dangers of the deductive method that Bacon had tried to counter. Coral reef theory had become slave to a tyranny of premise, and those such as Huxley and Dana who championed subsidence were indulging in something close to idealist thinking. "I cannot understand why Dana should . . . not see the force of the argument against subsidence," Alex wrote Semper, "and it is most confounding that Huxley [and Darwin] . . . should both be ready to call upon a 'deus ex machina' to account for what can so easily be explained by more simple causes."[19]

Perhaps most disturbing was the idolatry that the Duke had referred to—a personalization of theory that carried dangers to which Alex was particularly sensitive. Alex had seen Louis's defensiveness about species creation infect all his work; now he saw the defensiveness that Darwin's supporters had developed during the *Origin* controversy spread over anything the man said.

Alexander's sensitivity to such zeal was only heightened by his discovery, reading Darwin's *Life and Letters* in late 1887, that Darwin had been quietly but ferociously ambitious and constantly pushed his agenda behind the scenes. In a letter to Murray that December, a letter that he begins by expressing his dismay at Huxley's defense of Darwin's coral theory, Alex writes, "I was surprised . . . to see the elements of [Darwin] pushing his cause . . . brought out so persistently [in *Life and Letters*]. The one thing always claimed by Darwin's friends had been his utter unselfishness and absolute impartiality in his own cause. Certainly his correspondence with Hooker, Huxley, and Gray shows no such thing."[20] Alex was doubtless referring to the correspondence of the late 1850s and 1860s, when, along with cultivating his British allies and bulldogs, Darwin cheered Gray on in the American debates that so diminished Louis. It could not have helped to read of his father being ridiculed: "It is delightful to hear all that [Gray] says on Agassiz," Darwin wrote Hooker in 1854, in a letter reproduced in *Life and Letters.* "How very singular it is that so *eminently* clever a man, with such *immense* knowledge on many branches of Natural History, should write as he does." Alex, writing Murray in the midst of the Duke of Argyll flap, tries to forgive Darwin even as he points out these faults, saying it's a delightful book regardless. Yet there's no mistaking his sense of betrayal as he recognizes the self-serving behavior of the man who dethroned his father.

The tangle he had entered was wrapping its vines about him. To pursue good science, it seemed, was to take on his father's nemeses. With the coral reef controversy of the late 1800s—the polarization of opinion, the explicit layering of a methodological debate atop the consideration of evidence, the reentry of old *Origin*-era antagonists like Huxley and Dana—Alex's scientific and personal fates had merged. They had done so long before, of course. But this time he seemed to recognize it in ways he had not earlier.

And so amid the echo of Darwin and Dana's new editions, with the longest scientific discussion of reef theory to date leaving things unresolved, he decided to return to sea. He would sail in much the same spirit in which he had sailed to Florida and Hawaii, hoping to gather enough facts to outweigh the evidence of Darwin and Dana. But this time he would go to the very isles from which Darwin's theory had risen; he would go where Darwin and Dana had gone, see what they had seen, and cut the ground from beneath them.

There was another difference as well. When he had gone to Florida and Hawaii, the reef debate had been low-key, genial, and, as far as he could see, reasonably untainted by personalities and ideology. He had discussed the central points of contention cordially and productively with the man who had spawned the theory, a man who literally asked to be corrected—"knocked on the head," as he put it—if he was wrong. But after the blood spilled over the conspiracy of silence, the revelations of Darwin's own ambitiousness and backstage maneuverings, the insults delivered Murray by Huxley and himself by Dana, Alexander now understood quite well that he was entering an arena in which the lights were bright and the audience excitable, and in which everything, particularly the stakes, tended to be magnified. Though Darwin was dead, it was clear Alex would have to do more than knock him on the head with a few new facts. He had to bury him.

He lacked the youth that had blessed Darwin and Dana when they sailed. But he had time enough, immense expertise, and a great deal of money.

Part Three

CHAPTER FOURTEEN

To Sea

I

THE CORAL REEF expeditions Alexander Agassiz took over
the rest of his life, together with those he'd already taken to
Florida, Cuba, Yucatán, the Bahamas, Bermuda, the Galápagos, and
Hawaii, constitute one of the most comprehensive and wide-ranging
scientific investigations ever conducted. If to prove his case he had to
see more reefs than Darwin and Dana together had seen, he would
do so. He would sail to Tahiti, as Darwin had. He would travel to the
Fijis and the Ellice and the Marshalls, as Dana had. He would even
go to the Maldives, a huge Indian Ocean archipelago that neither
Darwin nor Dana had visited but that by the time Alex traveled
there, in 1902, remained the only major coral area he had *not* seen.
He spent altogether several years at sea, covering more than 100,000
miles. He passed thousands of days peering onto garishly colorful,
fish-filled reefs, sounding the depths of blue offshore banks and
apple green lagoons, hammering fossils from cliffs of limestone and
basalt, and squinting into microscopes to identify the tiny animals he
found imprisoned in island stone.

Few scientists ever covered more water. None saw more coral. As
the century turned, it was clear that this insistently empirical investigator intended not only to see more coral than anyone else (for he
accomplished that early in his quest) but to see every significant tropical coral reef formation on the globe. When he finished, there would
be no archipelago of which another could say he knew more. And

Alexander would harbor no doubt that Darwin and Dana, having gone before him, had seen poorly and spoken rashly. It was a mistake he would avoid perhaps too well.

2

Compared with his later journeys, Alex's first trips after the "conspiracy of silence" controversy and the latest editions of Darwin and Dana seem like practice runs. In 1891, following a plan long in the works, he sailed the U.S. Fish Commission's *Albatross* out of Panama on a general oceanographic journey to the Galápagos. For his coral reef work, the trip proved valuable mainly for showing him a set of islands sparse in coral despite a seemingly conducive site. The next winter, wanting to finish his Caribbean surveys before heading to the Pacific, he spent almost five months sounding banks off Cuba, the

Alexander Agassiz, center, about to examine
the catch from a trawl net

Bahamas, and the long string of islands that swing east-southeast off Florida's east coast out to the Turks and Caicos. In the winter of 1894–1895 he took what proved an ill-timed look at Australia's Great Barrier Reef. He wrote Murray that the Australia trip was the biggest bust he'd ever taken part in. The trade winds blew hard virtually every day, and because the ship he had leased, the *Croyden*, handled heavy seas poorly, he spent most of the time anchored in harbors, seldom reaching the reef banks he came to explore. What he did see, however, convinced him (as it did J. Stanley Gardiner soon after) that the 1,250-mile-long Great Barrier Reef rose not from a sinking island but by growing on current-formed banks.

His next destinations were obvious: the South Sea Islands, the scattered string of archipelagoes that bends in a seven-thousand-mile-long dogleg across the equator in the western Pacific, roughly halfway between Hawaii and Australia. These beautiful and remote islands, already deeply storied and romanticized by this time (Dana, fifty years before, had with reason feared becoming "long pig"—the local term for roasted European—there, while Gauguin was now there living his famously uninhibited life of "ecstasy, calmness, and art"), were the home ground of the Darwin-Dana theory. It was in Tahiti that Darwin experienced his epiphany, looking down from one island peak to see another framed "like an engraving" by its lagoon and reef. It was in the barrier islands and atolls of Fiji that Dana saw the "abundant evidence of subsidence" that convinced him Darwin was right.[1] Dana found more confirmation in the other Pacific archipelagoes—the Tuamotus, Tonga, the Ellice and Gilbert Islands. Here was the proving ground for Darwin's argument and, of necessity, for any theory that sought to displace it.

Alex might have chosen any of these island groups for his first South Sea expedition. On the advice of Dana and the British researcher William Wharton, he headed to Fiji. There, both men said (Dana arguing subsidence, Wharton otherwise), he would find numerous examples of every coral reef form. There were fringing reefs that skirted coastlines. There were barrier reefs that left sheltered lagoons between themselves and the shore. There were ring-shaped atolls on which surf broke from all directions around calm lagoons. The consistency with which the Fijis' several hundred islands took these three main forms helped persuade Dana that Darwin's was "the true theory of Coral Islands,"[2] and ever since then, Dana had cited Fiji as the subsidence theory's clearest and most complete illustration.

Alex went half hoping to find Dana wrong. But he also half expected to find Dana and Darwin confirmed in Fiji—but only there. He hoped that if the Fijian reefs did prove a perfect illustration of reefs formed through subsidence, it would be an illustration so markedly different from other reef systems that did *not* seem to conform to subsidence that Fiji would be the exception, as it were, to the many exceptions that Guppy, Bourne, Wharton, Gardiner, and others had found to Darwin's rule. They would be the nonexception that proved the rule wrong.

3

He almost didn't go. On October 5, 1897, as he was packing to leave the next day, Alex read newspaper reports that an Australian scientist named Edgeworth David, working on a project sponsored by London's Royal Society, had drilled into the coral of Funafuti (one of the Ellice Islands, one group north of Fiji) and penetrated over six hundred feet of coral without breaking through to anything beneath. "This information," as Alex put it later, "seemed to settle the coral question."[3] Continuous coral so thick strongly suggested an island that had thickened as it sank. The only way a nonsubsiding reef could create such a result was if the drill happened to pass through the long-accumulated talus that the reef had shed and then expanded outward upon. The newspaper story that Agassiz read, however, implied that the coral that the drill had passed through was too uniform to have been talus, that it was all one great thickness of continuous reef. Still, he knew better than to put much faith in preliminary reports, especially those in newspapers. He had already chartered a boat and shipped thousands of dollars of supplies to Fiji. So though he was tempted to stay home, "convinced that at any rate, whatever had been my experience in the West Indies, Australia, and the Sandwich Island reefs, yet that in a region of typical atolls in the Pacific the conditions of subsidence suggested by Darwin and Dana might exist," he decided to go anyway.[4] But the Funafuti results worried him. If the early reports were correct, if the drill had passed through six hundred feet of sunken reef rather than six hundred feet of talus, he might be spending a small fortune and several months simply to prove Darwin *right*.

It took almost a month to reach Fiji. Alex trained from Boston to Montreal, where he boarded a private railcar he had hired, then rolled over three thousand miles of Canadian Pacific track to Vancouver. There he boarded a steamship that took him over the nearly seven thousand miles of sea between Vancouver and Fiji. There was only one stop, in Hawaii, for coal and supplies. It was the longest stretch of water Alex had ever covered, and he was glad to have good weather and moderate seas.

When he arrived in Suva, the Fijian capital, he found waiting the *Yaralla*, the solid, well-appointed, fully crewed, twin-screw steamer he'd chartered out of Australia. The drilling, dredging, sounding, and collecting equipment he'd shipped months before were in crates on deck. He was received by friendly British officials, including a couple with whom he had steamed from Bombay to Naples a decade before (he had traveled enough to make the world rather small), one of whom was now the British commissioner in charge of relations with natives. Fiji had been made a colony in 1874, bringing a bit of British order after several decades in which European and American traders, whalers, and deserting sailors had disrupted the native tribal network into a chaos unsettling to the Empire's sensibilities and trade.* The intervening years had granted enough calm that Alex could travel free from dangers posed by other humans, though the subjugation of the native population, particularly its manipulation by missionaries, often depressed him.

The *Yaralla*, however, was just what he'd hoped for, a great

---

* The expedition on which Dana had been naturalist, the seven-ship U.S. Exploring Expedition of 1838–1842, had done a good part of this disrupting. Its commander, Lieutenant Wilkes, took it upon himself to levy harsh punishment on the Fijians for both hostility shown his own party and reported previous acts of cannibalism on two Europeans. (The Fijian's traditions of ritual cannibalism, in which they sometimes ate members of villages they conquered, had in some tribes loosened and expanded with the opportunities afforded by newly acquired firearms.) Wilkes carried out several cannon and rifle attacks against the allegedly offending villages, killing dozens of Fijians and sharpening hostilities for some time to come. When he was later brought before a court-martial for these excesses, he argued that however unfortunate the result of his authority's application, he had not clearly exceeded it, for along with being charged with trying at all times to create goodwill among the people he would visit, he had also been given broad authority to protect his crew and the interests of his country (which included the whaling industry that used the Fijis for trade), which he felt himself to be doing. His peers acquitted him.

improvement on the *Croyden*. It was skippered by a Captain Thomson, who had handled the difficult *Croyden* well off Australia, and piloted by a Captain Cox, who knew every wrinkle of every lagoon. Alex had also brought along a William Eyers of Michigan, the Diamond Drill Company's best drilling technician; Museum of Comparative Zoology staffers Alfred Mayer and William Woodworth, who looked after the zoological collections and assisted generally; and his son Maximilian, now in his mid-twenties and the expedition photographer. Alexander himself felt as fit as he had in years. His sea legs were nicely under him after the long passage, and he was strong from several weeks of riding in the Mexican highlands earlier that year, checking on mines. He was as tough as the mules he'd ridden there, he wrote Murray, "but I hope not as obstinate."[5]

After a few days of securing permissions, checking provisions, and unpacking and installing equipment, Alex had Captain Cox steer the *Yaralla* out of Suva and set off to survey the isles. He had already worked out a plan designed to bring him against reef formations and into lagoons with the sun behind him, shining into the water to illuminate navigational hazards and sea life and give good light for Max's pictures. Moving efficiently through the scattered archipelago required daily adjustments. Alexander took to rising at 5 a.m., when he would have a coffee and, still in his pajamas, walk the quiet deck and look out over whatever cove or lagoon they had anchored in. Then he would sit down before the charts and plan the day's run. After breakfast the work began. He, Max, Woodworth, and Mayer might go ashore to examine the island, paying special attention to any exposed limestone, or take a skiff over the reefs, dredging and fishing and peering down into the water, while Cox steamed the *Yaralla* around the island sounding the bottom contours. Alex often napped after lunch, resting during the worst of the heat, then worked until a late dinner. The scientists usually ate and did much of their work under a large awning that covered most of the deck; shaded but swept by any breeze, the deck stayed cooler than the cabins below. Alex did not scrimp on food or wine; he took great pleasure in these twilit dinners with his colleagues and son, surrounded by stars emerging in a sky darkening over volcanic ridges and the waves breaking phosphorescent on the sheltering reef.

As they steamed from place to place, they tended to have at least

one island in sight, though they sometimes passed through feature-
less ocean. Mountainous islands would emerge as dark teeth along
the horizon. Low atolls would appear as a dark stretch of horizon,
initially barely distinguishable from the wavering sea, that slowly
firmed into distinctive spires of coconut trees over dark brush and
bright sand. As the boat neared, Agassiz and his crew, looking out
from beneath the awning, would be able to see the breakers, then the
white-sand beach or any strip of island built by the waves—often
only a few yards across, rarely more than a half mile—and finally the
lagoon's calico water, the pale yellow-green of its sandy shallows alternating with blue depths spotted by patches of green, plum, and
orange coral.

"The corals here are superb," Alex wrote Murray. "I had no conception from the West Indian reefs of what a reef can be. The gigantic masses of the Astraeans, Meandrina, etc., dwarf the largest masses
of the Florida and Bahamas, and all within six to seven fathoms, so
that with a water glass one can see the whole reef."[6] The water glass
was a shallow half-barrel with a glass bottom; holding it over the side
of a boat with its base in the water gave a lens to all below. Alexander
loved using it almost as much as he loved using the big underlit glass
bowl in which he examined medusae and other plankton. To use it
he had to go to the calm side of an island or atoll on a still day, for
reefs to windward, which in the South Seas usually meant east, were
generally pounded by waves that made skiff work over the shallows
dangerous. The lagoons, however, were calm but in the most violent
gales.

Fish streamed all along, through, and around these isles and
reefs, and plankton bloomed in patterns sometimes so regular the
locals could plan harvests of them. At one point, having heard of a
great explosion of bololo, a reef-dwelling sea worm, Alex arranged to
be at the right island on the right morning, and with native guides
went out to meet the early bloom.

"We left the ship at three o'clock, bound for a spit named Bololo
Point," he wrote.

> We had scarcely reached the spot when our guide put his hand
> in the water and pulled out one of the worms. In a few minutes
> the water was full of them, canoes put out from the shore, men,

women, and children were wading on the reef exposed by the tide, with nets, and all kinds of utensils to catch Bololo. As the light increased, the Bololo increased, and at one time they were so plentiful that the water surrounding our boat must have been filled with them so thickly as to resemble vermicelli soup. A bucket put overboard seemed to contain nothing else. We made an excellent collection, and preserved a large number by different methods. We found, as we had expected, that their sudden appearance was connected with spawning; there were males and females swimming about full of eggs and of sperm. When in captivity they soon discharged these, the water became milky, and masses of dark eggs were left on the bottom of the dish. With the escape of the eggs came the collapse of the worm, and nothing was left by an empty skin scarcely visible. Thus the Bololo seems suddenly to disappear.[7]

Even aside from such sudden fluorescence, the waters were rich. "We constantly passed long windrows of Algae torn from the reefs, extended patches of a yellow Trichodesmium,* and masses of leaves and flowers, and branches of all kinds of trees, floating at the mercy of the winds and currents."[8] The fish were dense, and to his delight the water held many of the same medusae he'd found in the Caribbean; when he towed at night, he could tell which species were in the water by the color of the phosphorescence they fired as they passed through the net.

4

He found two kinds of islands mixed throughout the Fijis. The majority, composed of lava, had obviously risen into place through eruptions and possibly the sort of upheaval long associated with volcanic activity. Other islands were composed of or partially capped with great thicknesses of fine-grained limestone holding scattered fossils of mollusk and coral. This limestone seemed to have been lifted into place by the elevation that raised the volcanic isles.

---

* Trichodesmium is a planktonic cyanobacteria that gathers in large brownish or yellowish "blooms" in the South Pacific. In the 1770s Captain James Cook at first mistook them for sandbanks.

Alex could easily distinguish the two types of island or rock even from the boat, for "the gradual slopes of the volcanic peaks," as his son George put it, "contrast[ed] strongly with the flat-topped summits and precipitous cliffs of the limestone islands."[9] Volcanic isles took roughly conical forms cut by deep gorges and ravines; some still had craters clearly visible, and a few had craters that had become lagoons. Limestone isles or sections had more rectangular profiles, with flatter tops shearing off in pale bluffs. Big islands of either sort were usually surrounded by many small islands and islets, sometimes scattered randomly, sometimes threaded like beads along a line of reef. Surf and storm had carved many of these islets into spectacular shapes: anvils, tabletops, spires, and mushrooms.

Alex found a fairly typical collection of such islands in the Exploring Isles, a small archipelago along the Fijis' eastern edge. The group's dominating feature was the island of Vanua Mbalavu, a fat, backward *S* of lava and limestone surrounded by a low, narrow reef that circled off to the east and back like a tossed loop of string. Most of the reef was under water, detectable only by the surf breaking over it. Here and there rose cays colonized by brush and coconut trees. A few passes allowed entrance through the breakers.

The lagoon inside, miles across, made a superb and picturesque anchorage. At its western end, mountainous Vanua Mbalavu and two flanking islands rose hundreds of feet, the very picture of high, mysterious lava islands, with scores of wildly eroded islets clustered around them. The surf had carved caverns and holes into some of these islets, especially those made of the softer limestone; the tip of Ngillangillah, a limestone island on the lagoon's south side, "was merely a thin shell covering a huge cavern some 50 feet in diameter and rising to a height of nearly 100 feet, and full of stalactites."[10]

Alex spent several days working from this lagoon, thoroughly sounding it and its perimeter shores and taking a skiff out to examine the reefs. The more he saw, the more these islands seemed to deny Darwin and Dana. He was a bit stunned, or at least professed to be, for Dana had so often assured him that here in the Fijis subsidence showed itself as plainly and as variously as one could hope. Yet Alex could not line up his impressions with Dana's. Every single feature of the reef system seemed to contradict Dana's explanation.

It began with the lagoon in which he anchored. As Darwin and

Dana saw it, Vanua Mbalavu was a sinking volcanic mountain, and the barrier reef surrounding it was a ring of coral that had begun as a fringing reef before the island started its slow descent. The enclosed lagoon, by this explanation, must be fairly stagnant if it was not to get too deep—for if a subsiding lagoon was constantly swept clean by currents, its depth would match the extent of the subsidence, presumably hundreds of fathoms. The subsidence theory thus demanded a static view of lagoons.

Alex found just the opposite.

"There is no filling up of that lagoon," he would write in his report. "It is well scoured, and a strong current is constantly deepening the entrance and outlets at the western end."[11] He found the same throughout the area. In almost every lagoon he surveyed, he discovered currents and current-formed channels—moving water and a live bottom, as it were, instead of still water and accruing silt. In addition, the lagoons' bottoms clearly seemed carved by the currents. Subsidence not only wasn't needed to explain these lagoons, it couldn't explain them. Their genesis and maintenance seemed due to known, well-established forces: erosion, a bit of Murrayesque solution, and the universally recognized tendency of corals to grow faster to seaward, leaving a pool of protected water behind.

As to the islands and reefs themselves, Agassiz found abundant evidence of elevation but none of subsidence. Chief among this evidence were the great beds of limestone. The limestone cliffs, he wrote, "many hundreds of feet in height, plainly attest a great upheaval of the region."[12] This limestone appeared not to be coralline limestone, as Dana had concluded, but classic marine limestone, that is, sedimentary rock composed of the remains of zillions of tiny sea animals, mostly microscopic, single-celled foraminifera, that had long ago accumulated and then been calcified on the seafloor before being lifted, with larger shells of mollusks and occasional corals mixed in. Most limestone on land, from the White Cliffs of Dover to the Dolomite Mountains of the Italian Alps to the hill country of Texas, is made up of such material, which is marked by a fine texture inlaid with larger shells and fossils. This seemed the same stuff. True, the faces and sometimes the tops of these cliffs and slabs were thick with coral, suggesting old, upraised reefs. But some drilling or even a bit of hammering always showed this coralline outer layer to be a veneer over what appeared to be more classic marine limestone.

Alex backed up this interpretation by hiring an Australian geologist to drill and blast through the surface on several Fiji islands to examine the underlying limestone. The geologist confirmed that the thickly brecciated, coral-rich limestone surface was a mere cap over a more ordinary-looking marine limestone. Later, back in Cambridge, a mollusk specialist verified that the limestone's fossil mix was typical of that in very old limestone, and thus probably too old to be part of any coral formed in more recent times. The evidence seemed overwhelming. These limestone bluffs and hills were not old coral reefs that had subsided and then been raised; like limestone all over the world, they were upraised sea bottoms of sedimentary marine rock.

Alex knew that the question of how this limestone formed was crucial. Much of his reading of the Fijian reefs rested on his interpretation of the limestone, and his interpretation contradicted that of Dana, whom he had long recognized as a more able and experienced geologist. But he thought Dana wrong here. He had Dana's coral reef book on the boat, and he had read the short chapter explaining how coral limestone was often indistinguishable from ordinary marine limestone. According to Dana, most coral limestone (or reef rock, as Dana liked to call it) formed through calcification not of largely intact coral structures but of the sand into which coral reefs were constantly being beaten. After all, Dana argued, large areas in and around any coral reef structure are sand, so we should expect that when such an area becomes calcified, the resulting limestone should be largely fine-textured like ordinary limestone, with only occasional pockets of preserved coral breccia. Thus reef rock would often be "a fine white limestone, as compact as any secondary marble [which is limestone transformed by heat and pressure], and as homogenous in texture."[13]

While this made a certain amount of sense, it struck Alex as a justifying afterthought. It was even presented that way, delivered in a brief chapter that followed Dana's central argument for subsidence, which drew almost wholly on patterns of reef form and distribution rather than the islands' actual geology. Dana brushed aside, for

instance, the sharp contrast between the coral-rich, brecciated limestone that topped these limestone hills and the finer-grained limestone
that lay beneath it. His conclusions seemed to rise not from close
observation but from his eagerness to identify a dynamic that would
explain all reef forms. They were a search for an idea, not a response
to the landscape. Fascinated with the forms of the reefs and how they
seemed to express subsidence, he had underplayed and misinter-
preted the more direct geological evidence that would describe the
origin and history of these islands. He had succumbed to the "danger
of leaps" Alex had warned of in the margin of Dana's 1885 paper. He
had deduced, then pushed the facts to fit.

This was, as Alex would say, a very unsound way of working. If
you encountered what looked like classic sedimentary marine limestone, you couldn't just say that it was really reef limestone because
reef limestone would probably look like ordinary limestone; if you
wanted to use the limestone to bolster the reef argument, you had to
explain why it *had* to be reef limestone. You couldn't constantly
choose the least likely explanation and add a bunch of them up to
support your theory. Yet Darwin's theory seemed constantly to
demand such rationalization. Nothing was as it appeared. Rising
land was really falling land. Well-scoured lagoons were really inert,
debris-filled basins. Ordinary limestone was really coral limestone. It
surprised Alex that a geologist of Dana's stature should fall for all
this. Then again, Dana had been young at the time, only in his twenties and, by his own confession, enthralled with Darwin's theory.

The more Alex saw, the more certain he felt that Dana had erred.
By every appearance this "reef rock" was just ordinary limestone.
Indeed, the only reason to doubt that it was common marine limestone was to accommodate Darwin's theory. His certainty deepened
when, still in Fiji, he received a letter from Edgeworth David saying
that closer examination of the Funafuti drill cores showed a sharp
distinction between the coral of the first forty feet and the rock
beneath it, which might be marine limestone, coral, or coral talus
(David wasn't sure). So in Funafuti too, a limestone bed once
deemed all continuous coral now fell into question.

In several more weeks of zigzagging through the Fijis, Alex found
more of the same: limestone hills capped with coral rock; vibrant

lagoons being actively shaped by currents; abundant signs of elevation and none of subsidence.

He also found everywhere evidence of the force he came to believe played the major role in determining the form of these islands and reefs: erosion. Looking at the Fijis, he realized that just as the role of currents in creating lagoons had gone underrecognized, so erosion had been underestimated as a shaper of coral reefs and islands. The islands' deep gorges, sharply serrated ridges, and fantastically shaped peaks all declared how actively water and wind had sculpted the Fijis since they'd risen from the ocean two million years before. Significant erosion clearly occurred underwater too, as shown by the way the banks around the islands differed according to their exposure to current. Where currents brought little new material, banks were narrow. Where they brought abundant sand and silt, banks were wide. Their every dimension and contour appeared dictated more by the movement of the water against and around them than by the form of any supposedly subsiding underlying landmass. Eroded elevated banks, not subsiding mountains and isles, had formed the foundation for Fijis' reefs. Subsidence didn't figure.

Looking at the craters and loops of reef, Alex could even see how a volcanic crater could become an atoll without subsidence. Vanua Mbalavu, for instance, had only to finish losing its peak to erosion to become an atoll. The extinct, half-submerged crater that was the island of Totoya also illustrated this process. Totoya was but a jagged, circular rim that reached as high as twelve hundred feet and dipped down in one narrow spot, known as the Gullet, that allowed entrance into a lagoon filling the old crater. While Darwin and Dana saw this as an extinct volcano that had sunk below the surface, Alex saw it as a crater with a wall that had been eroded to let in the sea. Allow that possibility, he argued (and who could question the fact of erosion?), and you could see how the present Totoya, with its three peaks rising above the rest of the rim, would eventually be ground to sea level to form a classic atoll with surrounding banks. Here again, the known power of erosion replaced Darwin's hypothetical subsidence.

This vision of reef formation, in which the Fiji reefs grew on foundations lifted into place by tectonic elevations and then shaped by erosion, was original not in its parts but in the particular combination of forces it envisioned. Though it rejected the subsidence theory (and completely ignored Murray's theory of bank construction through planktonic accretion; this was Alex's theory now), it drew on almost every other reef theorist up to Alexander's time. The growth of reefs to seaward went back to Eschscholtz. The emphasis on tectonic elevation drew on a long association of uplift with volcanic areas going back through Geikie, Dana, Darwin, and Lyell to Humboldt. The stress on erosion echoed Lyell and expanded on ideas offered by William Wharton. The lagoon-formation model drew on Eschscholtz, Murray, Bourne, and Guppy. The reading of the limestone expanded on similar views and observations by Semper and Guppy. Alex put these ideas together with a set of emphases that was new but that stressed methods and ideas insistently not new: He proposed, in essence, that understanding reefs did not require any grand new theory but simply a better, more empirical consideration of how known forces worked together in particular places.

It was just the sort of theory he loved: specific, localized, tied to close observation, and with a grounded truth no global theory could hold. As he examined one atoll after another, the gradual accretion of his theory—the facts and observations slowly piling together into a sort of brecciate explanation—gave him a slower-growing version of the thrill Darwin took from his epiphanies. The more Alex saw in the Fijis, the more excited he became. By the time he returned to Suva the first week of December, he was feeling almost cocky.

"Hurrah!" he wrote Murray, a world away in Scotland.

I have been and gone and done it, as we say in Yankee slang. We have just come in from nearly a month's trip round the islands of the Fijis, and a more interesting trip I have never made. I have learned more about coral reefs and islands than in all my expeditions put together, and it looks to *me* as if I had got hold of the problem of deep [lagoons of] atolls, and of the history of the coral reefs of the group. But I'll not go into details now except to say that I am more than ever satisfied that each district must be judged by itself and that no sweeping theory as that of

Darwin can apply to coral reefs as a whole, or even to atolls. I don't believe from what I have seen that a single atoll in the Fijis has been formed by subsidence!—Darwin and Dana to the contrary notwithstanding. . . .

. . . I shall give them a dose they do not expect, and the theory of subsidence will, I think, be dead as a doornail and subside forever hereafter.[14]

5

After writing Murray, Alex set off for another two weeks of cruising and towing. The hardest of the work was behind him, however, as most of what he found now matched what he had already seen. He worked in the best of moods, almost boisterous in his enjoyment of the weather, the work, and the islands. By mid-December he'd seen all the reefs and islands he felt he needed to. He had Cox steer the *Yaralla* back into Suva on December 17, 1897.

That afternoon he found Max and Woodworth wreathing the main cabin in palm leaves and masses of flowers; it was Alex's sixty-second birthday, a marker he'd forgotten was coming. "You have no idea how prettily Max and Woodworth decorated the cabin," he wrote home to his stepmother. "There was not a piece of the woodwork to be seen."[15] Outside it was pouring, a third straight day of torrents, but the blowing sheets of gray did not dampen Alexander's spirits. As he had enjoyed weeks of good weather, missing only two days to squalls, the arrival of bad weather now, when they were back in port with the work done, only underlined what good luck had followed this expedition. It had been as decisive a trip as he could have hoped for. The bare revelatory power of what he saw—the seeming obviousness of the geology and bottom topography—had overwhelmingly validated his suspicion that Darwin and Dana had horribly erred. And for the first time he had his own theory of Pacific reefs, one based on the well-documented forces of elevation and erosion rather than indemonstrable subsidence.

With his confirmation he seemed to cross a line, both in his own confidence and in his attitude toward Darwin and Dana. His long-held respect for Darwin withered. Whatever genius Darwin had

shown in his other work—something Alexander never questioned—
his reef work was beginning to look like another Glen Roy.

"When I came here," Alexander wrote his old friend Wolcott
Gibbs,

> I took it for granted that Dana's and Darwin's premises about
> the coral regions of the Central Pacific were correct and that
> this group of islands (Fijis) was in an area of subsidence. You
> may judge of my surprise when I found that Fiji is an area of
> elevation. . . . I cannot understand how Dana ever made such a
> mistake, for he was in the group quite a while, but Darwin's
> observations were all theoretical and based upon cartographic
> study in his house, a very poor way of doing, and that's the way
> all his coral reef work has been done. He never was more than
> ten days in a region of reefs and thought out [beforehand]
> everything he has written. I never could see how his theory had
> got such a hold with so little holding ground.[16]

They stayed another three weeks in Suva, taking over a wing of
a hotel and using one end of the piazza as a laboratory and work-
space. Max, Woodworth, and Mayer packed specimens and developed photos. Alex, in no hurry to get back to Cambridge and happy
with weather "hot enough even for me," worked up his notes,
helped classify the more obscure specimens, and on calm days sometimes took a motor launch out onto the flat around Suva to do some
extra collecting.

On January 13 they departed for the States. On the way there,
during a stop in Hawaii, Alexander came upon one last piece of good
luck, taking a short outing that gave his new thesis the sort of confirmation he might only have dreamed about. It occurred when he
went out with a Mr. McCandless, one of Hawaii's more experienced
drillers. Both Alex and Dana had queried McCandless extensively
over the years about what his drills passed through in their hunt for
artesian wells. Agassiz had interviewed McCandless thoroughly
when he'd been in Hawaii thirteen years before, as had Dana twenty
years before that, and both had put much faith in his accounts.
McCandless had told them that he often punched through beds of
coralline limestone several hundred feet thick, sometimes several

hundred feet under the ground. Coral beds this deep and thick would seem to indicate subsidence, and that's how Dana interpreted them. But Agassiz, noting that the well drillers also sometimes struck pieces of old *trees* several hundred feet down, concluded that these buried reefs were just that—reefs that had been buried by eruptions from Hawaii's still-active volcanoes. The thicker reef beds were accumulated talus.

The active nature of Hawaii's volcanoes thus explained the buried coral limestones McCandless had described. Alexander had never doubted they existed. But when he went out now with McCandless, he found he should have. Working from a surface just above sea level, the drillers went through eighty feet of recent coral rock and then hit a different limestone with "but few corals," as Agassiz wrote later, and "composed almost entirely of the shells of mollusks"—a particularly shell-heavy sedimentary rock, seemingly formed on a shallow but noncoralline sea bottom, and quite different from the coral reef the drill had passed through first. When Alexander remarked on it, McCandless said it was always like this, and when Alex pressed him further, McCandless assured him that this lower limestone was identical to the limestones he had long described to both him and Dana as being reef rock. Alex was stunned and elated. Like a lucky gumshoe in a detective novel, he had stumbled across the true meaning of a misread clue.

"What [McCandless] calls an old reef," he wrote a friend that week, "is nothing but a mass of shells. This practically knocks out all the evidence there was in favor of subsidence derived from the [previous] boring holes. . . . All that was limestone they have called coral, so that both Dana and I were fooled, he in one way and I in another."[17]

6

While his *Blake* report had taken seven years to publish and his Hawaii report three, Alex wrote and published the Fiji monograph in just fourteen months.[18] The result—144 pages of text and several score photos, maps, and graphs occupying a full volume of the *Bulletin of the Museum of Comparative Zoology*—was unprecedentedly frank. Amid extensive descriptions and interpretation he made his conclusions uncharacteristically clear and emphatic. And in an impassioned voice familiar to his correspondents but rare in his publications, he gave vent to the pique he felt with Dana and Darwin.

The facts, of course, stood foremost. "These atolls and islands," he concluded, "have not been built (as is claimed by Dana and Darwin) by the subsidence of the islands they enclose. They are not situated in an area of subsidence, but on the contrary in an area of elevation. The theory of Darwin and Dana is therefore not applicable to the Fiji Islands."[19]

Rather, he said, the reef forms come from "causes which have acted during a period preceding our own. The islands of the whole group have been elevated and . . . exposed to a great and prolonged process of denudation and of aerial and submarine erosion." This erosion had created the submarine platforms upon which the reefs had grown. Lagoons were formed by the faster growth of seaward-facing coral and then further scoured and sculpted by currents.

This is the report's barest, plainest statement of both his negation of Darwin and Dana's theory and his own elevation-erosion model of how the Fijian reefs formed. It appears about three-quarters of the way through the monograph, a suitable place for a succinct statement of conclusions. He summarizes again at the end, reiterating his theory and insisting that "my observations in Fiji only emphasize what has been said so often, that there is no general theory of the formation of coral reefs . . . applicable to all districts, and that each district must be examined by itself."[20]

Alex, of course, was prominent among those who had been saying this so often, and his frustration that these continual efforts had not yet toppled Darwin's theory shows in the rest of the Fiji report, which, while mostly matter-of-fact and dispassionate, is peppered with jabs, plaints, indignant outbursts, and repetitions. He repeats his main assertions, for instance, close to a dozen times, as if he wants to make trebly and quadruply and quintuply sure, in this report that generally sticks so close to the facts, that not just his own reading of Fiji but his rebuttal of Darwin will finally get through to a group of peers that prefers a theory with, as he had written Gibbs, "so little holding ground." He seems to fear, given the past, that merely presenting evidence might not be enough, and that he must bludgeon the stubborn. Some of the reiterations are concise. Others are ponderous. The most labored reads like the closing statement from a courtroom lawyer determined to summarize every bit of evidence favoring his client.* At times his disgust comes through vividly.

"It is playing with words," he writes at one point,

> . . . to speak of the localities to which Darwin's theory . . . does not apply as exceptions to the rule. These exceptions now cover a good deal of ground. They include nearly all the coral reefs which have been examined by recent investigators,—from Semper in the Pelew Islands, Rein in the Bermudas, Murray in Tahiti and elsewhere, of Forbes, and of Bourne, of Guppy in the Solomon Islands, Kramer in Samoa, and others,—down to my own in Florida, the Yucatan bank, Cuba, Bermuda, the Bahamas, and West India Islands, as well as the Galapagos and Sandwich Islands, besides the exploration of the Great Barrier Reef of Australia, and of the Fiji Islands. Surely the list of investigators and localities is long enough. The negative evidence is now becoming overwhelming. . . . The Darwinian theory [has not] been proved to exist in a single location, either by a careful examination of the locality or by borings.

What on earth, you can hear him growl, *will it take to displace this poppycock?*

Despite this exasperation (or in its cause), he refused to apply his Fijian findings globally or even to the rest of the Pacific. He would not offer one overstretched theory to replace another. While his letters and the Fiji report reveal that he now believed that most other Pacific reefs had also formed on eroded, elevated sea bottoms, the

---

* Two pages after his most succinct offering, Alex produces this recapitulation: "From this evidence I am inclined to think that the corals of today have actually played no part in the shaping of the circular or irregular atolls scattered among the Fiji Islands, that they have had nothing to do in our time with the building up of the substructure of the barrier reefs encircling either wholly or in part some of the islands, that their modifying influence has been entirely limited in the present epoch to the formation of fringing reefs, and that the recent corals living upon the outer margin of the reefs, either of the atolls or of the barriers, form only a crust of very moderate thickness upon the underlying base. This base may be either the edge of a submarine flat, or of an eroded elevated limestone, or of a similar substructure composed of volcanic rocks, the nature of that base depending absolutely upon its character when elevated in a former period to a greater height than it now has; denudation and erosion acting of course more rapidly upon the elevated coralliferous limestones than upon those of a volcanic character."

closest he would come to saying so in the Fiji report was to gently (and just once) assert this probability: "It is well known that many of the [Pacific] islands are composed of elevated coralliferous limestones, and that is probably the composition of the substratum of many of the atolls of the Paumotos, Ellice, Gilbert, Tonga, and Fiji groups."[21] His caution expressed both his longtime assertion that each reef area was different and his conviction that "sweeping generalizations" were bad for science. He would not expose himself to the danger of leaps.

If he wanted to make global statements, he would have to see more of the globe. He hadn't yet seen even the entire Pacific.

CHAPTER FIFTEEN

The Last Archipelago

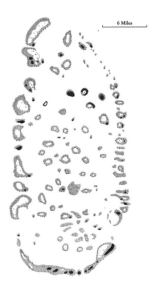

A typical group of atolls in the Maldives, the last major
archipelago that Alexander would visit

I

IN AUGUST 1899, just two months after publishing the Fiji report and sixteen months after returning to the United States, Alexander Agassiz, having procured use of the U.S. Fish Commission's *Albatross,* boarded the ship in San Francisco and set out to see the rest of the South Sea Islands.

He had essentially made up his mind about coral reefs by this time, concluding that they were built by elevation, erosion, accretion, and current, working in various combinations in different places. Where subsidence occurred, it was not the main cause but a supplement to these forces. This was the big picture. But science was in the details, and he wanted all of them before hazarding a comprehensive theory of the world's coral reefs. His theory's protean essence argued against applying it anyplace he hadn't seen. His was not, like Darwin's, a one-size-fits-all. And if he wanted to upend Darwin, he could not afford to overreach. He could not speak too soon or before he possessed every last gainable advantage. If you strike a king, you must kill him. Darwin had shown stunning resilience.

His journey of 1899–1900 covered essentially all of the South Sea Island groups, including a quick pass through the Fijis. He had spent much of the previous six months planning it, arranging for coal and food and other supplies to be delivered and stored at islands along the route; he figured to stay out as long as it took. As it happened, it took almost nine months, his longest expedition yet. Working east to west, he saw the Marquesas; the Tuamotus and Society Islands (also known as French Polynesia), which cluster together at the eastern end of the long dogleg of South Sea Islands; and then Tonga, or the Friendly Islands, which lie just below Fiji. After passing through Fiji he bent north toward the smaller, more scattered groups of the Ellice and the Gilberts, looped through the big oval of the Marshalls, and turned west through the loose line of the Carolines. From there he finished by heading north once again, hitting Guam before steaming out of the tropics and on to Japan.

Logistically it was not one of his smoother journeys, despite all his preparation. He found the crew of the *Albatross* just shy of incompetent; he once had to throw a line to the dock himself as half a dozen sailors stood inert because no one had ordered anyone to throw a line. The vessel was showing its age, with boilers so weak the ship could barely move upwind. Yet he enjoyed more than ever the scientific work and his ethnological tourism. He had always taken keen interest in the natives of the places he visited, and this long tour let him meet and see a greater variety than ever before. He was well aware that he was not seeing an untainted culture; in fact he found moving the struggles of the islanders to persist amid the presence of the various powers—mainly France, England, and Germany—that had colonized the archipelagoes. These were the islands of Melville's *Typee* and Conrad's *Lord Jim* (which Conrad was just finishing as

Agassiz hit the Marquesas), and Alex shared those authors' distress about what colonization inflicted on the inhabitants. He naturally harbored some of the condescension almost universal among white visitors. But his cynicism about authority (particularly religious), his democratic sentiments, and his habitual empathy for the underdog gave him a great sympathy for the islanders. He could smile at the idea of a Fijian eating a European and even joked that the practice might do well back home. He wrote of one queen in the Marquesas, "the wife of a celebrated chief, Toana (who conquered all the Marquesas); she must be eighty years old. . . . It is said that not liking her first husband she ate him and married the great chief. Would it not be a good recipe for Newport divorcees? It would lessen the later scandal so greatly and simplify matters."

He joked partly to cover the pain he felt at seeing their decimation. "The natives here are going fast," he wrote in the same letter, "dying off mainly with consumption [tuberculosis]; the adjacent valley, which held once three thousand warriors, has now fourteen inhabitants.* It seems too bad. Christianity is fatal to the South Sea Islanders—they cannot stand its restraints, and they die like sheep."[1]

He particularly disdained missionaries, whom he saw as coercing a debilitating superstition in service of a monopolistic trade.

What I never like in the South Pacific is to see the swell houses (comparatively speaking) of the missionaries. They always in all the islands have the very best of everything, and certainly don't show the natives any example of plain living, for they are most comfortable and have no end of servants. . . . I have been reading M__n [apparently an advocate for the missionary cause], and such twaddle passes my comprehension. It is nothing but an apology to join the European band of robbers in despoiling the barbarians, as we are pleased to call them, and compelling them to buy our goods and wares in addition to stealing their land—all in the name of spreading civilization. Just as the mis-

---

* According to a note in George Agassiz's *Letters and Recollections of Alexander Agassiz* (p. 354), this was the valley "Typee" of Melville's story, where a band of warriors was holding out against the corruptions of colonialism.

sionary swindles in the South Seas, who trades with natives, makes a lot of rules for them adapted to our uses, and compels them to do as we think right, all in the name of Christianity!— and if they resist, the missionary claims the protection of a Man-of-War of his country! What fun it would be for a man of energy and pluck to come among the islands and help them to resist such aggressions.[2]

This fantasy of helping liberate these oppressed natives emerges repeatedly in his letters home.

Alex was delighted when he found the occasional island that had been left mostly alone. One of his most pleasing visits was to the Fijian island of Kabara, where he had stopped two years previous in the *Yaralla* and where the village retained some economic and cultural independence. Despite having no common language with the villagers, he was received as an old friend. "It was very funny to see how pleased the natives were to see us again," he wrote home. "The old chief and his wife greeted us in a most stately manner, and after our return from the hill we called to bid him good-bye." Agassiz and the captain then hosted the chief and his wife and a large party on the *Albatross*, where some of the Fijians sang a song and then, accepting a few gifts from Agassiz, took their leave. Agassiz was heartened to have found them so well. "It is really refreshing to get to a village again where nobody can speak English, and where there are no missionaries or traders and the natives run themselves." It was the cleanest, healthiest, and most attractive village he had yet seen.

In the Marshalls, where the *Albatross* worked a month toward the end of the trip, trade and missionary work had badly diluted the native culture. Agassiz was depressed to see the native houses in many villages replaced by flimsy shacks with metal roofs. But he was thrilled to find that the islanders still made and sailed the best and most graceful outrigger sailing canoes in all the South Sea Isles. Many of them still knew how to navigate with the strange "charts" made of sticks lashed together that allowed them (inexplicably to Western navigators) to hit even tiny islands after days of open sea. He bought several of these instruments for Harvard's Peabody Museum of Ethnology.

2

Sailing in Dana's tracks, Alexander repeatedly found places the young geologist had misread. In the large lagoon of the Tuamotus' Rangiroa atoll, for instance, one of his first stops, he disembarked at an islet that Dana had described:

> I rushed across the islet to examine the limestone ridge which flanks the islets on the sea face, and which Dana saw from *shipboard* and described as elevated recent reef. I was tickled to death when I got there to find myself on familiar ground [that is, the limestone Dana had seen as reef rock appeared to be classic marine limestone]. . . . It is the same pitted, honey combed, eroded rock with which I had become familiar in Fiji. I think I have the key of the Paumotu coral reef problem, and it's only an expansion of what I have seen in Fiji; only this group is comparatively plain sailing and clear work, for Dana did not examine his islands very closely. As for Darwin, he only sailed through and never stopped at all, so that I am quite sure that unless something new and unforeseen turns up, I can chuck this group of atolls at the heads of the Darwin-Dana party and ask them for the next.[3]

Which is what he did, moving on from there to find one group after another contradicting Darwin's theory and fitting into his own broader, more multifaceted one. The Tahiti atolls proved much like Fiji, as did the Cook Islands and Tonga, which lay just below Fiji. The picture grew more complicated as they moved north to the Ellice and Gilberts and Marshalls, for the limestone beds there often appeared more coralline in nature, suggesting old coral reefs, and so thick he couldn't know how deep they went or what underlay them. These raised coral beds, he allowed, had probably been formed by subsidence—but did not play the role in shaping the present reefs that Darwin envisioned. Rather, they had slowly formed on subsiding bottoms more than two million years before and later been lifted into place, at which point they were shaped by erosion and current into today's reef foundations, just as volcanic and elevated marine limestone foundations elsewhere were. Thus subsidence helped create the material underlying the present islands and reefs, but it did not create the present reef forms. This, Alex concluded, was the usual end result of any localized subsidence, though he allowed there were doubtless a few cases in which an ongoing subsidence combined with erosion and current to help shape isolated islands or atolls.

This reading of the northern string of archipelagoes was strengthened by the oversights and misreadings of Darwin and Dana. Every group seemed to have marine limestone that Dana had misread as reef rock. As in the Fijis, the surrounding banks differed on windward and leeward sides, suggesting that erosion and current were the main shapers of reefs, for subsidence would not produce such a differential. Finally, the contours of most archipelagoes, as shown both by Alex's own soundings and others done since Dana's time, showed the bathygraphy as other than Dana and Darwin had assumed. His soundings made plain that while some atolls rose from great depths, as Darwin's model envisioned, many did not, resting instead on broad plateaus that stretched well away from the islands before falling off. This broader contour seemed far more consistent with elevation than continued subsidence; the deep ravines between some atolls were likely channels created by currents.

The evidence accrued. "I am gradually knocking out a lot of superstitions about atolls," he wrote home, "and it is really absurd that Darwin and Dana should have written such a lot of nonsense, all evolved from their brains or reading of what others have said and done."[4]

His dismissal of the sweeping nature of Darwin and Dana's theory deepened when he visited Funafuti, where in 1897 the Australian Edgeworth David had drilled through six hundred feet of some limestone-like substance that defied identification. David had returned in 1898 and shot another bore 1,114 feet deep, passing through similar material and still not reaching bedrock. The results remained controversial. Some of the investigators and members of the sponsoring Royal Society had declared them clearly supporting subsidence, while others who had examined the borings found them inconclusive. The Royal Society itself would later officially take a neutral stance on the results. Alexander, meanwhile, found the place consistent with his thoughts on elevation and erosion—and not particularly supportive of subsidence. Most striking to him was how different Funafuti was from other islands, and how foolish it seemed, given such variation among atolls, to draw sweeping conclusions before you'd seen them all.

"I found Funafuti just as different from other atolls as possible," he wrote,

> and . . . I begin to see how useless it is to discuss coral islands between people who have not seen the same thing. I could not make out what David, Sollas [another recent researcher], and Gardiner [who had been there two years before] meant until I had seen Funafuti—it's so different from all other atolls, and unless I had my experience to go upon it would be hopeless for me to give a natural explanation, and I should be groping round and talking in the air.[5]

From Funafuti they steamed north to the Gilberts, where the natives, complained Mayer, "insisted upon opening our jaws in order to admire the gold fillings in our teeth," and where Alex bought for the Peabody Museum a suit of coconut-fiber armor. They spent a full month in the Marshalls, a group of huge atolls with particularly thin rims surrounding immense lagoons, as if they had formed on particularly broad plateaus (or in Darwin's view, particularly large islands). Many a rim narrow enough to cast a stone across surrounded a lagoon so wide you couldn't see the other side. Alex did much sounding here, getting results similar to those from the Tuamotus and Ellice and Gilberts.

After coaling one last time in the Marshalls, the *Albatross* moved west through the Carolines. This last of the Pacific archipelagoes seemed to offer little new, being much like the Marshalls but on a smaller scale. He skipped through them quickly. Though he still had about two thousand miles to go to reach Japan and then the Pacific to cross, he was on his way home.

3

This transpacific trip expanded and solidified Alex's evolving model of reef building. It let him integrate for the first time the occasional incidence of subsidence in a way consistent with his central contention about how reefs were built. He had more confidence in this theory than ever, and there seemed few rocks left to turn over.

He set off to study the one major reef area he had not yet visited, the Indian Ocean. In December 1901 he crossed Europe and the Mideast to spend several weeks in the Maldives, a set of atolls that rise from a submarine peninsula extending several hundred miles southwest from India. Some five hundred miles long and eerily beautiful, the Maldives are perhaps the world's most singular reef archipelago. They had fascinated geologists ever since the British explorer Moresby charted their strange configurations in the mid-1830s. Most of the Maldives' twenty-six large atolls, particularly those in the northern archipelago's two-thirds, are composed of numerous smaller atolls, or faros, as they are called there, of which there are hundreds. Some of the faros have been built up into islands by wave-deposited sand and rock; others are largely or completely submarine, looking like ghost reefs and islands from above. Though some form open crescents, most are closed loops, and the loops take every conceivable shape: ovals, gourds, pears, beans, quarter-moons. The larger atolls, more consistently oval, are defined not by a continuous line of reef but by strands of spaced faros that on a chart look like water spots. The openness of these atoll rims lets the alternating seasonal monsoons (wet westerlies in summer, dry easterlies in winter) push water through and across them. This creates unusually rich lagoons that hold yet more faros and islets—far more than typically found in more classic atolls—and spectacular marine life.

Darwin, in one of his coral reef book's less convincing passages, described the Maldives as the remains of a single atoll that grew up around a huge, sinking island and was then slowly carved into its modern form by the monsoon currents. Since Darwin never saw the Maldives, Alex did not hesitate to differ. An actual look at the archipelago, he said in his report, showed that "the ingenious suggestions of Darwin regarding the formation of the Maldives are not borne out."[6] To begin with, the entire area showed signs of a slight elevation. The highly varying depths of the lagoons and surrounding plateaus further argued against an archipelago-wide subsidence, which could hardly be expected to differ so much across small areas. The breadth of the underlying peninsular bank also defied Darwin. On a finer scale, the faros all seemed molded less by any broadly consistent force than by the particular topographies of the knolls they grew upon and the currents that struck them.

Finally, rather than conforming to Darwin's vision of islands that evolved into barrier reefs and then atolls, these faros seemed to take an opposite course of development. When Alex compared what he observed to the reef forms in Moresby's 1830 charts, he saw that many curved reefs were becoming atolls and many atolls were turning into islands. One crescent-shaped reef had become a closed, circular reef with a shallow lagoon; several other crescents had extended their ends to come closer to forming circles; and some faros that Moresby showed as entirely submerged had grown islets on their rims. At least one small, closed faro had filled its lagoon in almost completely. Alex could virtually watch these reefs being built, and they were being built in a progression opposite Darwin's model. Alex, puzzling it out, concluded that the Maldives had begun as a submarine landscape of low hills and hummocks that bloomed into faros and atolls when either elevation or accrual had raised the higher elevations to reef-growing depths.

In their broad outlines, in their detailed variety, and in the development of their forms, the Maldives made the most striking contradiction yet to Darwin's theory, a fitting last piece to Alexander's quest to explain the world's reefs. A month after he turned sixty-six, still anchored amid the most beautiful and fascinating reefs he'd ever seen, he wrote Murray that he was finally done:

OFF NALANDU, SS *AMRA*,
MILADUMMADULU ATOLL, MALDIVES
JAN. 18, 1902

This will be the end of a most successful expedition, perhaps to me the most interesting visit to a coral reef group I have made—for certainly I have learned more at the Maldives about atolls than in all my past experience in the Pacific and elsewhere. I should never have forgiven myself had I not seen the Maldives with my own eyes and formed my own opinion of what they mean.

Such a lot of twaddle as has been written about the Maldives. It's all wrong what Darwin has said, and the charts ought to have shown him that he was talking nonsense. . . . I am glad that I always stuck to writing what I saw in each group and explained what I saw as I best could without trying all the time to have an all-embracing theory. Now, however, I am ready to have my say on coral reefs and write a connected account of coral reefs based upon what I have seen, and it will be a pleasure to me to write such a book.

CHAPTER SIXTEEN

A Connected Account

I

A LEX RETURNED from the Maldives the way he came, cross-
ing the Persian Gulf and the Mediterranean to Europe. He and
Max (who often traveled with him) reached Paris on March 1, 1902,
and, in what would become a sort of spring ritual over the next few
years, checked in for a long stay at the Hotel Athenée. He had no
desire to return to the dreary New England spring, and he was feeling tired and unwell—"used up," he told Murray. The return to civilization seemed to sap him. His appetite was so spare he lost
fourteen pounds his first few weeks there. His doctor in Paris told
him he'd been working too hard, and indeed he worked "like a
beaver" even in Paris, pushing hard to draft his Maldives report.
"Somehow I am feeling the effects of this trip," he wrote home.
Home replied with cables about how poorly the copper business was
going. Calumet seemed to need his attention, but he decided to
delay returning until May. "I don't want to go home if I can help it,"
he wrote Murray. "I could not stand one of our blizzards."

The other reason he couldn't go home yet is that he had promised
Murray he would give a talk on his Maldives findings at the March 31
meeting of the Royal Society of Edinburgh. Edinburgh's Royal Society (not to be confused with the better-known Royal Society of London) seemed a fitting place for Agassiz's first talk now that he'd
finished his coral explorations. It was Murray's home crowd, and in
the decade or so before the "conspiracy of silence" controversy moved

the coral reef discussion to the pages of *Nature,* the society's publications had been the main forum for those skeptical of subsidence.

Murray doubtless hoped Alex would now give an abstract of the "connected account" of reef development that he had promised in his letter from the Maldives. There's some possibility that he did—the society's proceedings hold only a notice of his talk, no transcript—but if so, it was only in a brief moment of candor. For Alex now returned to a reticence he hadn't shown in a quarter century, taking the sort of noncommittal stance he had occupied before he saw the Pacific. He clammed up. A year after returning, for instance, invited to give his views to London's Royal Society—given a chance to deliver a blow right in the lion's den—he gave a talk so short and insistently particularized that not even the most imaginative reviewers could call it a connected account of his views. Rather, it was the shortest summary (just two printed pages) of what he had seen. He merely presented descriptive synopses of the observable traits typical of the major coral areas and avoided almost anything that might seem an "all-embracing idea" about what dictated those forms. The closest he came to stating his theory was a single sentence, amid a dry description of the Carolines, offering that "denudation and submarine erosion fully account for the formation of platforms upon which coral reef and other limestone organisms may build, either barrier or encircling reefs, or even atolls."[1]

In terms of bare fact, this does describe the core of Alexander's theory. But while a statement so unemphatic might take hold if no prevailing theory existed, it could hardly be expected to displace a theory that had tenaciously held its ground for six decades. It had none of the spirited assertion of his Fiji report, for instance, and his attack on Darwin consisted of the comment that Alex had done his own studies "recognising that Darwin's theory did not explain the conditions observed."

His hesitance today seems perverse. It must have been maddening for his friends and colleagues, particularly Murray, who wanted not only to see the new theory advanced but to see Alex finally play his hand. His retreat seems inexplicable. Yet it was in fact a reluctance very much like the one Darwin had experienced for twenty years with his evolution theory. Knowing he would meet resistance, he sought to marshal every last fact and argument before he let loose;

and even when he'd marshaled every last bit, he hesitated. Darwin's hand was forced when he learned that Alfred Russel Wallace had developed the same theory. Alexander had no such prod. He could continue to indulge his caution.

2

Time passed, and not unpleasantly for Alex. His long research mission complete, he was free again to do other work and to travel more leisurely. He lived much as he had in the early 1880s, when for a few years he set aside the coral reef problem, before the Duke of Argyll flap convinced him his own efforts would be needed after all. As then, he was not now the only one working on the question. Of a new generation of reef researchers, J. Stanley Gardiner, who had closely preceded Alex both in the Fijis and the Maldives, was advocating a multifaceted theory much like Alex's, one that discounted subsidence and stressed the erosion of banks created by upheaval and accrual. Gardiner, just thirty at this point, lacked Alex's standing, but he had been looking at reefs virtually nonstop for almost five years and was willing to speak plainly. In the first few years of the 1900s, he published several papers that explicitly laid out his model as one that should replace Darwin's.[2] Wharton, Bourne, Guppy, and others lent support to this effort, as did the final reports of the Funafuti drillings, which were unambiguously inconclusive. The tug-of-war was looking more even, and as in the early 1880s, when Murray's theory was getting attention, Alex allowed himself to stand aside and let others pull.

He did not forget his plan to write a semipopular "connected account" of his coral reef theory. But neither did he push everything aside to concentrate on it. He tended to it among everything else—of which there was plenty. Having closed the Newport summer-research institute in 1897, he now spent his summers there working mainly in the morning, generally tending a mix of scientific publications and museum and mine business and—in his late sixties now, giving himself permission to slack a bit—passed most afternoons riding, golfing, boating, or entertaining. Winters he usually settled for a month or two or three in Paris, where he sometimes worked on the book between planning future trips and writing up reports from previous expeditions. (He still had research from the 1890s he hadn't written up.) Thus the coral reef book was usually set aside as a winter project, and the winters often got full.

Alex made slow progress. In Paris for the winter of 1903, for instance, he put the finishing touches on the Maldives report, which left, he wrote a friend, "only . . . a general résumé of the whole Coral Reef question, . . . which I hope to get out within the year."[3] The Maldives report was published, but not the reef book. He spent the winter of 1904 in Paris too, but he apparently devoted most of his time to planning an eastern Pacific expedition (mainly zoological) for the following winter. The Pacific trip itself occupied much of the winter of 1905. He spent the winter of 1906 in the Valley of the Kings near Luxor, Egypt, where his friend and Newport neighbor, archeologist Theodore Davis, had just discovered the tomb of the king and queen Yuya and Tjuyu. This was one of the most extraordinary finds in Egyptology, eclipsed only with the discovery sixteen years later of the tomb of King Tutankhamen, and it offered a world of distraction for anyone, especially an avid ethnologist like Alex. Winter of 1907 he went collecting in the West Indies. Winter of 1908, Africa.

He wasn't exactly making time for the thing. As the years passed, he admitted to Murray that he found the book a struggle. His only previous attempt at semipopular writing, the *Three Voyages of the "Blake,"* had occupied several years and two fat volumes, and being primarily descriptive it had not carried the much stiffer demand that now stood before him: explaining concisely and cogently the complex dynamics that produced the world's reefs. It seemed you had to write either a reductive aperçu, an approach that repelled him, or a tome that explained all the evidence driving the theory, which would be so massive and technical as to defeat the purpose. It was a slippery damn problem. How did you convey, in a work that by definition must be sweeping and summary, even a cumulative version of the vivid, particularized impact of the many pieces of evidence that proved Darwin wrong? The further he moved in space and time from the reefs, the less certain he seemed to become of what he'd seen there. Nowhere in any of his papers is he as adamant as he is in the letters he wrote from atolls, where it all seemed as clear as lagoon water. The reefs themselves must have started to seem a bit unreal—

particularly the lagoons, those calm circles of water surrounded by breaking surf and a world of ocean. They had once been quiet centers distant from everything: the cold of New England, the savagery of the letters in scientific journals, the dirty Cambridge snow and its horrid memories, the inexhaustible resistance of those who believed in subsidence, the maddening power of Darwin's baseless idea. In their bright, flat particularity, their surf-surrounded calm, the lagoons had been free of all that. Now, mashed together into a distant abstraction, they composed a vortex that drew it all in.

Castle Hill, the mansion that Alexander built at Newport,
Rhode Island, in the 1870s, and the only place where he felt at home

"I have started [again] on my coral-reef book," he wrote Murray in the late spring of 1907, "but it is a good deal more than I expected. If I stay at home I ought to make good progress." A few months later he wrote Murray that "I have made a fair beginning, and hope to keep the material within reasonable bounds and not allow it to run away with me."[4]

He worked on it that fall of 1909 in Newport and Cambridge and reported working on it in Naples, where he wintered that year. After his customary May visit to Calumet he took it up again that summer in Newport. But that fall, when he came back from his annual autumn check at Calumet, he was so dissatisfied with what he'd produced, he told Murray, that he set it aside, thinking he would ponder it over the winter and then in spring either salvage it or hatch a new version.

He planned to spend that winter traveling in Java. A flare-up of his old leg problems, however, convinced him he shouldn't be so far from doctors, so he decided to return to Egypt, where his neighbor Davis was working his way from one wondrous find to another. By the time he arrived, he had recovered well enough to get about and see Davis's discoveries. He found he had to nap more often. But despite feeling his age a bit, he enjoyed the winter keenly.

3

He stayed in Egypt through February, then returned to Paris. He and Max found the city still recovering from catastrophic floods that had swept through a month before. The Jardin des Plantes, France's foremost botanical museum, had been badly hit, with many specimens ruined and the work lives of his many friends there were disrupted. But Alex was heartened by how energetically the Parisians bounced back, particularly those in the poorer, lower districts who lost the most.

"The damage is stupendous," he wrote George's wife, and "all the small workmen who owned their houses in the banlieux . . . are cleaned out . . . ruined from one day to the next. . . . They ought to be crushed, but they rise to the occasion and get ready for the daily work, which, after all, has carried many a man over calamities which seemed unbearable." All these years later, his own grief was still close enough that he thanked work for burying it.

A week later he and Max left Paris for home, heading first to London to visit Murray. Murray asked Alex how the book was coming. Alex told him that though he had drafted it three different ways, he was still not quite happy with it. However, he said, he had hit on a more efficient plan and, having cleared his desk of other matters, he expected to get it written over the spring and summer.

On March 23, 1910, he and Max sailed out of Southampton on the giant passenger steamship *Adriatic II,* bound for New York. The fifth night out they had dinner, then spent the evening chatting in the smoking room before turning in. The next morning, Easter Sunday, Alex did not emerge for breakfast. When Max went to wake him, he found his father could not be roused. He looked like he was sleeping. But there was no breath or pulse. At seventy-four years of age, Alexander Agassiz had died.

Murray, back in London, was much aggrieved to hear of his friend's death. He was soon mortified at the further news relayed him by George and Max. They could not find the coral reef manuscript. They looked everywhere—the house in Cambridge, the mansion in Newport, every drawer, box, cabinet, and cranny of his museum quarters—but found no sign of the book. No outline, no organized notes, no hint of the three drafts he'd spoken of writing and setting aside. Only "extracts from other papers," reported George, "and a few rough notes, of no use to anyone but himself." It was, George noted with magnificent understatement, "an excellent example of his method of carrying his work in his head until the last moment."

CHAPTER SEVENTEEN

Eniwetok

I

GEORGE AND MAX never discovered whether the drafts their father spoke of existed only in his head, as George half-seriously suggested, or had been roughed out and discarded. The latter seems more likely. Alexander Agassiz tended to purge anything not meant for many eyes.

His failure to publish did not mean his ideas on reefs were lost, for his theory is evident from his publications and letters. But it meant he never entered a concise form of it into the coral reef debate. That argument was a half century old when Alexander died and would simmer another half century before being resolved. Might he have changed it had he delivered? It seems likely. Even in scattered form, Alex's theory exerted considerable influence; a succinct, well-argued version might have greatly magnified this influence, tilting further his way the balance that seesawed between Darwin's theory and his.

As it was, despite his reticence, Alexander Agassiz (along with others advocating theories similar to his) had already made their theory a near-equal to Darwin's. The editors of the renowned 1911 *Encyclopedia Britannica,* for instance, saw fit to assign the coral reef entry to G. C. Bourne, the Oxford geologist whose examination of the Chagos archipelago (south of the Maldives) had made him a Darwin doubter back in the 1870s. Bourne cited Agassiz's work as proof against the universality of Darwin's theory. Expressing what the editors presumably considered a judicious view of informed opinion, Bourne stated that in the face of Agassiz's findings

> it must be admitted that the subsidence theory of Darwin is inapplicable to a large number of coral reefs and islands. . . . In the present state of our knowledge it seems reasonable to conclude that coral reefs are formed wherever the conditions suitable for growth exist, whether in areas of subsidence, elevation, or rest . . . [and] the atoll or barrier reef shape is not necessarily evidence of formation during subsidence, [but] may be produced by the natural growth of coral, modified by the action of waves and currents in regions in which subsidence has certainly not taken place.[1]

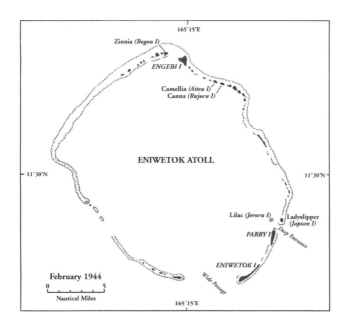

Eniwetok Atoll, in the Marshall Islands. Almost a half century after Alexander died, this small atoll, so classic in form, would yield critical information about the questions he had spent a quarter century investigating.

Bourne voices Alexander's main contention: Reefs take hold and grow not because they are on sinking bottoms but because depth and temperature allow, and their forms are created by erosion and local conditions. If Alex had not driven Darwin from the field, he at least had forced him to share it.

2

After Alex died, two main figures emerged to continue this debate, a third to complicate it.

Taking Alexander's side was J. Stanley Gardiner, the young British researcher who had just preceded Alex in both the Fijis and the Maldives. From 1897 to 1907 Gardiner saw as many reef areas as ever seen by anyone save Alex and perhaps Dana, and this, along with his fair-minded, lucid writing, made him one of his generation's most credible reef theorists. He advocated a theory in which three foundation-building dynamics operated in various places and pro- portions to build the world's reef platforms: a Murrayesque accretion of sediment; an Agassizian erosion of upraised islands or landmasses; and Darwinian subsidence, which as a direct genitor of atolls, he said, "has probably been a purely local phenomenon."[2] Gardiner eventually began to doubt that any of these theories could be applied with confidence, given the ambiguous and superficial nature of the observable evidence. As he put it in his 1930 *Coral Reefs and Atolls*, "If we regard the question of the formation of the foundation of coral reefs honestly, we are forced to admit that all our theories and con- siderations are mere camouflage for our lack of knowledge." In the 1910s and early 1920s, however, he advocated most strongly the erosion-elevation element of his trio, and he always agreed with Alex that Darwin's theory was overextended. Through his steady pressure in the 1910s and 1920s, Gardiner forced among scientists a grudging consensus that this was probably the case. In the 1930s, as Gardiner grew doubtful, the elevation-erosion theory was taken up by Harry Ladd and J. Edward Hoffmeister, among the most prominent reef scientists of *their* generation, as the "antecedent platform theory," which held that "any bench or bank . . . at the proper depth within the circum-equatorial coral reef zone can be considered a potential reef foundation, and . . . if ecological conditions permit, a reef could grow up to the surface without any progressive change in ocean- level"—an expression remarkably close to Alex's phrasings.[3]

Meanwhile emerged a new champion for subsidence. William Davis, fifteen years younger than Alex and twenty-two years older than Gardiner, had taught geology and geography at Harvard since 1885 but did not begin to study coral reefs intently until 1912, when he resigned his Harvard professorship at age sixty-two. A year later, at about the time he published a paper highlighting how Dana's embayed-valley insight supported Darwin, Davis's wife died. The next year, still grieving, he took a five-month tour of the South Pacific islands. He had formerly found a roughly evolutionary model helpful when studying the development of rivers, and now, like Dana, he was stunned by the explanatory power of Darwin's coral reef theory. From then until his death in 1935, he championed an aggressively deductive application of the theory, producing more than fifty publications culminating in the six-hundred-page *Coral Reef Problem* in 1928. Davis advocated what he quite seriously called the "home study" of coral reefs, insisting that the key to explaining coral reefs lay not in the reefs themselves but in large patterns of the sort visible on maps viewable in any living room. Darwin himself, of course, had done most of his theorizing over maps and charts (as Alex often noted with disdain) and considered his map showing the distribution of the Pacific atolls one of his strongest proofs.

But Darwin had worked when direct reef observations were few. Davis worked when more than two dozen experienced researchers had reported closely on reefs. His insistence that their evidence was secondary struck some as perverse. (One begins to understand why he didn't take this up while Alex was around.) He happily let powerful abstractions overrule observation and treated the latter as important when it supported subsidence but irrelevant otherwise. A later historian deemed his approach "research by debate." Gardiner could not abide this. In his 1930 *Coral Reefs and Atolls*, he dismissed Davis, who for two decades had been the most prolific writer on reefs aside from Gardiner, by mentioning him only twice. He led off his more lengthy mention (a paragraph) by calling Davis's *Coral Reef Problem* the book "wherein will be found almost all known facts that can be made to favour subsidence."[4]

It wasn't quite the Duke versus Huxley. But these two and their allies kept the coral reef controversy very much alive through the 1930s. A full century after it was posed, the debate over Darwin's theory still expressed an ambiguous body of evidence and a sharp divide over how to do science.

One more figure comes into play here. Reginald Daly, Canadian born, earned a Harvard geology doctorate in 1896 at age twenty-four, instructed there from 1898 to 1901, and after six years in the field with the Canadian International Boundary Commission and four teaching at the Massachusetts Institute of Technology returned to Harvard in 1912, at forty-one, to take Davis's place as the Sturgis Hooper Professor of Geology. He stayed another thirty years. Like Darwin, Daly was an avid field worker who valued imaginative, synthetic theorizing. In 1910 he offered a theory that threatened to completely rearrange things—and indeed would, though ultimately along lines different from what he expected.

In a 1909 visit to Hawaii, Daly had connected two key observations. First, he noticed that some of the high volcanic slopes bore the scrapes, gouges, and other marks of—of all things—glaciers. What Louis couldn't find in Brazil, Daly had found in Hawaii. This did not mean, as Louis had absurdly argued after finding much less credible glacial signs in Brazil, that glaciers once covered every inch of the globe. Hawaii was twenty degrees north of the equator, for one thing, and the marks were at high elevations; snow still occasionally fell on these peaks, so it wasn't stunning to find signs of former glaciers there. But this direct evidence made it clear that Hawaii had once been much cooler.

To Daly, this helped explain another thing that struck him: the relatively narrow width of the Hawaiian reefs, which suggested that they weren't very old, not nearly as old as the islands seemed. On the evidence of the glacial marks, he proposed that glacial periods had often cooled the water along the margins of the equatorial coral belt to below coral-friendly temperatures, temporarily halting coral reef growth there. He also knew, from the work of Alexander Agassiz and others, that many reefs in Hawaii and elsewhere showed signs of significant erosion—platforms, notches, and other irregularities of the sort often created by wave erosion and beaching—in the first thirty or forty fathoms below the surface. Taking his ice age insight a step further, he proposed that many glacial periods had consolidated enough seawater into polar ice caps and glaciers to drop the sea level as much as forty or fifty fathoms, exposing the reefs to the erosive power of waves at the same time the cooling water halted coral growth. When the ice ages ended, the waters would slowly rise and warm, and the reefs, altered by erosion, would resume growing. These repeated dunkings and slow risings allowed the reefs to periodically grow both upward and outward, thickening and broadening every cycle. In short, it wasn't sinking foundations that created the reefs; it was a slowly rising sea, or rather a series of sea rises.

This shook things up. It explained every subsidence-like effect not with an unproveable subsidence but via a glacial theory that was backed by bounteous evidence and almost a century of acceptance; and it explained oddities of reef form that Darwin's theory could not explain. Subsidence advocates didn't like this. They had trouble finding ground from which to attack the theory, however, for its chain of deductions was nearly as imaginative and elegant as Darwin's while resting on more empirical support. It was in fact the sort of theory Darwin would have loved. (One can imagine him dancing around a room on hearing it.) But some critics questioned Daly's estimates of the sea-level oscillations, and others thought he overstated the foundations' vertical stability. Davis, for instance, dismissed the theory as "largely invalidated by the evidence . . . of island instability."[5] But most subsidence advocates admitted the theory was formidable, and quite a few fence sitters moved to Daly's side.

The theory's implications for the Agassiz-Gardiner erosion-elevation theory were less clear. It seemed at once to contradict it, support it, and make it moot. From one way of looking at it, Daly was arguing that reefs were built much as Darwin had proposed, only with the sea rising (repeatedly) instead of the reef foundations falling—the same dance, but led by ocean rather than land. Yet you could also say that Daly's idea supported Agassiz. It accepted Alex's preexisting or elevated platforms and alternately brought them the two reef-shaping forces he emphasized: reef-friendly conditions in warm periods and erosive forces in cooler eras. Still, some wondered whether Daly bolstered Agassiz or simply replaced him. Daly himself saw his theory as a great boost to Agassiz's, calling the glacial-control hypothesis "a missing link in the chain of argument used by Semper, Rein, Murray, Agassiz, and Guppy against the wholesale-subsidence hypothesis."[6] "Correlating ice-caps and coral reefs, we use the great discovery of Louis Agassiz to support a principal conclusion of

Alexander Agassiz."[7] In the decades that followed, however, many saw Daly's theory as standing aside from Agassiz and Gardiner's.

So went the debate through the first half of the twentieth century. Three well-supported theories—the first and second mutually exclusive and a third seeming to replace the first and support the second—jockeyed for command over the same ambiguous body of findings. Clearly some definitive new piece of evidence was needed to settle the issue.

It had long been recognized that such evidence might be obtained by shooting a clean bore all the way through a coral reef's layers to "basement," or the original basalt that everyone agreed ultimately underlay all reef systems. But this peek under the floor proved elusive. The drills of the 1910s and 1920s couldn't go deep enough, and the few borings from those years improved little on the Funafuti results. Drilling technology advanced during the 1930s, but Japan had by then declared the Pacific off limits, so the drills couldn't be put to work where it mattered most. Reef science reached a sort of stasis. It was playing out nicely the prediction of geologist Arthur Holmes, who wrote in a 1916 review of Daly's work that "controversy will rage for many years on the problem . . . presented by the origin of coral reefs, for at present the data are still insufficient to provide an adequate basis for a complete explanation."[8]

3

The chance to drill deep finally came in 1950. The U.S. Navy, preparing to test nuclear bombs on several atolls in the Marshall Islands, assembled a team of reef geologists to do some deep core drilling as part of an elaborate pretest environmental survey of the area. The geologists, led by the United States Geological Survey's Harry Ladd (who with Hoffmeister had advocated an Agassizian "antecedent platform" theory since the 1930s), set up drills at opposite ends of Eniwetok, a circular atoll at the Marshalls' western edge. Drilling technology had advanced since Funafuti; the drills cut through the limestone with relative ease, bringing up one-and-a-half-inch cores. The results must have been sobering for Ladd and any other subsidence doubters present. The first cores were clearly reef rock, as expected. As the drill passed the first few hundred feet and out of coral reef depth, the cores changed little. They still appeared to be reef rock. Both the immediate shipboard and later laboratory analyses found that the granular stone held fossils of foraminifera, corals, and other life that grew only in shallow water, confirming that this was coral limestone. So it went as the drills cut deeper—500 feet, 1,000, 2,000, 3,000, 4,000. Finally, at 4,200 feet, the drills hit what was unequivocally basement, a greenish basalt, the volcanic mountain on which the reef had originated. Dating of the tiny fossils in the bottommost layer of coral showed that the reef had gotten its start in the Eocene. For more than thirty million years this reef had been growing—an inch every millennium—on a sinking volcano, thickening as the lava beneath it subsided. Darwin was right, Agassiz wrong.

As data from the Marshalls and elsewhere piled up over the months and years that followed, the balance fell decisively to Darwin's side. Drillings in the Tuamotus, at the other end of the South Sea Isles, produced results similar to those in Eniwetok, as did borings in the Caribbean and the Maldives, where a drill shot through sixty-five hundred feet of coral to basalt. Newly refined seismic techniques (first developed in the 1930s) established similar profiles in virtually all the Pacific archipelagoes. Echo soundings, which could continuously read the bottom topography, provided further proof of subsidence, showing that almost all these atolls were on steep-sided platforms, with valleys thousands of feet even between some closely spaced atolls; clearly these had not grown on available banks but had risen slowly atop their own thickening footprints. One after another of the world's reef areas—the Marshalls, the Ellice and Gilberts, the Taumotos, the Fijis and Hawaii, even most of the Caribbean reef systems—was found to follow Darwin's model. Only Florida, where Alexander started his quest and gathered his first impressions, showed itself to be built on the sort of current-shaped bank he proposed.

As for Daly, his glacial-control theory was found not to contradict Darwin's model but to complement it. New methods of sea-level analysis showed that the ocean oscillated even more than Daly envisioned. Over the previous two million years alone, the tropical oceans had undergone numerous oscillations of up to one hundred fathoms and temperature swings of five to ten degrees Fahrenheit. Even as the sea bottom slowly dropped, these fluctuations created

multiple surges of coral growth separated by intervals in which waves
created platforms, notches, and other erosive forms. The most recent
high-water drowning of reefs probably occurred in the Holocene,
only eight thousand years ago. The reef growth since then accounts
for the marked difference, emphasized so strongly by Alexander,
between modern, contiguous-looking corals and the underlying limestones. The window of growth for present-day reefs was far shorter
than Alexander or anyone else then imagined.

The structure was Darwin's, the topography Daly's. Separately,
neither theory could explain all reef areas; together they accounted
for almost all of them. Today this synthesis, sometimes called the
Darwin-Daly theory, is seen to fit hand in glove with the theory of
plate tectonics developed in the 1960s, for it is the movement of the
earth's huge plates that explains the subsidence of the Pacific and
many other reef areas. Darwin's theory seemed to be able to take in
anything. He had ignored a few details that had to be explained by
Daly. But he had gotten the big picture astoundingly correct.

4

We needn't ask how Alex missed all this. He faced an extraordinarily
difficult observational and theoretical problem, and it was another
half century before technology could reveal the evidence needed to
solve it decisively. With a few painful exceptions, he read the landscape in a defensible way, and his interpretations were shaped by an
empiricism true—perhaps too—to the tenets of his era. "Study
nature, not books," his father had famously urged, and Alex took to
heart this elevation of observation over theory. He was determined
that if he should err, it would be toward known facts and away from
the big picture.

As to the painful exceptions, it's clear now, after another century
of reef science, that Alexander made four crucial field errors that
allowed his misreading of atolls. Two were understandable. Two are
almost inexplicable.

The former first. Alex erred when he read the raised limestone
beds of Fiji and other Pacific atolls as old sedimentary limestone
rather than more recent reef limestone. His reading was encouraged
by the rock's clearly uplifted state (limestone can't be formed above

water); the marked difference between the chunky, coral-filled veneer and the finer conglomerate beneath it; and the reef rock's extreme similarity to older, marine limestone. This key misreading suggested to Alex a relatively large uplift (since marine limestones typically form in deeper water than coral limestones) and let Alex discard the implication of subsidence posed by a reading of the limestone as reef rock.

He also overestimated the effect and duration of subsurface erosion. Alex wasn't alone here; many of his colleagues struggled to explain the platforming, notching, and other erosive forms that complicated the idealized picture of smoothly contoured reefs, and no one really succeeded until Daly. Alex read these erosive patterns as evidence that the reef banks had been in place long enough to allow currents to create not just the topographical irregularities but the shapes of the reef foundations.

Both of these errors—his emphasis on the distinction between surface coral and underlying limestone and his vision of long periods of subsurface erosion—were attempts to interpret features that would be clearly explained only by Daly's glacial-control theory. Both were misreadings that other skilled observers might and did make.

More troubling are a pair of major errors that defy explication. One, the more amateurish, he made repeatedly in the lagoons of the archipelagoes that most strongly suggested subsidence (the Tuamotus in the east and the Ellice, the Gilberts, and the Marshalls in the north), where he mistook old, storm-deposited slabs of reef limestone, blackened by sun and algae and welded by calcification to the lagoon floors, for remnants of eroded volcanic islands. This allowed his mischaracterization of these islands as composed largely of volcanic rock, suggesting an island of lava that rose to the surface, rather than thickening reef limestone, which would indicate a slowly sinking island composed mainly of coral. The error astonishes trained geologists today. It seems the sort of mistake a neophyte or student might make. How did Alexander misread these slabs? It's possible he sampled them and made a misidentification. But it seems more likely that he looked too briefly. He kept a brisk pace through much of his longer Pacific trip and devoted much of the time to soundings. Rushed and having drawn fairly firm conclusions from his Fiji trip, he appears to have taken the shortcut for which he so disdained Darwin and Dana: From the deck of a boat at too great a distance, he observed poorly and concluded hastily.

His other inexplicable error was grossly misinterpreting his own soundings. He took considerable trouble to measure scores of depths in all the Pacific archipelagoes, yet he overlooked implications from the results that might have struck others as obvious. In almost all the archipelagoes, he found ravines up to forty-five hundred feet deep between many of the atolls—a finding that supported Darwin's theory and argued strongly against his own notion that most atolls grew from raised areas on broad banks. Yet he discounted these ravines by considering them very deep channels cut by current and chose to emphasize instead the shallower, inter-atoll banks he also discovered, which "go to show," as he wrote Murray, "that those atolls are not so immensely steep but rise from a great plateau."[9] He was practicing a Davis-like selectivity here, filtering his evidence to yield the interpretation most favorable to his own view.

That he would look too briefly, that he would strain evidence— these failures are harder to rationalize than his misreadings of geology. Indeed you can't rationalize them. Alex fell to the same fault he found so unforgivable in others: He saw what he wanted to see.

Was it some troubled awareness of this failure that kept him from writing up his theory? Did some part of him, realizing he was pushing the facts out of shape, balk at the sin he seemed to feel greatest, that of theorizing too soon and with too little proof? In 1904 he complained to Murray that a certain geologist carrying on an argument with Gardiner in the pages of *Nature* "is the kind of man who knows it all and has seen nothing of coral reefs. It really seems as if the less a man has seen the more anxious he is to write."[10] Perhaps at some level he recognized, as Gardiner would later, that there weren't really enough facts to go on.

It's stretching things, of course, to make his failure to publish his theory a virtue, the happy result of a healthy inhibition. That relieves him of the job he set out to do, which was to see reefs clearly and describe their genesis. If he saw the evidence as inconclusive, he should have said so. He can't be absolved of the obligation he carried, as so prominent, privileged, and experienced a scientist, as the man who had seen more reefs than anyone else, to declare his findings.

Epilogue

THAT ALEXANDER AGASSIZ did not publish his coral reef theory—that this most effectual of scientists and administrators, a man who completed countless projects started by both his father and himself, accustomed and even compelled to finish things, should fail to complete the most consuming work of his life—constitutes an irony of the sort usually reserved for scripted tragedy. It's only one among a long list of ironies painful to contemplate: that Alex, taking up a question seemingly made for him, should find himself locked in endless struggle with the man who destroyed his father. That every lesson Alex learned watching his father's destruction—his aversion to idealist thought and deductive method; his devotion to induction; his resistance to early conclusions or simple answers; his distaste for debate—should hamper him in his own battle with Darwin. That his conflict with Darwin should form a near mirror image of his father's, only this time with Darwin holding the lovely story and Alex the deep box of empirical ammunition, but Darwin winning anyway. That he should overlook the implications that his father's ice age theory held for reef formation, and that those implications should be seen and published by another even as he died.

Alexander Agassiz suffered these ironies partly because he was stubborn and partly because he was profoundly luckless. But these ironies also illustrate just how difficult a spot he stood in. He occupied a uniquely conflictual position during a time of immense contradiction and change. Both as a scientist and as a man, he was

Alexander Agassiz, in his mid-sixties, circa 1900

caught between the two figures who most excitingly personified the philosophical and methodological views that science was struggling to reconcile during the nineteenth century. Their conflict illuminated the starkness of the choice facing science and intellectual culture even as it hid the tangle of contradictions complicating that choice.

But if Alexander was more ensnared in these tangles than most, he was hardly alone. As science moved from the Victorian age to the modern, its great changes in method and philosophy and its immense gaps between orthodoxy and practice caused any number of scientists to be hoisted by their own petards. The comeuppances abound: Darwin, obsessed with oscillating landscapes, climbs too high at Glen Roy and falls when undercut by Louis's glacier theory.

Louis, thus emboldened, disastrously overextends both his glaciation and his speciation theory—and gets upended twenty years later by a Darwin wielding the empiricist principles Louis preached. Lyell, infecting Darwin with his vision of generative change, cheers as Darwin overturns his own coral reef theory and then flinches when his protégé proposes a blasphemous theory of selection. The devout Asa Gray, led by Darwin up his own careful stairway of evidence, arrives at the top to see a world purged of God. There was comedy as well: Lyell wishing Louis's lovely story were only true; Huxley turning Wilberforce's ape insult back on him; Huxley smeared with his own *Bathybius.* Hardly a notion or an action doesn't somewhere circle back to blindside its maker. It's as if every act and idea entered a warp and turned back on itself.

The distorting force, of course, was science's attempt to leave behind the idealist master it had so long served. This attempt had led to the Baconian method two centuries before and in Darwin's time to the argument between the Whewellians, who would have scientists collect evidence to build a theory, and the Herschel followers, who felt it acceptable to hatch a theory early and then buttress it with evidence. The Baconians and Whewellians stubbornly resisted the "danger of leaps" that Herschel's method seemed to invite. You had to climb the steps one at a time, and they all had to be visible. Thus Gray attacked Louis's creationism. Thus Alex, Murray, Geikie, and others balked at the speculative nature of Darwin's coral theory, which seemed a "simple and beautiful" idea until it faced the evidence.

The problem with so strict an inductivism, the reason it caught so many people in such agonizing binds, is that it ignores the way our minds operate. We see or experience a phenomenon, jump to conclusions about it, then (if we aspire to rigor) check our conclusions against more evidence. An idea rises not as the inevitable product of accumulated fact but as an early abstraction of experience. Its accuracy and utility reside not in its genesis but in how it tests out. This is the irony that underlies all the others: In their determination to create a method that could reflect only how nature actually works rather than how we *think* it should work, the inductivists prescribed a method that substituted the way they thought the mind *should* work for the way it actually does work. They pushed an idealist con-

ception of nonidealist theory generation. It tied them in knots.
Whewell, soaked in the history of great ideas, turned himself inside
out trying to explain, via his concept of "colligation," how a series of
observed facts accreted into an idea. He couldn't do it, because facts
don't mount to an idea. They require an act of imagination—or
recognition, if you'd rather—to fuse them into an explanation.

Herschel's model worked better. It relieved the scientist of proving that a theory rose from evidence and demanded only that evidence support it. It was okay to raise the shell and then fill in the
frame. It wasn't really inductive, but it was still empiricism, tied to
observation and testable experiment, and it allowed more powerful
theorizing.

This Herschellian model gave greater recognition to the role of
imagination, speculation, and the perception of broad patterns of distribution and change. It was a move toward the power of story. Explanations of complex dynamics naturally lean to narrative because they
have to explain not what is, as taxonomy does, but how something
happens. Thus the fates of the speciation theories of Louis Agassiz
and Charles Darwin. Louis's foundered because he overlaid an idealist story onto a science he claimed was descriptive; he lost his credibility when his fight with Darwin, who told a story driven by natural
processes, made it obvious that Louis told a story driven by divine
action.

Along with the elimination of divine cause, it was the acceptance
and emphasis of story—the focus on dynamic natural processes of
change rather than fixed descriptions of static things—that distinguished the shift in science that occurred during Darwin's and Alex's
time. It was only the purging of divine cause, of course, that made
storytelling safe. Even so, it took science another lifetime after Louis's
and Darwin's era to admit that it used stories (and many scientists
today would deny it yet). But the practical acceptance of empirical
story rather than description as science's main job began with the
acceptance of Darwin's ideas, and his first such story was not his evolutionary theory but his coral reef theory. Alex accepted the evolutionary theory because it was built on two decades of accumulated
fact and observation. It didn't come across as a story. He rejected the
coral reef theory because Darwin had published it on so little evidence and it was built on a foundation—and a flimsy one at that—

that seemed jerry-rigged after the fact. Alex had seen stories like that before.

THE ROLES of imagination, story, and even metaphor would expand further in the decades after Alex died. In particular the rise of physics, with its abstractions and elusive, hard-to-observe phenomena—subatomic particles, invisible forces such as gravity and energy, space-time and quanta—forced a revision not just of the rules of theory but of what a theory was. The concept of a theory as a definitive account of something—the sort of one "true theory" that Dana and Jukes saw in Darwin's coral reef hypothesis, for instance— yielded to the notion of a theory as a phenomenon's provisional approximation, and not necessarily the only approximation. Gravity was not just the force Newton described; it was also a curve in space-time. Light was at once wave and particle. This conception of theory acknowledged that we often see evidence partially or indirectly. It also acknowledged that, as Heisenberg's uncertainty principle suggested, observing a phenomenon can warp it. Heisenberg was referring to the way the process of locating a subatomic particle, which required bouncing a photon off it, could unpredictably alter the particle's location and path. But his principle expressed the growing awareness that observation sometimes failed and that even the most basic laws we perceive in the universe, such as those of gravity, are not complete accounts of a dynamic but our best working description of it. The notion of a theory, in short, changed much as the notion of species had, from something fixed to something provisional and capable of change, even expected to change.

This revised theoretical model was articulated eloquently in the 1920s and 1930s—by which time it carried the term "hypothetico-deductive theory"—by a German-born philosopher named Karl Popper. A sort of twentieth-century Herschel, Popper explored brilliantly how individuals wielded this method and how science or society tested the resulting theories (or failed to). Popper argued that we should not only be willing to accept a theory created deductively but that we should *expect* a theory to be created deductively, for that is how ideas come. He also argued that we should consider a theory scientific not simply because it is backed by evidence—for you can find evidence to back almost anything—but only if some observation or experiment could conceivably prove the theory false. He called this the "principle of falsifiability." Newton's theory of gravity, for instance, was a valid theory because it could potentially be proven false by a body that would not fall, and his laws of motion were valid because they could be falsified if some action produced no commensurate reaction. Accordingly, such theories as Freudianism or Marxism weren't scientific (though they might be useful) because you couldn't imagine any phenomena within their purviews that they couldn't explain. The great strength of psychoanalysis as an instrument of understanding—its ability to explain any human act or emotion—becomes its negation as a science.

A theory that could explain truly anything, then—that is, to which no conceivable exception could be imagined—was not scientific. A theory to which possible falsifications could be conceived and then attempted was scientific, for only attempted but failed falsifications could prove the theory's truth. Science thus progressed by a constant testing of theories for weaknesses (Popper called these tests "attempted falsifications") and the revision or replacement of the theory as necessary. Challenge, negation, and succession was science's proper course.

This model gives science an admirable rigor. But for scientists it envisions an antagonistic, almost gladiatorial world in which to work.

It was the bad luck of Alex, who abhorred open conflict, that one of the first ambitious and rigorous applications of the hypothetico-deductive method was Darwin's coral reef theory. Alex found himself chief challenger in an attempted falsification that lasted a century. He didn't see it that way, of course; he simply wanted to refute the results of a method he thought corrupt. He objected both on evidentiary grounds—because he saw so many things that seemed to disprove Darwin's theory—and because the theory was deductive on its face. Darwin was operating under the rules of an age still to come. Alex was applying those of his own era. At a time when scientists had good reason to forbid speculation from outrunning observable evidence, Alex, whose father had tripped himself up by doing just that, chose to take on a theory that by every rule of science he knew should be discarded. As Alex pointed out, Darwin's argument was ultimately circular, for he tried to explain reefs by a cause—subsidence—of which the reefs themselves were the main indication. The cause was to be its own proof. Accordingly, the theory rested not on direct evidence of subsidence but on reef forms and their distribution. William Davis had been right: The maps really were Darwin's best evidence. But Davis was the only one to admit this. Other subsidence advocates of Alex's time, citing the power of Darwin's argument and its "complete correspondence with observation" (Dana), fooled themselves when they called the theory good science, because by their own formal rules of science it wasn't. Even by Popper's rules it was more an interesting theory rather than one validated, for the only conclusive test was inaccessible: You could not imagine a reef or map that would contradict Darwin's theory. Until Eniwetok, definitive evidence lay in an untestable dimension.

As it happened, Eniwetok proved Darwin right. In the meantime Darwin's theoretical approach, boosted by his own evolutionary theory, the spectacular deductions of Einstein, and the explications of philosophers, was accepted, elaborated, codified, and given a long, ugly name. But in Darwin's and Alex's day, the hypothetico-deductive method was called speculation, and it was a dirty word. Alex's biggest mistake was truly unforeseeable: In coral reefs he addressed a problem that in his time remained unsolvable. He tested it as thoroughly as he could. But it was given to another age to find the answer.

ACKNOWLEDGMENTS

I am happy to thank the many people and institutions that helped me as I researched and wrote this book. I wish to thank, first of all, Victoria Wilson, my editor, and Charlotte Sheedy, my agent, for their sustained and sustaining enthusiasm for this project. Without them I could not have drawn this obscure story into the light. Kenneth Boss and Richard Johnson of Harvard's Museum of Comparative Zoology, where Louis and Alexander once roamed, gave this project a smaller but crucial early boost by hosting me at an afternoon tea, there among drawers holding tens of thousands of mollusks, and generously sharing their ideas and contacts on the history of the coral reef problem as well as their peerless company and good humor.

On the other side of Oxford Street, Harvard's Department of the History of Science granted me the invaluable status of visiting research associate. I thank Professor Everett Mendelsohn, Professor Robert Brain, and Michéle Biscoe, the department's coordinator of research studies, for so backing my research, and Judith Lajoie and the department's administrative staff for assisting me over various bureaucratic hurdles. The resulting privileges gave me full access to the incomparable resources of Harvard's library system. The staffs at Harvard's Widener Library, the Harvard Archives, Cabot Science Library, Kummel Library, and the Ernst Mayr Library at the Museum of Comparative Zoology all offered research help ably and with unflagging cheer. Particular thanks go to Dana Fischer of the Ernst Mayr Library for her aid in finding and viewing the extensive materials left in the library's special collections by Louis and Alexander Agassiz, and to Michael Currier of Widener for straightening out some potentially expensive due-date snafus. I also want to thank James McCarthy, the director of the Museum of Comparative Zoology, for his support.

The bibliography and reference notes suggest my debt to those who've written about this subject and its era. A handful of books and scholars, however, stand out as particularly critical to the knowledge and perspective needed to write this book. Edward Lurie's and A. Hunter Dupree's excellent biographies of Louis Agassiz and Asa Gray, respectively, were invaluable. And Louis Menand's *Metaphysical Club* revealed angles and not a few facts that might otherwise have escaped my view.

Less well known (and more scattered) are the writings of the distinguished geographer, reef researcher, and historian of science David Stoddart. Stoddart's work and insights on the history of the coral reef problem, particularly the genesis of Darwin's theory and the flaws and strengths of both Darwin's and Alexander's views, were vital to the development of my own perception of this strange history—and marvelously entertaining. He is a very funny geographer. His writings, his review of portions of this manuscript, and our discussion of its subject bolstered it critically.

A similarly crucial gift was provided by historian of science Mary P. Winsor, the director of the Institute for the History and Philosophy of Science and Technology at Victoria College, University of Toronto. Winsor not only provided the invaluable resources of her books and articles on Louis, Alexander, and the Museum of Comparative Zoology (see especially her *Reading the Shape of Nature*, 1991), she spent many hours discussing this project with me and generously (but ruthlessly, thank goodness) read and commented on the entire manuscript. She greatly expanded my knowledge of this particular story as well as the scientific and philosophical history of nineteenth-century science; through vetting the manuscript, she improved it immeasurably. I cannot thank her enough.

I benefited also from manuscript reviews by Richard Ober and Rick Weston, who supplied helpful feedback and suggestions as well as friendly support of my efforts throughout. I thank too the office mates from whom I rented my commodious work space: Rain Bainbury, Rich Cowart, Rich Sedano, and the aforementioned Mr. Weston, all of whom supplied welcome conversational diversion, quiet but continual encouragement, and the profound gift of never once asking when the book would finally be done.

As always, my family has provided my most elemental and central support. For long-distance, lasting affection and interest, I thank my siblings, Cynthia, Sarah, Ann, Allen, and Lynn; my late mother, Jane Preston; and my brother-in-law, John Colwell. For faith and support both spiritual and corporeal, I thank my father, Herman Dobbs, and my stepmother, Kathy Hall. And for interest, support, and generosity well beyond the call of in-law duty, I thank my wife's parents, James and Claudia Colwell.

Finally, I want to thank my sons, Taylor Allen and Nicholas James, who give my days and years an accruing splendor; and my wife, Alice Colwell, for casting the light.

NOTES

CHAPTER ONE: MAGPIE

1. Jules Marcou, *Life, Letters, and Works of Louis Agassiz,* vol. 1 (New York: Macmillan, 1896), ix.

2. Louis Agassiz to Rodolphe Agassiz, 14 February 1829, in Elizabeth Cary Agassiz, *Louis Agassiz: His Life and Correspondence,* vol. 1 (Boston: Houghton Mifflin, 1885), 98.

3. Quoted in Marcou, *Life, Letters,* 15.

CHAPTER TWO: NEUCHÂTEL

1. Alexander von Humboldt to Louis Agassiz, May 1835, Elizabeth Cary Agassiz, *Louis Agassiz: His Life and Correspondence,* vol. 1 (Boston: Houghton Mifflin, 1885), 255.

2. Louis Agassiz, *Recherches sur les poissons fossiles,* 5 vols. (Neuchâtel, 1833–1844), quoted in Edward Lurie, *Louis Agassiz: A Life in Science* (Baltimore: Johns Hopkins University Press, 1978), 83.

3. Adam Sedgwick to Charles Lyell, 20 September 1835, John Willis Clark and Thomas McKinney Hughes, *The Life and Letters of the Reverend Adam Sedgwick,* vol. 1 (Cambridge, 1890), 447, quoted in Lurie, *Agassiz,* 79.

4. Charles Lyell to Adam Sedgwick, 25 October 1835, *Life, Letters, and Journals of Sir Charles Lyell,* vol. 1, ed. Katherine M. Lyell (London, 1881), 457, quoted in Lurie, *Agassiz,* 79.

5. Quoted in Lurie, *Agassiz,* 99.

6. Charles Darwin to Charles Lyell, 9 August 1838, quoted in Martin Rudwick, "Darwin and Glen Roy: A 'Great Failure' in Scientific Method?" *Studies in History and Philosophy of Science* 5, no. 2 (1974): 117.

7.   See Janet Browne, *Charles Darwin: Voyaging* (New York: Knopf, 1995), 402, 426–27, 432–33, 436, 440–41.

8.   Charles Darwin to Charles Lyell, 6 September 1861, quoted in Rudwick, "Darwin and Glen Roy," 152.

9.   From F. H. Burkhardt et al., eds., *The Correspondence of Charles Darwin,* 9 vols. (Cambridge: Cambridge University Press, 1821–1861), 2: 322, as quoted in Browne, *Voyaging.*

10.   Francis Darwin, ed., *The Life and Letters of Charles Darwin,* vol. 1 (New York: Appleton, 1911), 49.

11.   George Agassiz, *Letters and Recollections of Alexander Agassiz* (Boston: Houghton Mifflin, 1913), 4.

12.   Ibid., 4, fn.

13.   Ibid., 7.

14.   Jules Marcou, *Life, Letters, and Works of Louis Agassiz,* vol. 1 (New York: Macmillan, 1896), 132.

15.   Charles Darwin to Joseph Hooker, 26 March 1854, in Darwin, *Life and Letters,* vol. 1, 403.

CHAPTER FOUR: CAMBRIDGE

1.   William James, "Louis Agassiz," *Science* 5 (19 February 1897): 285–89.

2.   Benjamin Silliman, Jr., to James Hall, 12 November 1846, James Hall Papers, New York State Museum, Albany.

3.   Henry Adams, *The Education of Henry Adams,* chap. 16, online edition available at http://www.bartleby.com/159/16.html.

4.   George Santayana, *Character and Opinion in the United States* (New York: Scribner's, 1921), 1–2, quoted in Edward Lurie, *Nature and the American Mind* (New York: Science History Publications, 1974), 19.

5.   Asa Gray to William C. Redfield, 13 October 1846, Asa Gray Papers, Gray Herbarium, Harvard University, quoted in Edward Lurie, *Louis Agassiz: A Life in Science* (Baltimore: Johns Hopkins University Press, 1978), 125.

6.   Ralph Waldo Emerson, *Journals,* quoted in A. Hunter Dupree, *Asa Gray* (Baltimore: Johns Hopkins University Press, 1988), 225.

7.   George Agassiz, ed., *Letters and Recollections of Alexander Agassiz* (Boston: Houghton Mifflin, 1913), 19.

8.   Ibid., 20.

9.   Ibid., 18–19.

10.   Alexander Agassiz, *Notes on the Described Species of Holconoti, Found on the Western Coast of North America* (Boston: George C. Rand & Avery, 1861).

CHAPTER FIVE: FIXITY

1. Harry Russell to Elizabeth Russell Lyman, 29 November 1862, Theodore Lyman letters, Lyman Family Papers, 1785–1956, Massachusetts Historical Society (microfilm, University of Michigan at Ann Arbor).

2. Alexander Agassiz to Theodore Lyman, 21 April 1862, Alexander Agassiz Papers, bAg 10.10.10.34, Ernst Mayr Library, Harvard Museum of Comparative Zoology.

3. As related in Anne Russell Agassiz to Elizabeth Russell Lyman, 26 November 1861, Lyman Family Papers.

4. Addison Verrill to Edward Morse, quoted in Mary Winsor, *Reading the Shape of Nature: Comparative Zoology at the Agassiz Museum* (Chicago: University of Chicago Press, 1991), 60.

5. I'm indebted to Ernst Mayr, and particularly his *One Long Argument* (Cambridge: Harvard University Press, 1991), for his lucid breakdown of the parts of Darwin's larger theory—a parsing with which I've taken a few minor liberties here.

6. Michael Shermer, "The Gradual Illumination of the Mind: The Advance of Science, Not the Demotion of Religion, Will Best Counter the Influence of Creationism," *Scientific American,* February 2002, online edition. Data is from a 2001 Gallup poll of Americans. About 10% believed in a strict creationism; just under 50% believed God somehow directed or influenced an evolutionary process; and just over 40% believed humans were shaped by a strictly natural evolution. The numbers for scientists were not radically different.

7. Asa Gray to J. D. Hooker, 21 February 1854, and 6 October 1855, quoted in A. Hunter Dupree, *Asa Gray* (Baltimore: Johns Hopkins University Press), 228.

8. Asa Gray, review of *Explanations: A Sequel to the Vestiges of the Natural History of Creation,* by Anonymous, *North American Review* 62 (1846): 465–506, quoted in ibid., 145–46.

9. Asa Gray to J. D. Hooker, 28 September 1858, quoted in ibid., 221.

10. Charles Darwin to Asa Gray, 25 April 1855, Francis Darwin, ed., *The Life and Letters of Charles Darwin,* vol. 2, (New York: Appleton, 1911), 420.

11. Asa Gray, "On the Botany of Japan, and Its Relation to North America, etc.," *Memoirs of the American Academy of Arts and Sciences* 6 (25 April 1859): 377–452.

12. Asa Gray to John Torrey, 7 January 1859, quoted in Dupree, *Asa Gray,* 253.

13. Ibid.

14. *Proceedings of the American Academy of the Arts and Sciences* 4 (1857–1860): 132.

15. Gray, "Botany of Japan," 445.

16. Quoted in Dupree, *Asa Gray,* 259.

17. Charles E. Norton to Elizabeth C. Gaskell, 27 December 1859, *Letters of Mrs. Gaskell and Charles Eliot Norton 1855–1865,* ed. Jane Whitehill (London, 1932), 42–43, quoted in ibid., 267.

18. Asa Gray, "Darwin on the Origin of Species," *Atlantic Monthly* 6 (1860): 109–16, 229–39, quoted in ibid., 295–297.

19. Asa Gray to Joseph Hooker, 31 March 1860, quoted in Edward Lurie, *Louis Agassiz: A Life in Science* (Baltimore: Johns Hopkins University Press, 1978), 295.

20. Louis Agassiz, review of *Origin of Species,* by Charles Darwin, *American Journal of Science* 80 (1860): 144, 154.

21. The 1861–1862 Lowell Lectures appeared as *Methods of Study* (Boston: Ticknor and Fields, 1863). The New York lectures, given at the Brooklyn Academy of Music, were published as *The Structure of Animal Life* (New York: Scribner's, 1865); they were essentially a popularization of Agassiz's 1861 *Principles of Zoology* (Boston: Gould and Lincoln), which was intended for college-level study. The series that ran in the *Atlantic Monthly* during 1863 and 1864 took book form as *Geological Sketches* (Boston: Ticknor and Fields, 1865.)

22. William James to Mary Robertson Walsh James, 31 March 1865, *The Correspondence of William James,* vol. 4, eds. Ignas K. Skrupskelis and Elizabeth M. Berkeley (Charlottesville: University Press of Virginia, 1992), 99.

23. Chauncey Wright to Susan Lesley, 12 February 1860, *Letters of Chauncey Wright,* ed. James Bradley Thayer, 43, quoted in Louis Menand, *The Metaphysical Club* (New York: Farrar, Straus, and Giroux, 2001), 209.

24. Chauncey Wright to Charles Eliot Norton, 10 August 1866, Charles Eliot Norton Papers, Houghton Library, Harvard University, bMS Am 1088 (8280), quoted in Menand, *Metaphysical Club,* 209.

CHAPTER SIX: TRANSMUTATION

1. Alexander Agassiz to Theodore Lyman, 25 February 1863, Alexander Agassiz Papers, bAg 10.10.10.34, Ernst Mayr Library, Harvard Museum of Comparative Zoology.

2. Alexander Agassiz to Theodore Lyman, 19 November 1863, ibid.

3. Alexander Agassiz to Theodore Lyman, 23 October 1863, ibid.

4. Alexander Agassiz to Theodore Lyman, 25 July 1864, ibid.

5. Alexander Agassiz to Fritz Müller, 17 January 1864, George Agassiz, *Letters and Recollections of Alexander Agassiz* (Boston: Houghton Mifflin, 1913), 48–49.

6. Alexander Agassiz to Theodore Lyman, 7 July 1865, Alexander Agassiz Papers.

7. Alexander Agassiz to Elizabeth Cary Agassiz, 17 July 1870, Agassiz, *Letters and Recollections,* 108.

8. Alexander Agassiz to Theodore Lyman, 16 November 1870, Alexander Agassiz Papers.

9. Quoted in Agassiz, *Letters and Recollections,* 97.

10. Charles Darwin to Fritz Müller, 1 December 1869, *More Letters of Charles Darwin,* vol. 2, eds. Francis Darwin and A. C. Seward (New York: Appleton, 1903), 357–358.

11. Alexander Agassiz to Charles Darwin, 4 March 1872, Agassiz, *Letters and Recollections,* 119–20.

12. Alexander Agassiz, "Revision of the Echini," *Illustrated Catalogue of the Museum of Comparative Zoology at Harvard College,* 7 (1872–1874): 17–18, quoted in Mary Winsor, *Reading the Shape of Nature: Comparative Zoology at the Agassiz Museum* (Chicago: University of Chicago Press, 1991), 152–54.

CHAPTER SEVEN: SELECTION

1. Alexander Agassiz to Theodore Lyman, 7 February 1872, Alexander Agassiz Papers, bAg 10.10.10.34, Ernst Mayr Library, Harvard Museum of Comparative Zoology.

2. Alexander Agassiz to Theodore Lyman, 16 March 1872, ibid.

3. Theodore Lyman diaries, 9 August 1874, Lyman Family Papers, 1785–1956, Massachusetts Historical Society (microfilm, University of Michigan at Ann Arbor).

CHAPTER EIGHT: A STILL GREATER SORROW

1. Theodore Lyman diaries, 24 December and 25 December 1876, Lyman Family Papers, 1785–1956, Massachusetts Historical Society (microfilm, University of Michigan at Ann Arbor).

2. Alexander Agassiz to Ernst Haeckel, 28 January 1874, *Letters and Recollections of Alexander Agassiz,* ed. George Agassiz (Boston: Houghton Mifflin, 1913), 127.

3. Theodore Lyman diaries, 15 January 1874, Lyman Family Papers, 1785–1956, Massachusetts Historical Society (microfilm, University of Michigan at Ann Arbor).

4. Theodore Lyman diaries, 12 July 1974.

5. Alexander Agassiz to Wolcott Gibbs, 8 August 1874, Agassiz, *Letters and Recollections,* 130.

6. Alexander Agassiz to Elizabeth Cary Agassiz, 19 January 1875, ibid., 133.

7. Alexander Agassiz to Elizabeth Cary Agassiz, 19 January 1875, ibid., 136.

8. Alexander Agassiz to Theodore Lyman, 16 February 1875, Alexander Agassiz Papers, bAg 10.10.10.34, Ernst Mayr Library, Harvard Museum of Comparative Zoology.

CHAPTER NINE: THE PLEASURE OF GAMBLING

1. Charles Darwin, *The Voyage of the "Beagle,"* vol. 29 (New York: Collier, 1909), 273–274.

2. Ibid., 270.

3. Alexander Agassiz to Elizabeth Cary Agassiz, 19 January 1875, *Letters and Recollections of Alexander Agassiz,* ed. George Agassiz (Boston: Houghton Mifflin, 1913), 136.

4. Charles Darwin to John Henslow, 18 April 1835, *The Correspondence of Charles Darwin,* vol. 1, eds. Frederick Burkhardt and Sydney Smith (Cambridge: Cambridge University Press, 1985), 440.

5. Charles Darwin, 16 August 1834, *Charles Darwin's "Beagle" Diary,* ed. Richard Darwin Keynes (Cambridge: Cambridge University Press, 1988), 253.

6. Francis Darwin, ed., *The Life and Letters of Charles Darwin,* vol. 1 (New York: Appleton, 1911), 37.

7. Ibid., 38.

8. Ibid., 39.

9. Ibid., 38.

10. Ibid., 42.

11. Ibid., 43.

12. Ibid., 47.

13. Ibid., 49.

14. Ibid., 50.

15. Ibid., 51.

16. Ibid., 52–53.

17. Charles Darwin to Leonard Horner, 29 August 1844, *More Letters of Charles Darwin,* vol. 2, eds. Francis Darwin and A. C. Seward (New York: Appleton, 1911), 117.

18. Darwin, *Life and Letters,* vol. 1, 52.

19. Ibid., 68.

20. Frederick Burkhardt and Sydney Smith, eds., *The Correspondence of Charles Darwin,* vol. 1, 236, cited in David Stoddart, "Darwin and the Seeing Eye," *Earth Sciences History* 14 (1995): 5. I'm indebted to this paper by Professor Stoddart for tracing and articulating much of the nature, history, and results of Darwin's attraction to Lyell's method, as well as for some of the quotes in this passage.

21. Burkhardt and Smith, *Correspondence,* vol. 1, 445.

22. Darwin, *Life and Letters,* vol. 1, 53.

23. Ibid., 52.

24. Stoddart, "Darwin and the Seeing Eye," 3.

25. Burkhardt and Smith, *Correspondence,* vol. 1, 232.

26. Ibid., 445.

27. Charles Darwin to J. S. Henslow, 18 April 1835, Darwin, *More Letters,* vol. 1, 20.

28. Darwin, *Voyage,* 320.

29. Charles Darwin to J. S. Henslow, 10–13 March 1835, Burkhardt and Smith, *Correspondence,* vol. 1, 436.

30. Charles Darwin to Caroline Darwin, 10–13 March 1835, Burkhardt and Smith, *Correspondence,* vol. 1, 434.

31. Both quotes 4 March 1835, Keynes, *"Beagle" Diary,* 302.

32. Ibid., 295.

33. 5 March 1835, ibid., 297.

34. Ibid., 302.

35. W. Knight, *Facts and Observations Towards Forming a New Theory of the Earth* (London, 1818), 258, 245, quoted in David Stoddart, "Darwin, Lyell, and the Geological Significance of Coral Reefs," *British Journal for the History of Science* 9 (1976): 199.

36. Darwin, *Voyage,* 493.

37. Darwin, *Life and Letters,* vol. 1, 493–94

38. Ibid., 58.

39. Charles Darwin, *Diary of the Voyage of the "Beagle,"* ed. Nora Barlow (Cambridge: Cambridge University Press, 1934), 399–400.

40. Charles Lyell to John Herschel, 24 May 1837, quoted in Darwin, *Life and Letters,* vol. 1, 293.

41. Ibid., 294.

42. Quoted in John Judd, introduction to Charles Darwin, *The Structure and Distribution of Coral Reefs,* 1889, *The Works of Charles Darwin,* vol. 7, eds. Paul H. Barrett and R. B. Freeman (London: Pickering, 1986), 11.

43. Henry Holland, review of *Narrative of the Surveying Voyage of H.M.S. Fly,* by J. B. Jukes, and *The Structure and Distribution of Coral Reefs,* by C. R. Darwin, *Quarterly Review* 81 (1847): 468–500, reprinted as "Australia—Coral Reefs," in Henry Holland, *Essays on Scientific and Other Subjects* (London, 1862), 350–385, cited in Stoddart, "Darwin, Lyell," 207.

44. B. Hall, review of *Narrative of the Voyages of H.M.S. "Adventure" and "Beagle,"* by P. P. King, R. Fitzroy, and C. R. Darwin, *Edinburgh Review* 69 (1839): 467–93, cited in Stoddart, "Darwin, Lyell," 207–8.

45. Darwin, *Life and Letters,* 58.

46. The most direct discussion of the two theories' similarities, to which I'm indebted for these parallels, is Howard Gruber and Valmai Gruber, "The Eye of Reason: Darwin's Development During the *Beagle* Voyage," *Isis* 53 (1962): 186–200.

CHAPTER TEN: TO LIGHT: MURRAYS REEFS

1. Alexander Agassiz to Wolcott Gibbs, 3 March 1875, *Letters and Recollections of Alexander Agassiz,* ed. George Agassiz (Boston: Houghton Mifflin, 1913), 148.

2. Theodore Lyman diaries, 4 June 1876, Lyman Family Papers, 1785–1956, Massachusetts Historical Society (microfilm, University of Michigan at Ann Arbor).

3. Alexander Agassiz to John Murray, quoted in John Murray, "Alexander Agassiz: His Life and Scientific Work," *Science* 33 (9 June 1911): 882.

CHAPTER ELEVEN: A QUESTION OF SCIENCE

1. Alexander Agassiz to Wyville Thomson, 23 January 1877, quoted in John Murray, "Alexander Agassiz: His Life and Scientific Work," *Science* 33 (9 June 1911): 879.

2. James Dwight Dana, *Corals and Coral Islands* (New York: Putnam, 1872), 7; and *On Coral Reefs and Islands* (New York: Putnam, 1853), 89.

3. Charles Darwin, *The Structure and Distribution of Coral Reefs,* 1889, *The Works of Charles Darwin,* vol. 7, eds. Paul H. Barrett and R. B. Freeman (London: Pickering, 1986), 125.

4. The italics are Darwin's.

5. James Dwight Dana, *United States Exploring Expedition During the Years 1838, 1839, 1840, 1841, 1842, Under the Command of Charles Wilkes, U.S.N. Zoophytes* (Philadelphia: Sherman, 1846), 83, 84.

6. Ernst Haeckel, *Ziele und Wege der heutigen Entwickelungsgeschichte* (*Goals and Paths in the History of Development Today*) (Jena, Germany: Dufft, 1875), 78–85. I'm grateful to Alice Colwell for translating this document.

7. Alexander Agassiz to Ernst Haeckel, 11 December 1875, MCZ Archives, as related in Mary Winsor, *Reading the Shape of Nature: Comparative Zoology at the Agassiz Museum* (Chicago: University of Chicago Press, 1991), 54, note. I'm grateful to Dr. Winsor for drawing this reply to my attention.

8. Alexander Agassiz to Alexander Braun, 28 January 1874, *Letterbooks of Louis and Alexander Agassiz,* vol. 5, Houghton Library, Harvard University.

CHAPTER TWELVE: ACCRUAL

1. John Murray, "On the Structure and Origin of Coral Reefs," *Proceedings of the Royal Society of Edinburgh* 10, no. 107 (1879–1880), 505–18. The same article also ran in *Nature* 26 (1880): 351–55. I've cited the latter in following quotations, since it's easier to find.

2. Murray, "Structure and Origin," 353.

3. Charles Lyell, notebook entry for 30 June 1856, *Sir Charles Lyell's Scientific Journals on the Species Question,* ed. L. G. Wilson (New Haven, Conn.: Yale University Press, 1970), 108, cited in David Stoddart, "Darwin, Lyell, and the Geological Significance of Coral Reefs," *British Journal for the History of Science* 9 (1976): 212.

4. Alexander Agassiz to Charles Darwin, 16 April 1881, *Letters and Recollections of Alexander Agassiz,* ed. George Agassiz (Boston: Houghton Mifflin, 1910), 281–82.

5. Charles Darwin, *The Structure and Distribution of Coral Reefs,* 1889, *The Works of Charles Darwin,* vol. 7, eds. Paul H. Barrett and R. B. Freeman (London: Pickering, 1986), 266.

6. Charles Darwin to Alexander Agassiz, 5 May 1881, *More Letters of Charles Darwin,* vol. 2, eds. Francis Darwin and A. C. Seward (New York: Appleton, 1903), 197–98.

7. Alexander Agassiz to Charles Darwin, Agassiz, *Letters and Recollections,* 285.

8. Alexander Agassiz to James Dwight Dana, 7 April 1885, *Agassiz Letterbooks,* vol. 7A (1880–1885), Houghton Library, Harvard University.

9. Gilbert Bourne, "The Atoll of Diego Garcia and the Coral Formations of the Indian Ocean," *Nature,* 5 April 1888: 546–50; and H. B. Guppy, "Notes on the Characters and Mode of Formation of the Coral Reefs of the Solomon Islands," *Proceedings of the Royal Society of Edinburgh, 1885–1886,* 857–904.

10. James Dwight Dana, "Origin of Coral Reefs and Islands," *American Journal of Science* 30 (August/September 1885): 171.

11. Ibid., 190.

12. Mary Winsor's *Reading the Shape of Nature: Comparative Zoology at the Agassiz Museum* (Chicago: University of Chicago Press, 1991) evocatively describes this lab and its workings on pp. 198–12.

CHAPTER THIRTEEN: "A CONSPIRACY OF SILENCE"

1. Leonard Huxley, *Life and Letters of Sir Joseph Dalton Hooker,* 2 vols. (London: John Murray, 1918), quoted in David Stoddart, "The Duke, the Professors, and the Great Coral Reef Controversy of 1887–1888," *Earth Sciences History* 7 (1988): 92. Professor Stoddart's paper remains the best account of the controversy, and I'm grateful to him both for pulling together the many threads of this story and for his many insights, such as the Duke's being ahead of his time in making the point that science, as both a social and an intellectual enterprise, was vulnerable to errors driven by personalities and politics.

2. W. S. Lilly, "Materialism and Morality," *Fortnightly Review* 40 (1887): 575–94; Thomas H. Huxley, "Science and Morals," *Fortnightly*

Review 40 (1887): 788–802; and "Scientific and Pseudo-scientific Realism," *Nineteenth Century* 21 (1887): 191–205; Duke of Argyll, "Professor Huxley on Canon Liddon," *Nineteenth Century* 21 (1887): 321–39; and Thomas H. Huxley, "Science and Pseudo-science," *Nineteenth Century* 21 (1887): 481–98. All quotes and citations here are as quoted in David Stoddart, "Coral Reef Controversy," 90–98.

3. Susan Schlee, *The Edge of an Unfamiliar World: A History of Oceanography* (New York: Dutton, 1973), 162.

4. John W. Judd to Thomas H. Huxley, 10 October 1887, Thomas Huxley, "Science and the Bishops," *Nineteenth Century* 21 (1887): 625–41.

5. Thomas H. Huxley, "The Duke of Argyll's Charges Against Men of Science," *Nature* 37 (9 February 1888): 342.

6. William J. Wharton, "Coral Formations," *Nature* 37 (1888): 393–95; Gregory C. Bourne, "Coral Formations," *Nature* 37 (1888): 414–15; and Henry B. Guppy, "Coral Formations," *Nature* 37 (1888): 462.

7. Guppy, "Coral Formations," 462.

8. Alexander Agassiz, *Three Cruises of the "Blake,"* vol. 1 (Boston: Houghton Mifflin, 1888), 78.

9. Alexander Agassiz, "The Coral Reefs of the Hawaiian Islands," *Bulletin of the Museum of Comparative Zoology* 17 (1889): 125.

10. Ibid., 133, 141.

11. Ibid., 138.

12. Ibid., 136.

13. Ibid., 121.

14. Ibid., 132.

15. Alexander Agassiz to Carl Semper, 12 April 1888, *Letterbooks of Louis and Alexander Agassiz,* vol. 9, Houghton Library, Harvard University.

16. James Dwight Dana, *Corals and Coral Islands,* 3d ed. (New York: Dodd, Mead, 1890), 309.

17. Thomas G. Bonney, "Summary of the Principal Contributions to the History of Coral Reefs Since the Year 1874," appendix 2 in Charles Darwin, *The Structure and Distribution of Coral Reefs,* 1889, *The Works of Charles Darwin,* vol. 7, eds. Paul H. Barrett and R. B. Freeman (London: Pickering, 1986).

18. John W. Judd, introduction to Darwin, *Structure and Distribution.*

19. Alexander Agassiz to Carl Semper, 12 April 1888, *Agassiz Letterbooks.* vol. 9.

20. Alexander Agassiz to John Murray, n.d. December 1887, *Agassiz Letterbooks,* vol. 9.

CHAPTER FOURTEEN: TO SEA

1. James Dwight Dana, "Origin of Coral Reefs and Islands," *American Journal of Science* 30 (August/September 1885): 99.

2. James Dwight Dana, *On Coral Reefs and Islands* (New York: Putnam, 1853), 98.

3. Alexander Agassiz, "The Islands and Coral Reefs of Fiji," *Bulletin of the Museum of Comparative Zoology* 33 (1899): 1–167, plus plates: 72.

4. Ibid., 47.

5. Alexander Agassiz to John Murray, 16 May 1897, *Letters and Recollections of Alexander Agassiz*, ed. George Agassiz (Boston: Houghton Mifflin, 1913), 323.

6. Alexander Agassiz to John Murray, 16 May 1896, Agassiz, *Letters and Recollections*, 317.

7. Agassiz, "Islands and Coral Reefs of Fiji," 16.

8. Ibid., 15.

9. Agassiz, *Letters and Recollections*, 337.

10. Agassiz, "Islands and Coral Reefs of Fiji," 91.

11. Ibid., 15.

12. Ibid., 337.

13. Dana, *On Coral Reefs*, 110.

14. Alexander Agassiz to John Murray, 3 December 1897, Agassiz, *Letters and Recollections*, 328–29, 330.

15. Agassiz to unspecified recipient, December 1899, ibid., 334.

16. Alexander Agassiz to Wolcott Gibbs, 15 December 1897, ibid., 333.

17. Alexander Agassiz to unspecified recipient, January 1888, ibid., 336.

18. Agassiz, "Islands and Coral Reefs of Fiji."

19. Ibid., 135.

20. Ibid., 144.

21. Ibid., 109.

CHAPTER FIFTEEN: THE LAST ARCHIPELAGO

1. Alexander Agassiz to unspecified recipient, 15 September 1899, *Letters and Recollections of Alexander Agassiz*, ed. George Agassiz (Boston: Houghton Mifflin, 1913), 354.

2. Alexander Agassiz to unspecified recipient, n.d. November 1899, ibid., 364.

3. Ibid., 358.

4. Ibid., 362.

5. Ibid., 368.

6. Alexander Agassiz, "The Coral Reefs of the Maldives," *Memoirs of the Museum of Comparative Zoology* 29 (1903): 11.

CHAPTER SIXTEEN: A CONNECTED ACCOUNT

1. Alexander Agassiz, "On the Formation of Barrier Reefs and of the Different Types of Atolls," *Proceedings of the Royal Society of London* 71 (1903): 413.

2.   See, for instance, J. Stanley Gardiner, "The Formation of Coral Reefs," *Nature* 69 (18 February 1904): 371–73.

3.   Alexander Agassiz to Ernst Ehlers, 2 February 1903, *Letters and Recollections of Alexander Agassiz,* ed. George Agassiz (Boston: Houghton Mifflin, 1913), 408.

4.   Quoted in John Murray, "Alexander Agassiz: His Life and Work," *Science* 33, no. 858 (9 June 1911): 882.

CHAPTER SEVENTEEN: ENIWETOK

1.   "Coral Reefs," *Encyclopedia Britannica,* 1911 ed., available at http://1911encyclopedia.org/c/co/coral.htm.

2.   J. Stanley Gardiner, "The Formation of Coral Reefs," *Nature* 69 (18 February 1904): 373.

3.   Harry S. Ladd and J. Edward Hoffmeister, "A Criticism of the Glacial-Control Theory," *Journal of Geology* 44 (1936): 74–92.

4.   J. Stanley Gardiner, *Coral Reefs and Atolls* (London: Macmillan, 1931.

5.   William D. Davis, "Coral Reefs," *Encyclopedia Britannica* 1950.

6.   Reginald A. Daly, "Pleistocene Glaciation and the Coral Reef Problem," *American Journal of Science* 30 (1910): 298.

7.   Ibid., 308.

8.   Arthur Holmes, "Coral Reefs and the Ice Age," *Geographical Journal* 48 (16 November 1916): 414–15.

9.   Alexander Agassiz to Elizabeth Cary Agassiz, 16 October 1899, *Letters and Recollections of Alexander Agassiz,* ed. George Agassiz (Boston: Houghton Mifflin, 1913), 362.

10.   Alexander Agassiz to John Murray, 3 May 1904, in *Alexander Agassiz Letterbooks,* vol. 14, Houghton Library, Harvard University.

SELECT BIBLIOGRAPHY

"Borings into a Coral Reef." [Review of the Atoll of Funafuti: Being the Reports of the Coral Reef Committee of the Royal Society.] *Nature* 69, no. 1799 (21 April 1904): 582–585.

"Prof. Agassiz' Expedition to the Maldives." *Geographical Journal* 19, no. 4 (April 1902): 483–83.

Adams, Henry. *The Education of Henry Adams.* Oxford: Oxford University Press, 1999.

Agassiz, Alexander, and Louis Agassiz. Letterbooks of Louis and Alexander Agassiz, 1859–1910. Houghton Library, Harvard University.

Agassiz, Alexander. "On the Formation of Barrier Reefs and of the Different Types of Atolls." *Proceedings of the Royal Society of London* 71 (1902–1903): 412–14.

———. "The Coral Reefs of the Hawaiian Islands." *Bulletin of the Museum of Comparative Zoology* 17 (1888–1889): 121–70.

———. "The Coral Reefs of the Maldives." *Memoirs of the Museum of Comparative Zoology* 29: 1–168, 82 pl.

———. "The Coral Reefs of the Tropical Pacific." *Memoirs of the Museum of Comparative Zoology* 28: 1–410, 238 pl.

———. "The Tertiary Elevated Reefs of Fiji." *American Journal of Science* 4, no. 6: 155–67.

———. Alexander Agassiz Papers. Ernst Mayr Library, Harvard Museum of Comparative Zoology.

———. "Islands and Coral Reefs of Fiji." *Bulletin of the Museum of Comparative Zoology* 33: 1–167, 120 pl.

———. *Notes on the Described Species of Holconti, Found on the Western Coast of North America.* Boston: Rand & Avery, 1861.

———. *Revision of the Echini.* Cambridge: University Press, 1872.

————. *Three Cruises of the "Blake."* 2 vols. [full title: *Three Cruises of the United States Coast and Geodetic Survey Steamer "Blake" in the Gulf of Mexico, in the Caribbean Sea, and Along the Atlantic Coast of the United States, from 1877 to 1880.*] Boston: Houghton Mifflin, 1888.

Agassiz, Elizabeth, ed. *Louis Agassiz: His Life and Correspondence.* Boston: Houghton Mifflin, 1890.

Agassiz, George, ed. *Letters and Recollections of Alexander Agassiz.* 1st ed. Boston: Houghton Mifflin, 1913.

Agassiz, Louis. "Evolution and Permanence of Type." *Atlantic Monthly,* January 1874: 92–101.

————. "Prof. Agassiz on the Origin of Species." In *Science in America: Historical Collections.* Edited by John Burnham. New York: Holt, Rinehart and Winston, 1971. Originally appeared in *American Journal of Science and Arts* 80 (1860): 142–54.

Argyll, Duke of. "A Conspiracy of Silence." *Nature* 37: 53–54, 246, 293.

————. "A Great Lesson." *The Nineteenth Century* 22: 293–309.

Bechtel, William. "The Nature of Scientific Integration." In *Integrating Scientific Disciplines.* Edited by William Bechtel. Boston: Martinus Nijhoff, 1986.

Bonney, Thomas G. "Coral Reefs." *Nature* 40: 222.

————. "Summary of Professor Edgeworth David's Preliminary Report on the Results of the Boring in the Atoll of Funafuti." *Proceedings of the Royal Society of London* 62 (1897–1898): 200–202.

————. "The Structure and Distribution of Coral Reefs." *Nature* 40: 125.

Bourne, Gregory C. "Coral Formations." *Nature* 37: 414–15.

————. "Coral Reefs." In *Encyclopedia Britannica,* 1911 ed. Online at http://1911encyclopedia.org/c/co/coral.htm.

————. "The Atoll of Diego Garcia and the Coral Formations of the Indian Ocean." *Nature* 37: 546–50.

Bowlby, John. *Charles Darwin: A New Life.* New York: Norton, 1990.

Burkhardt, Frederick, and Sydney Smith, eds. *The Correspondence of Charles Darwin.* Vol. 1: 1831–1836. Cambridge: Cambridge University Press, 1985.

Clark, Hubert Lyman. "The Purpose and Some Principles of Systematic Zoology." *Popular Science Monthly* 79 (1911): 261–71.

Crews, Frederick. "Saving Us from Darwin, Part II." *New York Review of Books,* 18 October 2001: 51–55.

Daly, Reginald A. "Pleistocene Glaciation and the Coral Reef Problem." *American Journal of Science* 30 (1910): 297–308.

————. "The Glacial-Control Theory of Coral Reefs." *Proceedings of the American Academy of Arts and Sciences,* 51, no. 4 (November 1915).

Dana, James Dwight "Origin of Coral Reefs and Islands." *American Journal of Science* 30 (1910): 89–105, 169–81.

————. *On Coral Reefs and Islands.* New York: Putnam, 1853.

————. "Agassiz's Contributions to the Natural History of the United States." *American Journal of Science* 25 (1858): 321–41.

————. *Corals and Coral Islands.* New York: Putnam, 1872.

Darwin, Charles. *The Structure and Distribution of Coral Reefs. The Works of Charles Darwin.* Vol. 7. Edited by Paul H. Barrett and R. B. Freeman. London: Pickering, 1986.

————. *The Voyage of the "Beagle."* Vol. 29 of the Harvard Classics, edited by Charles Eliot Norton. New York: Collier, 1909.

Darwin, Francis, ed. *The Life and Letters of Charles Darwin.* 2 vols. New York: Appleton, 1911.

————, and A. C. Seward, eds. *More Letters of Charles Darwin.* 2 vols. New York: Appleton, 1903.

Davis, William D. "Coral Reefs." In *Encyclopedia Britannica,* 1950 ed., 1950.

————. "The Home Study of Coral Reefs, Parts 1–3." *Bulletin of the American Geographical Society* 46 (1914): 561–77, 641–54, 721–39.

————. "The Formation of Coral Reefs." *Scientific Monthly* 27, no. 4 (October 1928): 289–300.

————. *The Coral Reef Problem.* New York: American Geographical Society (Special Publication No. 9): 1928.

Dexter, Ralph W. "An Early Defense of Darwinism." Letter, *American Naturalist* 93 (1959): 138–39.

Dupree, A. Hunter. *Asa Gray: American Botanist, Friend of Darwin.* 1959. Reprint, Baltimore: Johns Hopkins University Press, 1988.

Gardiner, J. Stanley. *Coral Reefs and Atolls.* London: Macmillan, 1931.

————. "The Formation of Coral Reefs." *Nature* 69 (18 February 1904): 371–73.

————. "The Formation of the Maldives." *Geographical Journal* 19, no. 3 (March 1902): 277–96.

Geikie, A. "The Duke of Argyll." *Nature* 62: 13–14.

————. "The Origin of Coral Reefs II." *Nature* 29: 124–28.

————. "The Origin of Coral Reefs." *Nature* 29: 107–200.

Ghiselin, Michael T. *The Triumph of the Darwinian Method.* Berkeley: University of California Press, 1969.

Goodale, George Lincoln. "Alexander Agassiz, 1835–1910." In *Biographical Memoirs of the National Academy of Sciences.* Vol 7. Washington, D.C.: National Academy of Sciences, 1912.

Gray, Asa. "Darwin's Theory on the Origin of Species by means of Natural Selection." *American Journal of Science and Arts,* 79 (1860): 153–84. Slightly abridged in John C. Burnham, *Science in America: Historical Selections.* New York: Holt, Rinehart and Winston, 1971.

————. "Darwin on the Origin of Species." *Atlantic Monthly* 6 (1860): 109–16, 229–39.

Gray, Jane Loring, ed. *The Letters of Asa Gray.* 2 vols. Boston: Houghton Mifflin, 1893.

Greene, J. C. "The Kuhnian Paradigm and the Darwinian Revolution in Natural History." *Perspectives in the History of Science and Technology.* Edited by D. H. Roller. Norman: University of Oklahoma Press, 1971.

Gruber, H. E., and V. Gruber. "The Eye of Reason: Darwin's Development During the *Beagle* Voyage." *Isis* 53 (1962): 186–200.

Guppy, Henry B. "Coral Formations." *Nature* 37: 462.

————. "Notes on the Characters and Modes of Formation of the Coral Reefs of the Solomon Islands." *Proceedings of the Royal Society of Edinburgh* 13: 857–904.

————. "The Structure and Distribution of Coral Reefs." *Nature* 40: 53–54.

————. "Coral Formations." *Nature* 37: 604.

Haeckel, Ernst. *Ziele und Wege der heutigen Entwicklungsgeschichte.* (*Goals and Directions of the History of Development [Biogenetics] Today.*) Jena, Germany: Dufft, 1875.

Hanson, Raymond N. *Patterns of Discovery: An Enquiry into the Conceptual Foundations of Science.* Cambridge: Cambridge University Press, 1958.

Holmes, Arthur. Review of *Coral Reefs and the Ice Age,* by Reginald Daly, *Geographical Journal* 48, no. 5 (16 November 1916): 411–15.

Huxley, Thomas H. "Science and the Bishops." *The Nineteenth Century* 22 (1887): 625–41.

James, Preston E. "On the Origin and Persistence of Error in Geography." *Annals of the Association of American Geographers* 57 (1967): 124.

Jones, O. A., and R. Endean, eds. *Biology and Geology of Coral Reefs.* Vols. 1 and 4. New York and London: Academic Press, 1973.

Judd, John W. "A Conspiracy of Silence." *Nature* 37 (1887): 272.

————. "The Duke of Argyll's Charges Against Men of Science." *Nature* 37 (1887): 317–18.

Keynes, Richard Darwin, ed. *Charles Darwin's "Beagle" Diary.* Cambridge: Cambridge University Press, 1988.

Kuhn, T. S. *The Structure of Scientific Revolutions.* Chicago: University of Chicago Press. 1962.

Kuklick, Bruce. *The Rise of American Philosophy: Cambridge, Massachusetts, 1860–1930.* New Haven, Conn.: Yale University Press, 1977.

Ladd, Harry S. "Reef Building." *Science* 134, no. 3481 (15 September 1961): 703–15.

Ladd, Harry S., and J. Edward Hoffmeister. "A Criticism of the Glacial-Control Theory." *Journal of Geology* 44 (1936): 74–92.

Ladd, Harry S., and J. Tracey, Jr. "The Problem of Coral Reefs." *Scientific Monthly,* November 1949: 297–305.

Lee, Hermione. "Tracking the Untrackable." *New York Review of Books.* 12 April 2001: 53–47.q

Lightly, J., "Error in Geography." In *The Story of Human Error*. Edited by J. Jastrow. New York: Appleton, 1936.

Losee, John. *A Historical Introduction to the Philosophy of Science*. Oxford: Oxford University Press, 1972.

Lurie, Edward. *Louis Agassiz: A Life in Science*. Baltimore: Johns Hopkins University Press, 1988.

———. *Nature and the American Mind: Louis Agassiz and the Culture of Science*. New York: Science History Publications, 1974.

Lyell, Charles. *Principles of Geology*. London: Murray, 1830–1833.

Lyman, Theodore. Letters. Lyman Family Papers, 1785–1956. Massachusetts Historical Society. (Microfilm, University of Michigan at Ann Arbor.)

Marcou, Jules. *Life, Letters, and Works of Louis Agassiz*. New York: Woodworth, 1915.

Mather, Kirtley F. "Reginald Aldworth Daly." In *Dictionary of Scientific Biography*. Edited by Charles C. Gillespie. New York: Scribner's, 1971.

Mayer, Alfred Goldsborough. "Alexander Agassiz, 1835–1910." *Popular Science Monthly* 77 (November 1910): 419–58.

Mayr, Ernst. "The Nature of the Darwinian Revolution." *Science* 176 (1972): 981–89.

———. *One Long Argument: Charles Darwin and the Genesis of Modern Evolutionary Thought*. Cambridge: Harvard University Press, 1991.

Meade, T. Mellard. "The Theories of the Origin of Coral Reefs and Islands." *Nature* 37 (1887): 54.

Medawar, Peter. *Induction and Intuition in Scientific Thought*. Philadelphia: American Philosophical Society, 1969.

Menand, Louis. *The Metaphysical Club: A Story of Ideas in America*. New York: Farrar, Straus and Giroux, 2001.

Montgomery, William. "Charles Darwin's Theory of Coral Reefs and the Problem of the Chalk." *Earth Sciences History* 7: 111–20.

Morin, Richard. "Can We Believe in Polls About God?" *Washington Post*, 1 June 1998. Online at http://www.washingtonpost.com/wp-srv/politics/polls/wat/archive/wat060198.htm.

Munson, Ronald. Review of *The Philosophy of Biology*, by Michael Ruse. *Studies in History and Philosophy of Science* 5 (1974): 73–85.

Murray, John, and R. Irvine. "On Coral Reefs and Other Carbonate of Lime Formations in Modern Seas." *Proceedings of the Royal Society of Edinburgh* 17: 79–109.

Murray, John. "Alexander Agassiz: His Life and Scientific Work." *Science* 33 (1911): 873–87.

———. "Coral Formations." *Nature* 37 (1887): 438.

———. "Structure, Origin, and Distribution of Coral Reefs and Islands." *Nature* 39 (1889): 424–28.

———. "On the Structure and Distribution of Coral Reefs and Islands." *Proceedings of the Royal Society of Edinburgh* 10: 505–18.

Oeser, Erhard. *Historical Earthquake Theories.* http://www.univie.ac.at/
    Wissenschaftstheorie/heat/heat.htm.

Paton, Lucy Allen. *Elizabeth Cary Agassiz.* Boston: Houghton Mifflin, 1919.

Popper, Karl R. "Conjectures and Refutations." In *Introductory Readings in
    the Philosophy of Science.* Edited by E. D. Klemke et al. Buffalo, N.Y.:
    Prometheus Books, 1988.

———. *The Logic of Scientific Discovery.* London: Hutchinson, 1959.

Price, George M. "Geology and the Recapitulation Theory: A Study in Cir-
    cular Reasoning." In *Report on Evolution.* Malverne, N.Y.: C. William
    Anderson, 1971.

Rosen, Brian Roy. "Darwin, Coral Reefs, and Global Geology." *BioScience*
    32, no. 6 (1982): 519–25.

Rudwick, M. J. S. "Darwin and Glen Roy: A 'Great Failure' in Scientific
    Method?" *Studies in the History and Philosophy of Science* 5 (1974):
    97–185.

Ruse, Michael. "Charles Lyell and the Philosophers of Science." *British
    Journal of History of Science* 9 (1976): 121–31.

———. "Darwin's Debt to Philosophy: An Examination of the Influence
    of the Philosophical Ideas of John. F. W. Herschel and William
    Whewell on the Development of Charles Darwin's Theory of Evolu-
    tion." *Studies in History and Philosophy of Science* 6 (1975): 159–81.

Ryan, Alan. "The Group." Review of *The Metaphysical Club: A Story of Ideas
    in America* by Louis Menand. *New York Review of Books,* 31 May 2001:
    16–20.

Santayana, George. *Character and Opinion in the United States.* New York:
    Scribner's, 1921.

Schlee, Susan. *The Edge of an Unfamiliar World: A History of Oceanography.*
    New York: Dutton, 1973. Schlee's highly readable book, unfortunately
    out of print, is a solidly researched overview of the science. I am partic-
    ularly indebted to Schlee for her accounts of the *Challenger* findings,
    John Murray's interest in sedimentation, and the 1887–1888 controversy
    over the "conspiracy of silence."

Shermer, Michael. "The Gradual Illumination of the Mind: The Advance
    of Science, Not the Demotion of Religion, Will Best Counter the
    Influence of Creationism." *Scientific American,* February 2002, online
    edition: http://www.sciam.com/2002/0202issue/0202skeptic.html.

Skrupkelis, Ignas K., and Elizabeth M. Berkeley, eds. *The Correspondence of
    William James.* 10 vols. Charlottesville: University Press of Virginia,
    1992– .

Snyder, Laura J. "William Whewell." In *Stanford Encyclopedia of Philosophy.*
    Online edition. http://www.plato.stanford.edu.

Sollas, W. J. "Report on the Coral Reef at Funafuti." *Nature* 55, no. 1425 (18
    February 1897): 373–77.

Stanford Encyclopedia of Philosophy, s.v. "Popper, Karl." Online at http://plato.stanford.edu.

Steers, J. A., and David R. Stoddart. "The Origin of Fringing Reefs, Barrier Reefs, and Atolls." In *Biology and Geology of Coral Reefs.* Vol 4. Edited by O. A. Jones and R. Endean. London: Academic Press, 1977.

Stoddart, David R. "Darwin and the Seeing Eye: The Iconography and Meaning in the Beagle Years." *Earth Sciences History* 14, no. 1 (1995): 3–22.

———. "Theory and Reality: The Success and Failure of the Deductive Method in Coral Reef Studies, Darwin to Davis." *Earth Sciences History,* 13 (1994): 21–34.

———. "Coral Islands, by Charles Darwin, with an Introduction, Map, and Remarks." *Atoll Research Bulletin* 88 (1962): 1–20.

———. "Coral Reefs: The Last Two Million Years." *Geography* 58 (1973): 313–23.

———. "Darwin, Lyell, and the Geological Significance of Coral Reefs." *British Journal for the History of Science* 9 (1976): 199–218.

———. " 'This Coral Episode': Darwin, Dana, and the Coral Reefs of the Pacific." In *Darwin's Laboratory: Evolutionary Theory and Natural History in the Pacific.* Edited by Roy MacLeod and Philip F. Rehbock. Honolulu: University of Hawaii Press, 1994.

———. *On Geography and Its History.* Oxford: Blackwell, 1986.

———. "The Duke, the Professors, and the Great Coral Reef Controversy of 1887–1888." *Earth Sciences History* 7 (1988): 90–98.

———. "Alexander Agassiz and the Coral Reef Controversy." Manuscript courtesy of author, 2003. An earlier version was read at the 17th Pacific Science Congress, Honolulu, 1991.

Thornton, Stephen. "Karl Popper." In *Stanford Encyclopedia of Philosophy,* online edition. http://plato.stanford/edu/entries/popper/#pred.

Weiner, Jonathan. *The Beak of the Finch.* New York: Vintage, 1995.

Wharton, William. "Foundations of Coral Atolls." *Nature* 49 (1897): 390–93.

Whewell, William. *The Philosophy of the Inductive Sciences.* 2 vols. London: Cass, 1967.

Wiens, Harold. "Atoll Development and Morphology." *Annals of the Association of American Geographers* 49 (1959): 31–54.

Williams, David B. "A Wrangle Over Darwin." *Harvard* (September 1998). Online at http://www.harvard-magazine.com/issues/so98/darwin.html.

Winsor, Mary P. "Agassiz's Notion of a Museum: The Vision and the Myth." In *Cultures and Institutions of Natural History.* Edited by Michael Ghiselin and A. E. Leviton. San Francisco: California Academy of Sciences, 2000.

———. "Louis Agassiz and the Species Question." *Studies in the History of Biology* 3 (1979): 89–117.1

———. "Non-Essentialist Methods in Early Taxonomy." In press, 2004.

———. *Reading the Shape of Nature: Comparative Zoology at the Agassiz Museum.* Chicago: University of Chicago Press, 1991.

———. *Starfish, Jellyfish, and the Order of Life: Issues in Nineteenth-Century Science.* New Haven, Conn.: Yale University Press, 1976.

Wright, J. K. "A Plea for the History of Geography," *Isis* 8 (1926): 447–479. Reprinted in *Human Nature in Geography,* by J. K. Wright. Cambridge: Harvard University Press, 1966.

Yonge, C. M. "Darwin and Coral Reefs." *A Century of Darwin.* Vol. 1. Edited by S. A. Barnett. Cambridge: Harvard University Press, 1963.

INDEX

A NOTE ON THE TYPE

This book was set in Adobe Garamond. Designed for the Adobe Corporation by Robert Slimbach, the fonts are based on types first cut by Claude Garamond (c. 1480–1561. Garamond was a pupil of Geoffroy Tory and is believed to have followed the Venetian models, although he introduced a number of important differences, and it is to him that we owe the letter we now know as "old style." He gave to his letters a certain elegance and feeling of movement that won their creator an immediate reputation and the patronage of Francis I of France.

Composed by North Market Street Graphics, Lancaster, Pennsylvania
Printed and bound by Berryville Graphics, Berryville, Virginia